ROOSEVELT
AND
ROMANISM

RECENT TITLES IN CONTRIBUTIONS
IN AMERICAN HISTORY

Series Editor: Jon L. Wakelyn

Contributions in American History, No. 47

ROOSEVELT AND ROMANISM

Catholics and American Diplomacy, 1937-1945

George Q. Flynn

GREENWOOD PRESS
Westport, Connecticut • London, England

For Sean, Kathleen,
and Margaret

Library of Congress Cataloging in Publication Data

Flynn, George Q
   Roosevelt and romanism.

   (Contributions in American history; no. 47)
   Includes bibliographical references and index.
   1. Catholics in the United States—History. 2. Roose-
velt, Franklin Delano, Pres. U.S., 1882-1945. 3. United
States—Foreign relations—1933-1945. I. Title.
BX1406.2.F58   282'.73   75-35343
ISBN 0-8371-8581-5

Library of Congress Catalog Card Number: 75-35343.
ISBN: 0-8381-8581-5

First published in 1976

Greenwood Press, a division of Williamhouse-Regency Inc.
51 Riverside Avenue, Westport, Connecticut 06880

Printed in the United States of America

CONTENTS

ACKNOWLEDGMENTS

This study, as is frequently the case, rests upon the contributions of many individuals. The more formal sources are discussed in the appropriate footnotes and in the bibliographical essay. Here I would like to thank those friends who played a more personal role in making the book a reality. Naturally, the book represents my own interpretation and many suggestions had to be ignored. But I benefited greatly from the advice of Robert Ferrell of Indiana University and James Patterson of Brown University, both of whom read the manuscript and suggested many helpful revisions. My thanks go also to the Texas Tech University Library, the Indiana University Library, the Interlibrary Loan Department at the University of Miami Library, the faculty research funds of Seattle University and Texas Tech University, the staff at the Franklin D. Roosevelt Library, research assistants at the National Archives, and librarians at the Catholic University of America Library. A number of individuals aided me on research trips, including the late Reverend Thomas McAvoy of the University of Notre Dame and archivists at Marquette University and at the University of Wyoming. In Washington, I benefited immensely from the hospitality of

Norman Melun and Lawrence Henneberger and their families. My wife, Mary Reising Flynn, helped with the typing and proofreading. I hope that the following pages serve as a modest recompense for all of their efforts.

The author also wishes to thank the *Catholic Historical Review* for permission to reproduce the sections of Chapter 4 on the Vatican, portions of which first appeared in that journal.

INTRODUCTION

Writing about Catholics and foreign policy presents problems. One may
ask what a religion has to do with foreign policy. Yet the American
Catholic church did have a foreign policy, and church leaders vigorously
debated United States diplomacy from 1937 through 1945. Before the
war, they swayed between isolationism and interventionism in their
debate. Their theology recognized the principles of a just war. The Vatican
stood as a symbolic repudiation of nationalism and isolationism. The
Catholic church taught the Christian brotherhood of all men and the duty
of each citizen to respond to calls of national defense. Such notions should
have conditioned American Catholics to accept international involvement
by their government. But other factors pulled them in the opposite direction. Ironically, the Vatican also served as a force for isolationism.[1]

1

During the 1930s, the Holy See sought desperately to find a formula
for peace; American Catholics could help by preventing the United

States from being entangled in European rivalries. An international conflict would only lead to one branch of the church fighting another.[2] The
ethnic background of American Catholics also encouraged isolationism.
The Irish were anti-British, while German- and Italian-Americans feared
another confrontation with the land of their ancestors. Even the church's
strong anticommunism had ambiguous implications. It encouraged a
blindness to all noncommunist threats and also led some American
Catholics to preach an apocalyptic struggle with Marxism or with any
state—Germany, for example—that sought to destroy religion.

On a theoretical level, American Catholics had ample rationale for
either a vigorous interventionism or isolationism. Much depended upon
the leadership of President Franklin Roosevelt, upon the substance of
his foreign policy, upon the character of American Catholic and Vatican
leadership, and upon the secular tensions of the period. The following
pages will reveal how American Catholics during the years from 1937 to
1945 moved from an attitude of opposition to European involvement by
the United States to active cooperation with Roosevelt and strenuous
support of the war effort. The book also seeks to explain why arguments
used to reject entanglement in the 1930s had no effect by 1941. When,
in 1945, Catholics began to reject Roosevelt's diplomacy, they did not
return to isolationism. Catholic isolationism had passed away between
1937 and 1945. In part, this transformation reflected a desire by church
leaders to remain within the Roosevelt coalition and to avoid appearing
antagonistic to what a popular president defined as the national interest.
Arguments for noninvolvement made little impression on prelates dedicated to affirming the identity of Catholicism and Americanism. These
prelates had become nervous over the apparent split between church and
state which appeared in the 1928 election, in assessment of the Spanish
Civil War, and in attitudes toward the Soviet Union. Franklin Roosevelt
played a major role in helping to nationalize the Catholic church in
America. This nationalization process reached fulfillment during the
war as leading churchmen identified the cause of the United States with
the cause of Christianity. By the end of the war, however, the moral consensus forged by Roosevelt had collapsed before the Russian question.
Catholics became internationalists, but by late 1945 "internationalism"
had become a synonym for "anticommunism."

2

The study of the interaction between religion and politics has been neglected in the United States. Perhaps this omission of a causal role for religion in politics reflects a larger commitment to the Enlightenment. Early rationalists emphasized the reasonableness of the world. Religious questions appeared to be mere historical oddities which could be expected to fade away before the illumination of science, mysticism having no place in a scientific world. Later, thinkers such as Marx saw religion as a rationalization of more basic motives. To explain human behavior in terms of religion, however, was to mistake shadow for substance, argued these modern philosophers.

Despite such opinions, religion continued to be used in explaining society; it would not do to ignore the sacred or dismiss it as irrelevant.[3] Men such as Georg Simmel, Alexis de Tocqueville, and Emile Durkheim became increasingly aware of the enduring religious dimension of any society; it would not do to ignor the sacred or dismiss it as irrelevent.[3] As a modern political scientist put it, "as an important value-generating institution and source of status and power, religion cannot exist without seriously affecting the nature of political discourse."[4] Religion is one of the means by which men attempt to give meaning to the world around them; it seems reasonable to suggest that the religious commitment of an individual will have a bearing on his political actions. In European history, the association of a religious affiliation with a particular political posture has been so frequently observed as to become a truism.

America's historical experience has further confused our understanding of the causal role of religion in political activity. The extreme religious diversity of the United States and its cultural pluralism guaranteed not only religious toleration but also religious neutralization. An overt political maneuver by any one religious group could be expected to produce counter-moves by other religious groups. The political means of overcoming such a conflict was to promote religious freedom by seeing that all churches had equal standing in the nation. In practice, this came to mean that all churches achieved equality by agreeing not to affect political life in a formal or institutional way. An implicit contract emerged by which institutional religion became ostracized from the public arena in exchange for the adoption by the government of a cultural quasireligion based on vague Judaeo-Christian principles. By the twentieth century, it was considered bad form for a cleric to play politics. But, simultaneously, all politicians had to have some religious identity. The 1928 presidential campaign demonstrated that, despite the First Amendment and the implicit contract, religion was still a factor in politics, but the way it was expressed in this case only strengthened those who argued that it should not mix with government. As Harold Ickes, secretary of the interior, put it during the 1930s, a good American had to compartmentalize his political and religious responsibilities.[5]

If we accept the notion of human integrity, it will be difficult to subscribe to the notion of a religious self functioning independently of a political self. Still, the folk prejudice against religious interaction with public life continues. Undoubtedly influenced by Protestant emphasis on the internalization of religious belief and a consequent depreciation of any corporate dimension to Christianity, this attitude has been widely supported in modern America. Scholars spoke of a religious revival in the early 1950s. The religion described, however, appeared to be more a consensus of moral cliches adding up to the American way of life than an institutional church preaching a transcendent faith. People were embarrassed by such terms as a "Catholic" and "Jewish" vote. The narrowness of religious institutional identification contrasted vividly with the public religion of patriotism. Since presumably all Americans shared in the covenant of the American way of life, it was not a source of separatism as the old religious institutions had been. Americans wanted their leaders to be religious but not to permit the institutionalized representation of their religion to affect their view of reality (witness the confused debate between candidate John Kennedy and the Protestants of Houston). Such a split presents psychological problems since questions of state policy have as much moral content as any other type of human decision.[6]

Despite these secularizing and de-institutionalizing trends, there is some evidence that the "old time" religion is alive and well. Despite the embarrassment generated by religious identification in the public arena, institutional churches continue to flourish in modern America. They function in our modern cities not merely as communal groups but also as vehicles for understanding transcendent faith and dogma.[7] Furthermore, the evidence of a religious factor in politics is very convincing, and no one church group has a monopoly on the inclination to seek political support for its moral position. Often, membership in a particular church helps to determine what political party one joins. The church can affect a man's political decisions by establishing an ethical code to insure that secular decisions are disposed toward a particular interpretation of social reality. Church membership may also affect political decisions by helping to establish the class status of an individual, since religious groups have as much status dimension as economic groups. If a political issue has religious significance in a formal way, one can also expect religious identity to have an impact on the political decision.[8] In such circumstances, it would not be surprising if the formal leaders of the church took an active role in political debate and thereby insured that religious identity was a determinant of political action.

The history of the Catholic church in America is filled with such examples of political activism. Ironically, at the same time there is a general tendency on the part of Catholics to deplore suggestions that they make secular decisions on the basis of religious motives. The psychology of compartmentalization recommended by Ickes finds public endorsement by Catholics. Perhaps Catholic sensitivity to the notion of religious motivation is a result of the authoritarian reputation of the church. The old charge of Catholics being priest-ridden has not been without its impact within the church. While clerical and hierarchical direction over religious matters was accepted, until recently, as a matter of course, this capitulation on one level has led to a rather vigorous protest of independence in secular matters. But despite Catholic assertions that they are perfectly free in secular matters, such does not appear to be the case. The suggestion itself rests upon a very narrow idea of how the church shapes the value system of an individual. Is it not unreasonable to argue that an individual can accept from a priest guidance and direction involving the most intimate and profound aspects of existence and at the same time reject this same cleric when he passes an opinion on a political topic? Some Catholics may distinguish between the formal teachings of the church and an expression of opinion by a priest, but one wonders how well this theoretical point functions in practice. In the normal course of decision making, there seems good reason to believe that clerical leaders play a considerable role in shaping the opinions of Catholics. If a man is a serious Catholic, he will read one of the 134 Catholic newspapers or one of the 197 Catholic magazines published by the church. Similarly, when the bishop makes a public statement on a controversial political issue, the Catholic layman will be aware of it. While he might reject the primitive notion that this statement is now part of official church teaching, he will still grant it a reverence traditionally due the position and character of its author. While it is granted that a study of the actions and attitudes of prelates and leading laymen tells us more about the leaders of Catholicism than about the average Catholic, this limitation is balanced by the guarantee that the opinions articulated are self-consciously Catholic.[9]

The student of the interaction of Catholicism and politics also faces the danger of confusing religious identity with ethnic identity. Somehow, national origin seems more legitimate as a causal factor than religion. We explain a Boston politicians's behavior by his Irish-American background, not by his Catholicism. But mass migrations of Irish and Italians formed the bulk of early church membership, and national origin cannot be ignored in a study of American Catholics. Yet is it as powerful a motivational factor among Catholics as their religious association?[10] While first-generation groups huddled together to protect themselves from a hostile religious climate, their church as well as their secular culture was being reinforced. Second- and third-generation American Catholics, however, were seldom interested in promoting their ethnic uniqueness, but their religious identity was constantly being drilled into them by attendance at mass and in parochial schools. Ethnic associations were vehicles for romance or entertainment, while religious association continued to inculcate serious values. One study shows that third-generation Catholics are "more active devotionally and doctrinally orthodox" than recent immigrants. There is a positive correlation between Americanization and church attendance even when the national-origin factor is held constant among Catholics.[11]

The economic-class factor also fails to explain Catholic political behavior fully. No one can question economics as a motive force, but, until very recently, in America an overwhelming majority of Catholics, leaders and followers, shared the same lower-class status. This makes it difficult to use a class variable to distinguish behavior among Catholics.

Yet, even when class is held constant, there seem to be significant differences in the behavior of Catholics and non-Catholics. Furthermore,
Catholics, like members of other religious groups, are very conscious
of their relative status in the nation, and "the denial of equal honor and
respect . . . may be as powerful a factor in stimulating political discontent
as the denial of economic advantages."[12]

Catholics live by bread just as everyone else. Only an extreme reductionism would attempt to explain all Catholic political behavior in
religious terms. Religious determinism appears just as short-sighted as
economic determinism. Both notions do injustice to the pluralism of
American culture and the depth of human personality. But there seems
no danger of the religious factor being overplayed in recent histori-
ography; indeed, it is all too often ignored. Yet historical change is
impossible to explain without some attention to a realm of human
endeavor concerned with such fundamental questions as justice and
morality. Religion deals with that sphere "within which the most
fundamental types of social change will have their origins, . . . the context within which material changes are transmuted into motivations
and values that have wide urgency."[13] Religious associations in the sense
of a doctrinal and institutional type of Catholicism are significant in the
United States. To ignore the impact of such groups on politics and foreign
policy is to impoverish historical reality.[14]

The American Catholic church did have an impact on foreign policy
in the Roosevelt years. Similarly, Catholicism was influenced by events
of American diplomacy. Catholic leaders, clergy and lay, took stands on
public issues and attempted to win support for their views from coreligionists. Catholic leaders influenced the flock by issuing manifestos and,
more subtly, by being disposed to favor one pattern of response over
another through long-term religious education. Catholic attitudes about
communism fit this description. Canonically, only the pope and bishops
are teachers of the church, and then only in the realm of faith and morals.
Very seldom is an issue of policy decided by the official teaching of the
church. Theoretically, a political statement by a bishop has no more institutional sanction than a statement on theology by a layman. Practically,
however, a bishop will defend his secular position on the basis of his understanding of the official teaching of the church in an area where that teach-

ing is merely implicit and derivative. The hierarchical and dogmatic dimensions of the Catholic church enhance the ability of clerical leaders to transmit their values to the faithful even when the topic considered is not intrinsic to the faith. Another source of reinforcement in the past was that Catholic leaders were representative of their followers in class, education, and ethnic background. This fact contributed to the effectiveness of clerical leadership.[15]

American Catholics tended to be members of the Democratic party. The church leaders voted for Roosevelt in 1932. After all other variables were isolated, there was still a large difference between the political responses of Catholics and other Americans. In the presidential elections of 1936 and 1940, vote returns indicated that Catholics consistently voted for Roosevelt in larger percentages than Protestants within the same economic class.[16] Studies of attempts of Catholic leaders to influence the vote of their coreligionists reveal that they had some success.[17] Such political "clout" was a truism to professional politicians even before modern social research isolated it. Franklin Roosevelt was constantly aware of a Catholic vote. As an Eastern politician, he needed no one to tell him about the power of the church to influence the outcome of an election. An ambitious politician in an Eastern metropolis found it *de rigueur* to know all the priests in his electoral district and to know what they were thinking and saying. Ethnic balance on a ticket was important, but so was religious balance. The religious factor was never ignored by the men who had to win elections in Catholic districts.[18] As the narrative of this book demonstrates, the church also affected foreign policy decisions. Thomas Bailey, a noted historian of diplomacy, was right when he wrote some time ago that "if religion is important to us, and if foreign policy is also important to us, each is bound to have some influence on the other, for the two cannot be compartmentalized in our thinking."[19]

American Catholics represented one-sixth of the total population of the nation in the 1930s. Geographical and historical factors had made them an important element in the Democratic coalition of Franklin Roosevelt. Finally, a number of foreign policy problems which arose during the 1930s, such as the Spanish Civil War, aid to Communist Russia, and relations with the Vatican, had special meaning to Catholics. To ignore the interest of Catholic leadership in the diplomatic issues from 1937 through World War II would be to operate in a historical vacuum.

NOTES

1. B. Fensterwal, Jr., in "The Anatomy of American 'Isolationism' and Expansion," *Journal of Conflict Resolution* II (June and December 1958), p. 136, argues that American Catholics were isolationists due to Vatican influence but supplies no evidence for this assertion.

2. James O'Gara, in "The Catholic Isolationist," *Catholicism in America: A Series of Articles from the Commonweal* (New York, 1954), pp. 106-110, writes that Catholic dogma has had little effect on the political views of the faithful since, despite papal condemnation of nationalism, American Catholics remain chauvinistic.

3. Robert A. Nisbet, *The Sociological Tradition* (New York, 1966), p. 222.

4. Seymour M. Lipset, "Religion and Politics in the American Past and Present," in *Religion and Social Conflict,* edited by Robert Lee and Martin E. Marty (New York, 1964), p. 70.

5. Harold L. Ickes, *The Secret Diary of Harold L. Ickes*, 3 vols. (New York, 1953-1954), vol. 2, p. 605. Ickes lamented the defection of Frank Murphy from the liberal side in the Spanish Civil War controversy by writing, "I had thought that Murphy was one Catholic who could rigidly keep his religion and his politics in separate, airtight compartments, and I am disappointed" (vol. 2 p. 605).

6. Will Herberg, in *Protestant, Catholic, Jew* (New York, 1960), formed the classic statement of the growth of Americanism as a religion.

7. Nisbet, *The Sociological Tradition*, p. 230; see also Gerhard Lenski, *The Religious Factor: A Sociological Study of Religion's Impact on Politics, Economics, and Family Life* (Garden City, N.Y., 1963), pp. 18-20 and 319-326, who makes a clear distinction between the church as a communal group and as an associational group. He presents evidence that American Catholicism is thriving on both levels in at least one major metropolis.

8. Lipset, "Religion and Politics," pp. 102, 105, 107, and 118; Lenski, *The Religious Factor*, p. 168; George Q. Flynn, *American Catholics and the Roosevelt Presidency, 1932-1936* (Lexington, Ky., 1968), pp. x-xv.

9. Figures on the Catholic press are from the *National Catholic Welfare Conference News Service*, June 7, 1937 (microfilm, The Catholic University of America, Washington, D.C.), which indicates a newspaper circulation of 2,396,516 and a magazine circulation of 4,604,141; here-

after this source will be cited as *NCWC News Service*; David O'Brien, *American Catholics and Social Reform* (New York, 1968), p. viii (also in doctoral thesis format, University of Rochester, 1965). For more on the problem of studying leadership as a key to mass opinion, see Flynn, *American Catholics*, pp. xii-iv.

10. The literature on ethnic politics is vast. Most studies tend to lump religious affiliation, national origin, and race together under the term "ethnic." There is overwhelming evidence of the potency of the ethnic factor in American politics, but few studies have attempted to segregate its various dimensions. See especially Harry A. Bailey, Jr., and Ellis Katz, editors, *Ethic Group Politics* (Columbus, Ohio, 1969), and Moses Rischin, *Our Own Kind: Voting by Race, Creed or National Origins* (Santa Barbara, Cal., 1960). Scott Greer, "Catholic Voters and the Democratic Party," in Bailey and Katz, *Ethnic Group Politics*, pp. 170-186, studied the 1956 election in St. Louis. He held constant the variables of generation in America, country of origin, education, and geography and still found that "religion seems to have independent discriminating power; when variables which are supposed to explain Catholic preference for the Democratic Party are controlled, it still makes an important difference" (p. 184). His hypothesis is that "differential association among Catholics . . . continues to be very important (a) because the Church is itself an organizational and associational matrix, providing a framework for social life which includes religiously segregated schools, religious endogamy, and a wealth of organized activity" (p. 185). Referring to the post-World War II period, Will Herberg, in "Religious Group Conflict in America," in Bailey & Katz, *Ethnic Group Politics*, p. 21, writes, "within the three fold American scheme of race, ethnicity, and religion, a shift has taken place from ethnicity to religion as the dominant form of self identification." See also Sam Bass Warner, *Urban Wilderness* (New York, 1972), p. 156ff., for support of Herberg's thesis that race and religion have displaced ethnicity as an identification symbol.

11. Lenski, *The Religious Factor*, pp. 37-38, 58n, 138, and 180; Lipset, "Religion and Politics," pp. 102-104, also points out that there is more evidence of ethnic strength among German-Americans because of the belligerent status of their homeland in two world wars.

12. Lenski, *The Religious Factor*, p. 173; Lipset, "Religion and Poli-

tics," pp. 92, 93, and 94, compared Protestant and Catholic votes in 1936, 1940, and 1944. Holding constant the occupational variable, he found that Catholics supported Democrats more often than did Protestants. The percentage differences were as follows: in 1936, Catholics +31 percent; in 1940, Catholics +31 percent; in 1944, Catholics +27 percent.

13. Nisbet, *The Sociological Tradition*, p. 230.

14. Lenski, *Religious Factor*, p. 319.

15. Lipset, "Religion and Politics," p. 70; Nisbet, *The Sociological Tradition*, p. 222; Lenski, *The Religious Factor*, p. 285. As might be expected, those laymen who are most involved in the church are most susceptible to clerical leadership, but this is merely saying the more Catholic, the more priest-led. Naturally, receptiveness to clerical intervention in politics is also influenced by basic agreement or disagreement with the clerical stand on the issue at hand. Many Catholics objected to Father Coughlin's politicizing, but explained their opposition in a way which makes one suspect that they really objected to the cause he was advocating; see P. H. Callahan to Rev. John A. Ryan, November 4, 1939, John A. Ryan Papers, Catholic University of America, Washington, D.C.

16. See note 12. The following figures are indicative of Roosevelt's voting strength in centers of American Catholicism:

City	Percentage Demo. Vote in Presidential Elections 1936/1940	Pop. of Catholics in City (in Diocese), 1936		Total Pop. in City, 1940	Percentage of Pop. Catholic
Hartford	70.0/65.0	61,885*	(632,671)	166,267	27
Providence	62.7/62.1	133,265*	(346,423)	253,504	52
Boston	69.9/63.3	308,512*	(1,044,359)	770,816	40
Newark	72.6/62.2	193,585*	(645,000)	429,760	45
New York	75.4/61.2	1,551,296	(1,000,000)	7,454,995	20
Pittsburgh	70.7/61.6	238,691*	(661,826)	671,659	35
Baltimore	68.3/64.0	189,407*	(384,710)	859,100	22
Philadelphia	62.1/60.0	528,824*	(852,000)	1,931,334	27
Cleveland	76.5/69.9	281,839*	(548,403)	878,336	32

Detroit	68.9/63.0	335,628*	(502,316)	1,623,452	20
Chicago	66.9/58.5	896,565*	(1,400,000)	3,396,808	26
Cincinnati	59.2/49.9	91,857*	(250,000)	455,610	21
Milwaukee	82.1/64.1	175,087*	(475,000)	587,472	29
St. Louis	67.0/58.1	206,237*	(440,000)	816,048	25
St. Paul	73.8/58.1	86,106*	(306,796)	287,736	29
New Orleans	91.3/85.7	191,933*	(330,000)	494,537	38
San Antonio	73.5/70.8	73,712*	(195,326)	253,854	29
Louisville	62.1/59.4	75,384*	(106,311)	319,077	23
Denver	66.2/52.8	41,368*	(140,702)	322,412	12
San Francisco	75.0/60.3	176,169*	(430,000)	634,536	27
Los Angeles	71.3/61.1	169,077*	(317,549)	1,504,277	11

*Cities where Catholicism ranks first in total number of members.

Sources: American Institute of Public Opinion, *The Gallup Political Almanac for 1948* (Princeton, N.J., 1948), pp. 272-274; *The Official Catholic Directory, 1940* (New York, 1940); and U.S. Bureau of the Census, *Religious Bodies,* 2 vols. (Washington, D.C., 1941), vol. 1, pp. 70-71. In 1936, of the fifty largest cities, Roman Catholicism ranked first in population in forty-one.

---

17. John H. Fenton, *The Catholic Vote* (New Orleans, 1960), p. 56.

18. See, for example, the 1939 files of Representative John J. O'Connor New York Democrat, which contain a list of all the Catholic churches in his congressional district, with the names and rank of all personnel (file, 1939, O'Connor Mss., Lilly Library, Indiana University, Bloomington, Ind.); another example of the same sensitivity to the Catholic vote occurred in 1944 when Ed Flynn rejected the vice-presidential aspirations of James Byrnes because the latter had left the Catholic Church. See Byrnes's comments on this issue in James Brynes, *All in One Lifetime* (New York, 1958), pp. 118-120. New York politicians referred to the archbishop's residence as "the Powerhouse"; see William D. Hassett, *Off The Record with FDR* (Warm Springs, Ga., 1958), p. 103.

19. Thomas Bailey, *The Man in the Street* (New York, 1948), p. 199.

ROOSEVELT
AND
ROMANISM

1

NEUTRALITY

The small band of Catholics who followed Leonard Calvert, the brother of Lord Baltimore, to America in 1634 had grown into an impressive establishment of twenty million by the 1930s. This transformation came from the high birth rate—Catholics, like all of the settlers, followed a course of replenishing and multiplying—and from tremendous infusions of Irish, Germans, Italians, and Poles in the nineteenth and early twentieth centuries. Faced with a Protestant majority possessing a keen sense of its Reformation heritage, American Catholics at first had turned inward. They thought they were defending themselves against Know-Nothing groups, Maria Monk propaganda, and the American Protective Association. Throughout the nineteenth century, the leaders of American Catholicism strove to reconcile the faith with customs of their adopted land. But integration remained illusory. The Ku Klux Klan in the 1920s and the 1928 presidential campaign dispelled any naive assumptions that Catholics were members of the American community. The arrival in the White House of Franklin D. Roosevelt and the advent of the New Deal, however, did make a difference. President Roosevelt had great rapport with the leaders of

American Catholicism. The New Deal was for all Americans. Some
bishops even thought they saw signs of papal influence in this social
legislation; the future appeared bright for Catholics as Roosevelt began
his second term.

American Catholics in 1937 represented a vigorous religious community led by 132 bishops and 33,500 priests.[1] Most of these leaders
were native-born and had risen to power through service in the United
States. Most of the bishops came from middle-class families of either
Irish or German background. Theoretically possessing the independence
of medieval barons and subject only to the pope, they varied widely in
their church and secular power. The rulers of rich and populous areas
generally had a greater effect on church policy than did the bishops of
small, isolated districts. The cardinals—William O'Connell of Boston,
George Mundelein of Chicago, William Dougherty of Philadelphia,
Patrick Hayes and later Francis Spellman of New York—were a major
force in the religious and secular life of Catholics who lived in big cities.
Urban concentration guaranteed that such archbishops as John T. Mc-
Nicholas of Cincinnati, Samuel A. Stritch of Milwaukee, Michael T.
Curley of Baltimore, John J. Glennon of St. Louis, John Cantwell
of Los Angeles, Edward A. Mooney of Detroit, and John J. Mitty of
San Francisco would possess political power. Below this level were
bishops with more than local influence. Joseph Schrembs of Cleveland,
Gerald Shaughnessy of Seattle, Robert E. Lucey of Amarillo, Edwin V.
O'Hara of Great Falls, Montana, Joseph F. Rummel of New Orleans,
Francis J. L. Beckman of Dubuque, Karl J. Alter of Toledo, John F.
Noll of Fort Wayne—all were outspoken in their views of secular society
and quite willing to evaluate trends and present the church's attitude.

These leaders had available an energetic press as the means of propa-
gating their policies. A formidable institution by any standard, the
Catholic press in 1937 had 134 local or diocesan papers which were
read by some 2,396,516 subscribers, and 197 periodicals or journals
which reached 4,604,141 Catholics. Here was a network of impressive
dimensions. Radio programs, such as the weekly "Catholic Hour" based
in New York, supplemented the press. Like the bishops, these organs
differed radically in influence, coverage, and sophistication. Each bishop,
no matter how modest his diocese, usually had a paper to keep his people
informed. The more influential papers included the *Catholic Review* of

Baltimore, the *Tablet* of Brooklyn, the *Tidings* of Los Angeles, the *New World* of Chicago, the *Pilot* of Boston, the *Catholic Herald* of Milwaukee, the *Catholic Messenger* of Davenport, Iowa, the *Monitor* of San Francisco, and the nationwide *Our Sunday Visitor* of Fort Wayne, Indiana. These papers were full-scale journalistic enterprises featuring regular editorials and extensive commentary on secular events. They shared the national news services provided by the National Catholic Welfare Conference and also tapped the regular wire lines.

Catholic magazines also reached a wide spectrum of readers. The more devotionally oriented Catholics read the *Sacred Heart Bulletin* or the *Ave Maria*. The leading journals in circulation and influence were those which confronted the secular world and sought to provide a Catholic explanation to political and diplomatic problems. Preeminent in this type of journalism were *America*, published by the Jesuits; the *Commonweal*, supported by a group of New York liberal laymen; and *Catholic World*, published by the Paulist Fathers in New York. Theoretically independent of hierarchical control, these journals seldom published anything objectionable to ecclesiastical leaders. When they did take an independent tack (the *Commonweal* was best known in this regard), episcopal pressure either pushed them back into line or cut their circulation.

On yet another level, the public life of the church flourished through the many national organizations of lay Catholics. The Knights of Columbus, the National Conference of Catholic Men, the Catholic Alumni Association, and others all enjoyed large memberships during the 1930s. Most of the time, these groups concentrated on apostolic and spiritual missions, but they also provided the hierarchy with attractive and convenient forums for statements on public issues. The leaders of these groups could be expected to work with the bishops to resolve a public problem.

No picture of American Catholicism in the 1930s would be complete without some understanding of the National Catholic Welfare Conference (NCWC). As a center of American Catholicism, the NCWC was both unique and paradoxical. Church law insisted upon a direct channel of authority from the pope to each bishop, and the NCWC had no canonical standing. Indeed, the Vatican had been suspicious when the organization grew out of the collaboration of American bishops during World War I. The bishops ignored Rome's displeasure because they saw a need to unify, coordinate, and organize Catholics of the United States in such fields as education and social welfare. By the late 1930s, the NCWC had permanent headquarters on Massachusetts Avenue in Washington, D.C., an elaborate staff, and committees dealing with social action, education, press relations and legal problems. Congressmen had come to expect staff members of the NCWC to testify on pending legislation when the church thought its interests were at stake. The general secretary of the NCWC during the late 1930s, Monsignor Michael J. Ready, established communication with President Roosevelt, members of the cabinet, and the Department of State.

The Catholic church apparently had arrived at a modus vivendi in America. But now, late in the 1930s, a whole new set of issues arose out of the pressure of international affairs. Catholic leaders soon had to respond to a series of critical questions about the mission of the United States in a world torn by strife. The church's new-found security and its position of some respect in American life appeared to be in jeopardy.

1

Americans, Catholic and non-Catholic, had responded to threats from abroad during the 1930s by adopting an isolationist position. While the term "isolationism" involved a whole series of ideas, at the center of the notion were two postulates: the United States should avoid war and should avoid any long-term association with a foreign nation. The motives which inspired isolationists varied. Some, such as the noted historian of the economic origins of the Constitution, Charles A. Beard, were moved by a concern for fulfillment of domestic reform, sure to be forgotten during a military adventure. Others, including the Republican senator from Ohio, Robert A. Taft, feared a collapse of the established order in the wake of another war. Senator Gerald P. Nye of North Dakota opposed war on pacifist principles. William E. Borah of Idaho refused to sacrifice any American sovereignty to a program of collective security. Unlike the rather theoretical isolationism of the 1920s, during the depression the movement associated itself with responses to particular threats to the peace. Perhaps most Americans never understood the implications of their isolationism since they easily discarded it when confronted with the prospect of a Europe dominated by Germany or an Asia controlled by Japan, but before the disaster at Pearl Harbor, few observers possessed enough foresight to predict such a response.[2]

One small group of American Catholics accepted isolationism because they based their attitude toward diplomacy on a philosophy of pacifism. To these men and women, religion and war were mutually exclusive ideas. Since diplomatic involvement with Europe would surely lead to war, these Catholics urged isolationism. Some Catholic authors, such as the Reverend John LaFarge, S. J., insisted that only "a physical attack upon our shores" would justify war. No such qualifications bothered the *Catholic Worker* and its editor Dorothy Day. She and her followers held to an uncompromising pacifism, opposed all preparedness, and repeatedly denounced collective security. Miss Day and the members of her organization represented the purest form of pacifism within Catholicism. Many of them applied for and were granted conscientious objector status during World War II.[3]

Most American bishops frowned upon such Christian idealism. Over the years, the church had come to terms with man's warlike disposition. Catholic bishops emphasized that the church did not condemn all wars. Instead, it asked certain questions about any conflict to help a Catholic determine the justice of the affair. Were the moral goals of the combatants clear? Was it impossible to see clearly who was in the right? Had all legitimate means for a peaceful settlement been exhausted? Was the war being fought with humane weapons? Could we be sure the war would not lead to an even greater evil as a consequence of the fighting? If a Catholic could answer such questions affirmatively, he could be sure the conflict was just and merited support. Above all, the bishops taught that, in cases of doubt, one must accept the wisdom of the state in such matters. In the absence of a direct episcopal prohibition, American Catholics should accede to the wishes of the state.[4]

During the 1930s, Catholic writers also spent much time discussing how to keep the peace. The most important writing on this subject came from the Catholic Association for International Peace (CAIP). This organization represented the most sophisticated and consistent attempt by a Catholic group to form a religious outlook on foreign policy questions. The CAIP was formed in 1926 with the three-fold purpose of keeping the United States out of war, ending war everywhere, and encouraging American participation in a system of collective security. Closely related to other idealistic peace groups which proliferated during the 1920s, the CAIP was primarily concerned with educating Catholics on the need for international cooperation. Throughout the 1930s, it functioned under

the general auspices and supervision of the Social Action Department of
the NCWC and never had more than 500 members. Charles G. Fenwick
of Bryn Mawr College directed the CAIP, and his work drew endorsement from such Catholic spokesmen as Father John Ryan of Catholic
University, Monsignor Michael J. Ready, professors Parker T. Moon and
Carlton J. H. Hayes of Columbia University, and Senator Joseph C.
O'Mahoney of Wyoming. Chronic indebtedness forced Fenwick to rely
for support on contributions by idealistic nuns throughout the country.
The CAIP's work consisted primarily of public relations and education
among Catholics, but Executive Secretary Elizabeth Sweeney also mailed
literature to isolationist congressmen (such as Nye) in the Senate.[5]

Most of the pamphlets published by the CAIP during the 1930s
carried the same message. Catholics should work for international peace.
They should pray and support the League of Nations. CAIP literature
often emphasized international economic cooperation, a policy similar
to the reciprocity notions of Secretary of State Cordell Hull, as a path
to peace. By the late 1930s, Fenwick had become critical of the league
because he thought it only defended the status quo instead of working
to redistribute the world's resources and to open markets. In addition,
the CAIP consistently warned against relying upon neutrality laws as a
means of avoiding American responsiblity in international affairs.[6]

Like the proposals of many semi-pacifist groups during the 1930s, the
CAIP's program had contradictions. Fenwick and others encouraged internationalism, but they denounced any American intervention in a European
conflict. After war began in Europe, the CAIP endorsed aid to victims of
aggression. CAIP members such as Ryan, Hayes, and Moon worked with
groups promoting aid to the Allies. Simultaneously, the CAIP denounced
spending for armaments. The United States was supposed to assist victims
of aggression but also to renounce war and stop manufacturing arms. The
CAIP hoped that peace would be secured in Europe but failed to suggest
concrete tactics or ways in which the United States could promote international accord other than through nebulous moral precepts. The group
kept emphasizing the need for the United States to take part in a new
world organization for peace, but the old organization had proved inadequate. The dilemma remained. No one could argue with the CAIP for
encouraging peace and international cooperation. But something a trifle
stronger than this encouragement seemed to be needed to frustrate aggression, something which might require the manufacture of arms.[7]

A special problem with the CAIP approach was the tendency of its leaders to identify personal morality with international relations. Assuming that a nation was merely a collection of individuals, they also assumed that the morality of individual relations could apply to international relations. They failed to appreciate the distinction Reinhold Niebuhr made between moral man and immoral society. Perhaps this tendency was natural in a movement which rested upon a religious view of the world, but it did not encourage the hardheaded analysis of mundane issues which might lead to a workable arrangement between imperfect world powers.

While such notions did stand as alternatives for those who sought a larger view of international responsibility than those provided by American isolationism and nationalism, few Catholic leaders accepted the CAIP program. The American bishops did not share the CAIP's internationalism and the organization had little influence upon the hierarchy of the church.[8] Instead, the CAIP had its greatest effect upon the young idealistic Catholic who could not accept the uncompromising pacifism of the Catholic Worker movement but still wanted to inject morality into international relations. At the same time as the rush to rearm in Europe, the CAIP organized Catholic Peace Clubs. By 1937 the movement had spread to 87 colleges and universities across the nation. Sweeney even solicited support for the movement from President Roosevelt. After checking with James A. Farley and the Reverend John J. Burke of the NCWC, the president sent a note endorsing the clubs and applauding student interest in international affairs.[9] Roosevelt's confidence in these young men and women was soon rewarded. When college and high school students throughout the country held a peace strike on April 22, 1937, they concluded their celebration by taking an oath not to assist the government in any future war. This type of unequivocal pacifism was condemned by the CAIP and by the National Catholic Alumni Federation. Most Catholic students boycotted the celebration, appalled as much by the sponsorship of Marxist groups, such as the American League Against War and Fascism, as by the ideas expressed.[10]

A cross section of the Catholic press in the 1930s expressed the same interest in peace but a distaste for any attempt to commit the United States to organization with other nations for collective security. The Catholic Press Association of the United States went on record in 1938 as opposed to "any action or conduct on the part of the Government, groups or individuals tending to involve us in affairs of any foreign government." Frank A. Hall, director of the *NCWC News Service,* urged the Catholic press to wage a campaign against "the sinister forces in the United States that are seeking to entangle our government . . . in international conflict." Such sentiments were supported in the *Buffalo Echo, America, Catholic World,* and the *Catholic Messenger* of Davenport. The Catholic Daughters of America, meeting in Atlantic City, boldly declared that "no power on earth short of invasion shall draft us into war." The National Council of Catholic Women heard Bishop Joseph M. Corrigan, rector of the Catholic University of America, declare that a "patriotism of peace" was needed in the country.[11]

Most American Catholics agreed that the United States should stay out of foreign adventures. They agreed for different reasons. In some cases religious platitudes against war justified neutrality, but a few spokesmen were more concrete. A surprising number of Catholics objected to intervention because of their memory of World War I. The leader in this school was the Reverend James Gillis, editor of the *Catholic World,* who repeatedly filled his columns with warnings of how Roosevelt was pursuing the same disastrous course followed by Woodrow Wilson. Like Wilson, Roosevelt was ignoring the Senate and the people and taking sides in the European controversy. Gillis was not the only one to use the analogy of World War I. Archbishop Michael Curley of Baltimore consistently argued that we had gained nothing from our earlier intervention and another crusade would lead to economic collapse. Cardinal O'Connell of Boston reminded his followers of the results of the Paris Peace Conference and warned against another trip into the pit of power politics. "We had enough of it in 1917," wrote the editor of the *Brooklyn Tablet.* Such sentiments found support in diocesan newspapers.[12]

Lurking within this disillusionment over World War I and international collaboration was a distrust of association with Europe. To the San Francisco *Monitor,* there were two sides to "the [present] quarrel in Europe, and . . . both sides are bad." Gillis repeatedly warned against the "European city-slickers" who would make a fool of poor Uncle Sam again. Charles C. Tansill of Georgetown University, a controversial student of the American entry into World War I, told the Holy Name Society in New York City that "America is great because she has remained aloof from the evils of Europe." Archbishop Beckman of Dubuque and Archbishop Mitty of San Francisco both contended that there was no just side in the European struggle. Critics often dismissed much of this anti-European bias as a mere cover for the traditional anti-British feeling of the Irish clergy in the United States. Undoubtedly there was some anglophobia. During the earlier Ethiopian crisis of late 1935, the Reverend Ralph L. Harps, rector of the North American College in Rome, which trained many prominent American clerics, wrote presidential assistant Frank Walker, warning against being misled by British propaganda. The American hierarchy was dominated by men such as Cardinal O'Connell and Archbishop Curley, who had no love for England. But such sentiments did not exhaust the general distrust of European involvement. This distrust also appeared related to fears that intervention would mean the end of American democracy. Tansill and Reverend Ignatius W. Cox of Fordham made this point clear in their public analyses.[13]

Non-Catholic Americans shared these same feelings of disillusionment with World War I and distrust of Europe. Catholic suspicions derived distinction from the inordinate influence of anticommunism in their interpretation of the world around them. It is difficult to exaggerate the distrust of the communist movement which pervaded Catholicism during the 1930s. At first glance, it would appear that a resolute fear of communism might stimulate an aggressive view toward the world by Catholics rather than a desire to remain disengaged. Yet, repeatedly, Catholics condemned communism and simultaneously demanded that the United States remain free of entanglements and wars. Many Catholics suspected that no matter what the issues in Europe, only the communists would benefit from a war. The United States must be kept protected from a conflict which would make it an easy prey for a communist takeover. As Patrick J. O'Shea, national chairman of the Catholic Students Peace Federation, wired Congressman John J. O'Connor in 1939, "The youth of America must never be called upon to fight, suffer and die for the triumph of Red Democracy and world Atheism." When Father John Ryan of the Catholic University loaned his name to attempts to revise the Third Neutrality Act, he was accused of aiding the communists and breaking the "clerical front." Fear of communism caused many Catholics to urge withdrawal of the United States from international affairs lest it be contaminated.[14]

Catholics also justified their neutralism and noninvolvement by using both the heritage of their nation and the teachings of their pope. Frequently, noninterventionists buttressed their appeals with a quote from the farewell address of Washington. Catholics reassured themselves of their national identity and promoted noninvolvement at the same time. Because they realized the foolishness of calling upon the United States to adopt a foreign policy on the basis of the pope's teachings on international cooperation, justification for isolationism had to be located within the national tradition; George Washington was a perfect source. Editors of such publications as the *Boston Pilot*, the *Brooklyn Tablet*, and *Extension Magazine*, were united by their familiarity with the warnings of Washington against entangling alliances. Catholic isolationism sought roots in the nation's past.[15]

Paradoxically, however, the Catholic hierarchy realized that excessive isolationism could breed rampant nationalism. This fear was given some voice when Charles G. Fenwick and John Schuler of the CAIP conceived the idea of a joint statement by the American hierarchy on the importance of peace. Such a statement would also serve to dramatize the cause of the CAIP, which was being neglected by the bishops. Finally, it would be a great opportunity for the bishops to provide moral guidance for the average Catholic on international affairs. After a year of debate on how to solicit such individual statements, a form letter was finally mailed to about forty-one important bishops. Their replies arrived during 1938. The results were disappointing, as Schuler himself admitted. Perhaps as many as one-half of the bishops failed to respond at all. Those who did answer sent statements filled with banalities about the evils of war. If there were any general themes to the responses, they were a sincere distrust of the extreme nationalism which would develop during a war and a similar distrust of international communism. A few bishops warned that American involvement in Europe would mean the end of social progress at home. Archbishop John T. McNicholas of Cincinnati warned his flock against so-called peace propaganda which might lead the nation into war. He urged Catholics to consider the formation of "a mighty league of conscientious noncombatants." There was unanimity about the importance of a self-defense program, but if Fenwick and Schuler were expecting a dramatic position paper from the American hierarchy, they must have considered their effort a waste of time. There was little in the individual statements that either an interventionist or isolationist could argue over.[16]

Such fears of war did not mean Catholic bishops ignored or accepted what was happening in Europe. After all, the church was a vulnerable part of European civilization. The anti-Christian actions of both Germany and the Soviet Union worried the American church. No other news source in the world gave closer attention to the everyday doings of the League of Militant Atheists than the *NCWC News Service.* In 1937 and 1938 Catholic criticism of Hitler's Germany was equally negative and even went beyond the expressed views of the Roosevelt administration. In March 1937, Pope Pius XI issued an encyclical on the intolerable religious situation in Germany and condemned the insidious racial doctrines manifested by National Socialism. In the United States, the American hierarchy supported this criticism of Germany. Perhaps the most outspoken member of the hierarchy was George Cardinal Mundelein of Chicago. The cardinal used the occasion of a quarterly clergy conference on May 22, 1937, to attack Hitler for his antireligious actions. Mundelein called the Fuehrer "an inept paper hanger," among other things. A large group of American bishops joined the denunciation.[17] When the German press attacked Mundelein, even Pius XI came to his defense. The Catholic Press Association at its annual convention in Rochester affirmed its support for the cardinal and condemned all forms of totalitarianism.[18]

German persecution of the Jews acted as a stimulant for Catholics to concern themselves with international affairs. American church leaders brought pressure to bear on the Roosevelt administration to become involved in this European problem. Moral imperialism was apparently reconcilable with general noninvolvement in international politics. Martin H. Carmody, supreme knight of the Knights of Columbus, wrote the president expressing the deep distress his organization felt for the fate of German Jews and urged the administration "to use its influence to preserve in its full meaning, force, and intent, the Palestine Mandate." Two months later, in December 1938, the Reverend Maurice S. Sheehy of Catholic University wrote Roosevelt, suggesting the establishment of a special commission of prominent Catholic leaders to coordinate a grand campaign in Latin America against Nazi harassment of the Jews. Monsignor Ready of the NCWC, ex-Governor Al Smith, and leaders of the hierarchy spoke out against German pogroms on network radio in November 1938. Archbishop Mooney, as episcopal chairman of the NCWC administrative board, the largest representative body of the American hierarchy, joined with Protestant leaders in condemning the persecutions. As early as 1936 Mooney also helped establish a Committee for Catholic Refugees from Germany. Catholic leaders such as Archbishop John G. Murray of St. Paul and Cardinal Dougherty of Philadelphia also urged Roosevelt to protect the rights of Jews and to help them find a new home if they were forced to leave Germany.[19]

Catholic awareness of international affairs again manifested itself most clearly in support for Pan-Americanism and the Good Neighbor Policy. Although suspicious of contact with Europe, Catholics seemed very trustful toward Latin America. Despite unfortunate friction between American Catholics and the administration over anticlericalism in Mexico in 1935, by Roosevelt's second term most prelates were enthusiastically endorsing the Good Neighbor Policy. Catholics applaude the president for seeing the historic and geographic unity of the hemisphere, an approach which could also be interpreted as segregating the nation from European affairs. Indeed, the Good Neighbor Policy itself could be read as a form of isolationism. As Monsignor Ready announced over the National Broadcasting Company, "there is in it [the Good Neighbor Policy] no hypocritical fallacy of race superiority preached by senseless prophets of absurdity." The various inter-American conferences held at Buenos Aires (1936), Lima (1938), and Panama (1939) appeared to be important steps in developing a hemispheric unity to face the growing threat of European totalitarianism.[20]

Roman Catholics united behind an active Latin-American policy because they envisioned a special role for the church in any alliance. As Senator Dennis Chavez of New Mexico said in his address to a Holy Name Society meeting, the Catholic church was the key to promoting inter-American friendship. Because of its historic roots in South American culture, the church "is in a strategically important position to foster and cement improved relations." The means to promote good will were the twenty million Catholics in the United States who should be encouraged to become agents for the Good Neighbor Policy. Chavez's ideas found support from a wide range of Catholic sources. Reverend Joseph F. Thorning, a prominent Catholic educator and something of an isolationist with respect to Europe, returned from a trip to Latin America praising the success of Roosevelt's policy and predicting that the means of cementing ties would be "Catholic Christianity." Reverend Dr. Howar J. Carroll, assistant to Ready at NCWC, also publicly praised the Good Neighbor idea. Catholics in the United States could be instruments in activating this diplomacy because they shared a common religious heritage with Latin America. Others with the same view included Reverend Dr. Edwin Ryan of Catholic University, M. Pauline Casey, vice-president of the National Council of Catholic Women, and Dr. Martin R. P. McGuire, dean of the Catholic University Graduate School. The *NCWC News Service* took up the notion in its editorials. Occasionally, the thesis led to simplistic outbursts, as when Charles Fenwick of CAIP wrote his executive secretary: "Why doesn't Roosevelt have a Catholic in the State Department? I could have stopped that war between Bolivia and Paraguay two years ago." Fenwick even lobbied to induce the president to appoint a CAIP man as part of the United States delegation to the Buenos Aires meeting of American states.[21]

After the war broke out in Europe, the Reverend James A. Magner of the Ibero-American Institute at Catholic University wrote of the dangers of ignoring the role the church could play south of the border. He specifically objected because only one Catholic was appointed to the newly-established Commission for American Republics under Nelson Rockefeller. "In fact," Magner complained, "the entire State Department as related to Latin America is deficient in Catholic personnel." Rejecting a religious test for office, Magner still felt that the president could pick men who would "appreciate and sympathize with the cultural and religious values of these people."[22]

Magner exaggerated. Roosevelt always knew of the special status of the Catholic church in Latin America and he understood how American Catholics could serve the cause of inter-American understanding. As early as April 1937 Assistant Secretary of State Sumner Welles had contacted Monsignor Ready of the NCWC about maintaining a constant information exchange on matters in Latin America, especially in Mexico. During the course of the next few years, both men promoted a clandestine collaboration of church and state. Roosevelt helped host a meeting of a Eucharistic Conference in the United States, to the delight of Latin American delegates. In turn, when Father Rosendo de Jesus Valenciano, a Costa Rican radical, published violently anti-American and pro-German pieces, copies of this literature were sent to Ready by the Department of State, with hints that religious pressure should be used to silence such a nuisance. Similarly, Welles remained in constant communication with the Apostolic Delegate, Ameleto Cicognani, regarding the Vatican's efforts to restore peace to Peru and Ecuador. Monsignor Ready frequently made use of State Department sources to check out rumors of anticlerical activities in Latin America.[23]

The administration by 1939 was making direct use of American Catholics in the conduct of Latin American diplomacy. Reverend Maurice Sheehy of Catholic University, an administration stalwart, had originated the collaboration by suggesting in a letter to the president that a mission of prominent Catholic prelates be sent to Latin America to sell the Good Neighbor Policy to native ecclesiastics. The Americans could also warn local priests against the dangers of totalitarianism. Sheehy thought they could help stem German penetration of South America. Roosevelt, Hull, and Welles all approved the idea of a clerical peace corps, and Bishop James H. Ryan of Omaha, Sheehy, and others soon shipped out. Welles publicly praised these prelates for promoting hemispheric defense.[24]

One wonders if Welles was serious about the Catholic contribution. Some clerical reports on Latin America appear naive. Reverend John F. O'Hara, president of Notre Dame University, had made a trip there, and his subsequent report to Roosevelt reached some rather surprising conclusions. After speaking at length with leading officials in at least three Latin American nations, including Venezuela, O'Hara found that all of these men favored "vigorous action" by the United States toward Mexico for its expropriation of American and British oil property. In the eyes of these men, forbearance by the United States in this case could only encourage communist agitation in other nations. As O'Hara explained to Roosevelt, Latin Americans liked the Yankee oil companies and thought they were doing much good. Such information clashed with Department of State estimates. The president replied to O'Hara that the goal of the administration was a peaceful and mutually acceptable resolution of the Mexican conundrum.[25]

Whatever the practical effect of this visit, American Catholics supported Roosevelt's Latin American strategy. Before the United States went to war, prominent Catholics such as the Reverend Dr. George Johnson and William F. Montavon of the NCWC, Charles Fenwick of CAIP, Dr. Martin P. McGuire of Catholic University, and George N. Shuster of Hunter College were working with Nelson Rockefeller's State Department office for the coordination of commercial and cultural relations. Catholic bishops from Latin America visited the United States to attend religious functions with the aid of money supplied by Rockefeller. Obviously, the administration was reaping benefits in its collaboration with American Catholics for the promotion of interhemispheric harmony.[26] But there were limits on the use of Catholicism to promote American foreign policy. When Myron Taylor, Roosevelt's special representative to the Vatican, hinted in 1940 that the pope could play a role in deterring fascist penetration of Latin America, he met a cold response. Cardinal Maglione, Vatican secretary of state, emphasized that Roosevelt's role was "paramount in South America."[27]

2

Catholic thinking on American foreign policy in the late 1930s reflected many different streams. One could argue that there was no unified Catholic position on foreign policy at this time. Pacifists, nationalists, disillusioned World War I crusaders, anglophobes, and League of Nation proponents, all found a home in American Catholicism. Although Catholics could reflect an enthusiastic willingness to promote international understanding between the United States and Latin America, they could also resist attempts to become involved with Europe. When Roosevelt turned away from this hemisphere and toward Europe, he found more Catholic leaders responding in a negative fashion. The main issue of 1939 became attempts by the administration to revise neutrality legislation that limited the role the United States could play in European affairs. The story of how the president and Congress combined to erect a legal facade of neutralism for the United States before 1939 has already been told in detail. In 1935, 1936, and 1937, a series of neutrality laws designed to avoid the supposed mistakes made by Woodrow Wilson was passed.[28] Reflecting a highly mechanistic view of how a nation becomes involved in war, these laws sought to erect automatic safeguards to prevent another crusade to Europe. Roosevelt consistently desired more discretionary power than Congress was willing to give him in the implementation of this legislation. Yet he did share the desire of Congress to avoid becoming involved in war through trade entanglements. Only the rush of events in Europe in 1938 and 1939 convinced him of the need for a more active collaboration by the United States to keep the peace.[29]

Many American Catholics shared the sentiments which produced the neutrality legislation of the 1930s. Pacifist and religious groups had been

instrumental in promoting the idea of neutrality. The hearings of Senator
Nye on munitions sales and foreign policy had fed this same enthusiasm.
American Catholics did not play an active role in the initial lobbying, but
they soon came to regard the system of neutrality laws with as much
reverence as the original sponsors. Even the *Commonweal,* usually sympathetic to presidential prerogative, liked the idea of legally repudiating
intervention and neutralizing American military power. The image of
World War I returned to frighten the editors of such Catholic papers as
the *Boston Pilot*, the *Monitor*, and the *Brooklyn Tablet*. They sought
justification in congressional limits on presidential initiative by reminding their readers of the Wilsonian experience. An arms embargo might be
just as effective as soldiers in influencing the course of world events. When
a cash-and-carry principle was incorporated into the embargo in 1937,
Catholics denounced it as a sell-out to Great Britain and proof that the
United States was still under British influence. Few Catholic neutralists,
however, viewed the laws as a means of complete separation from the
world. They saw the measures as an attempt to avoid the mistakes of
World War I rather than as a rejection of all international responsibility.[30] Furthermore, to such people, the laws were wholly consistent
with traditional notions of American neutrality. To those who complained
that cash-and-carry sacrificed freedom of the seas, one Catholic authority
replied that the notion "has not been discarded, but has been wrapped up
and put away for future use, like a precious heirloom that ought not be
altered with every changing whim."[31]

One small group of Catholics criticized the neutrality laws because
they prevented the United States from playing a more active role in
European politics. Their position was a mixture of two ideas: the United
States could not hope to remain insulated from international affairs, and
the Catholic church in the United States was in a position to promote
Christian ideals in American diplomacy. Like their coreligionists, these
men also wanted the United States to remain at peace, but they saw little
hope for that if war engulfed Europe. Not surprisingly, they had also supported the domestic program of the New Deal even after the first crisis of
the depression had been overcome. The group included George Cardinal
Mundelein, Bishop Robert Lucey, Father John Ryan, and representatives
magazines such as the *Commonweal* and organizations such as CAIP. Bishop
John J. Swint of Wheeling and Thomas C. O'Reilly of Scranton even went
far as to urge Roosevelt not to recognize the previous German annexation

Austria.[32] To Charles Fenwick and Father Ray McGowan of the NCWC,
American neutrality laws were defective and dangerous because they were
designed to avoid international responsibility and to reject collective security. The laws made no provisions for distinguishing between the aggressor
and the victim, an intolerable situation to Bishop Lucey and the *Commonweal*. Another weakness was the tendency of such measures to straitjacket
the president in his constitutional task of conducting foreign relations.
After Roosevelt's problems in 1937 over how to avoid applying the neutrality law in East Asia where it would help Japan, many of these liberal
Catholics dismissed such legislation as silly.[33]

Fenwick criticized the 1937 act in particular because it discriminated
in favor of the nations which controlled the sea, made no provisions for
the transshipment of goods from a neutral to a belligerent, would hurt
our trade, and rested on a "narrow conception of national interest." By
failing to distinguish between victim and agressor, the act aspired to moral
neutralism, a suicidal step in a shrinking world.[34] From a religious point
of view, the neutrality legislation argued for a narrow vision of world
events, a vision against which the life of the church stood as testimony.
The church taught the unity of men under God and the mutual responsibility of all for the peace of the world.

The president did not share the doctrinal universalism of Catholicism,
but he did want the support of Catholics as he sought to change the neutrality law. From late 1937 until the outbreak of war in September 1939,
he moved quietly toward a greater involvement in European affairs. The
traditional picture of an internationalist-minded president struggling
desperately to pull Congress and the public into the real world distorts
both Roosevelt's commitment to collective security and the public's dedi-
cation to isolationism. Yet on a number of occasions before Germany
invaded Poland, the president drew attention to the dangerous course of
events in Europe. In October 1937 he spoke of the need for peace-loving
nations to quarantine aggressors. One Catholic evaluation of this speech
revealed an apparent anti-English bias. The *Boston Pilot* complained that
Roosevelt was now adopting the line long advocated by Great Britain;
Irish anglophobes feared we would once again become the dupes of John
Bull. In the eyes of others, the president had just signaled the end of neutrality and the beginning of collective security.[35]

Yet Roosevelt also had reason to believe that American Catholics
supported his quarantine speech. The *Commonweal* endorsed the idea of

coordinated efforts by peace-loving nations to opposed aggressors. The executive committee of the CAIP sent letters to Roosevelt to publicly condemn the aggressors and use economic sanctions. In the long run, the CAIP really favored an international economic policy which would make wars unnecessary. Few Marxist thinkers had greater faith in the importance of economic factors.[36]

More important than the CAIP, George Cardinal Mundelein supported Roosevelt's program. As part of his trip to Chicago, the president made a point of dining at the cardinal's residence, a history-making event, according to the Catholic press. During what reporters referred to as a "social call," the president discussed a wide variety of topics with the cardinal, including the possible appointment of an American mission to the Vatican. But the real import of the meeting was twofold: Roosevelt wanted to show some appreciation for the repeated occasions when Mundelein had supported his domestic program, and he wanted to enlist the cardinal's support for the initiative outlined in the quarantine speech. Roosevelt explained that his plan did not call for military action but rather for the severance of all communication with the aggressor. Although the deterrent ability of such a policy seems questionable, Mundelein appeared enthusiastic and even urged the apostolic delegate to recommend Vatican endorsement of the program. The cardinal wrote Roosevelt that "you can count on us here to hold up your hands . . . in all your undertakings for the good of our own country and of humanity."[37]

The president reciprocated with special treatment for the cardinal. Mundelein planned to travel to Rome in 1938 to report on a recently completed Eucharistic Congress. The president took great pains to set up an elaborate reception for the cardinal by the American ambassador to Italy, William Phillips. As Roosevelt wrote Hull, he wanted "emphasis given to the fact that the American Ambassador is accompanying Cardinal Mundelein." After several gala receptions, Phillips explained the pageantry to the press as in keeping with the cardinal's unique position in America and because he was held in high regard in the Midwest and by the president. As we shall see in Chapter 4, Mundelein was also negotiating about a presidential mission to the Vatican. But Roosevelt, in a rather off-handed way, also wanted to make clear that special recognition was in store for those Catholic leaders who endorsed his foreign policy. The Department of State, however, could not but wonder at the cost of this endorsement. Officials were confronted with the task of answering many inquiries by irate Protestants who condemned such treatment as a violation of the Constitution's separation of church and state.[38]

Catholics also came to the president's aid when he called upon Congress to increase spending for the army and navy. With few exceptions, Catholics supported the call for preparedness. Only such extreme pacifists as the Catholic Worker group came out against defense appropriations, arguing that they were designed for war. Most Catholic leaders who favored defense spending, it is true, footnoted their endorsements with qualifications that the arms be used solely for the defense of our own shores.[39]

Roosevelt, however, was mistaken if he confused support for preparedness and endorsements by Mundelein, the CAIP, and a few liberals with the commitment of American Catholics to direct intervention in Europe. Catholics might support spending to strengthen our army and navy, but the limits of their commitment appeared in 1939 when Roosevelt attempted to revise the existing neutrality law by repealing its automatic arms embargo provision. Such a revision would have allowed the United States to aid victims of expected German aggression. New York Representative Sol Bloom sponsored the legislation in early 1939 as war clouds gathered across the Atlantic. The administration took heart about Catholic sentiment when Al Smith, long since disenchanted with the New Deal, publicly backed neutrality revision. Smith's recent visit to Europe had convinced him of the dangers to democracy and of the need for a strong American foreign policy.[40]

Al Smith was an exception in his support of neutrality revision. Traditional isolationist elements among American Catholics denounced it. Father Charles Coughlin of Detroit, a consistent opponent of American involvement in Europe, went on the radio to warn against a measure which would, in his view, give Roosevelt unlimited power to get the United States into war. In Coughlin's mind, passage of this measure would repudiate the tradition of Washington and help the forces of communism and British imperialism. Dorothy Day echoed these sentiments in a symposium on neutrality sponsored by the *Commonweal*. Rather than allow the president to sell arms to victims of aggression, Miss Day urged a total embargo and even nationalization of the munitions industry if necessary. Segments of the Catholic press opposed the Bloom bill largely on the grounds that it would allow the president to implement his known pro-English bias and thereby implicate the United States in a European war. No one sympathized with German aggression, but many felt that the entire affair was simply another round in a never-ending series of European struggles. Herbert Wright of Catholic University argued that it was silly to change a neutrality law which kept us out of both the Italo-Ethiopian war and the Spanish Civil War. Bishop John F. Noll of Fort Wayne warned against revision, hinting that it would surely get us into war. The hierarchy avoided any official statement, but one historian came away from his study impressed with Catholic opposition to the Bloom bill.[41] Such isolationist sentiment affected Congress and the bill died in committee.

The president decided to try another tack in mid-April 1939. He sent messages to the European dictators, asking them to guarantee the existing territorial boundaries of Europe. The administrative board of the NCWC, including all of the leading bishops of the nation, issued a statement at their Washington meeting commending Roosevelt's efforts to bring the disputants to the peace table. Father John Ryan and other Catholic internationalists were delighted at the bishops' message because it appeared to be a decided rebuke to the isolationist wing of Catholicism and to men such as Father Coughlin. But such an interpretation exaggerated the bishops' internationalism. No one could sensibly argue with a call for peace. As it was, elements of the Catholic press lamented the one-sidedness of the president's appeal and lectured Roosevelt on the futility of such grandstand gestures. The *Commonweal* and *America*, among others, felt that Roosevelt's call, which singled out Germany and Italy, ignored the "wrongs committed by post-war England and France." The *Buffalo Echo* predicted that history "will condemn President Roosevelt." To these Catholics, Roosevelt's statement had merely exacerbated an already tense situation. The appeal was in "bad taste." As the *Brooklyn Tablet* wrote, "all the dictatorship and all the imperialism should not lead to the shedding of one drop of American blood in distant lands."[42]

American Catholics, it appears, shared the sentiments of their fellow citizens in endorsing neutrality, distrusting Europe, and desiring to avoid another world war. Even their suspicion of communism was shared by most Americans. Cardinal Mundelein and a few others campaigned for collective security, but not even Roosevelt took an interest in such notions before 1939. Domestic priorities and the sordid evaluations of the committee of Senator Nye about how the United States got into World War I contributed to the neutralism of Catholics as it did to that of a majority of Americans.

Still, the picture appears too clear, the story too simple. Catholic views on foreign relations from 1936 to 1939 did not merely mirror those of their fellow citizens. Particular episodes during this period affected the church's view of international relations in a way which helped to distort the Catholic view of American neutrality.

NOTES

.1. In the organization of the Catholic church, the two basic "ranks" are *priest* and *bishop.* An *archbishop* is simply a bishop responsible for a larger diocese. The title of *cardinal* is an honorary designation which, while bestowing certain privileges, does not enlarge the basic sacramental powers of priest and bishop.

2. On the general subject of isolationism in the 1930s, see Selig Adler, *The Isolationist Impulse: Its 20th Century Reaction* (New York, 1957), p. 219; Manfred Jonas, *Isolationism in America, 1935-1941* (Ithaca, N.Y., 1966), pp. 1-90 passim; Donald F. Drummond, *The Passing of American Neutrality, 1937-1941* (Ann Arbor, Mich., 1955). On congressional isolationism, see Robert A. Divine, *The Illusion of Neutrality* (Chicago, 1962). On Roosevelt, see Robert A. Divine, *F.D.R. and World War II* (Baltimore, 1969). The most recent study of Roosevelt's diplomacy, which accepts most of the traditional findings, is that of James M. Burns, *Roosevelt: The Soldier of Freedom, 1940-1945* (New York, 1970).

3. The bishops often argued that in the absence of a moral directive, the Catholic's duty was to obey the state. See David O'Brien, *American Catholic Social Thought* (New York, 1968), for a discussion of the Catholic Worker Movement; *Commonweal,* October 23, 1936, p. 613; also important is Patricia McNeal, "Origins of the Catholic Peace Movement," *Review of Politics* 35 (July 1973), pp. 346-374. LaFarge quoted in Thomas F. Doyle, "To War or Not to War," *Catholic World* 150 (December 1939), p. 273.

4. Philip Hughes, "War and the Christian Tradition," *Catholic Mind* 37 (October 22, 1939), pp. 869-876; William F. Drummond, S. J., "Pacifism and War," *Catholic Mind* 38 (June 22, 1940), pp. 241-243, re-

jects the analogy of individual moral responsibility and the responsibility of the state. (For a discussion of the morality of war, see Chapter 6.) Doyle, "To War or Not to War," pp. 266-273.

5. D. H. McArthur, secretary to Nye, to Sweeney, July 8, 1936, Series 3-a, Box 7, Catholic Association for International Peace Mss., Marquette University Archives, Milwaukee (hereafter cited as CAIP Mss.); Sweeney to Norman McKenna, editor of *Christian Front*, June 25, 1936, Ser. 3-a, Box 2, CAIP Mss.; *Boston Pilot*, July 31, 1937, p. 12; *Commonweal*, November 3, 1939, p. 21; Sweeney to Rev. D. Ed. V. Stanford, January 27, 1937, Ser. 3-5, Box 2, CAIP Mss.; McNeal, "Origins of the Catholic Peace Movement," p. 359.

6. CAIP, *Obligations of Catholics to Promote Peace* (Washington, D.C., 1940); James M. Eagan, *The Pope's Peace Program and the United States* (Washington, D.C., 1940); CAIP, *America's Peace Aims* (Washington, D.C., 1941).

7. CAIP, *America's Peace Aims*.

8. *National Catholic Welfare Conference News Service:* March 20, 1937; July 19, 1937; July 29, 1940; April 25, 1938, on microfilm at The Catholic University of America, Washington, D.C. (hereafter cited as *NCWC News Service*); *Commonweal*: August 23, 1937, p. 404; October 24, 1937, p. 623; *Catholic World* 145 (April 1937), p. 109; CAIP Mss., Box 1 and Box 5; William Drummond, "Pacifism and War," p. 241ff.

9. John Stuart, Democratic National Campaign Committee, to Steve Early, October 23, 1936, in *Selected Materials from the Papers of Franklin D. Roosevelt Concerning Roman Catholic Church Matters,* microfilmed at the Roosevelt Library, Hyde Park, 3 reels, Louisiana State University Library (hereafter cited as *Sel. Materials*).

10. *Commonweal:* March 27, 1936, p. 605; November 20, 1936, p. 100; October 29, 1937, p. 16; March 11, 1938, p. 550; *Catholic Herald Citizen* (Milwaukee), November 21, 1936, p. 1; *NCWC News Service,* April 26, 193

11. *Commonweal*: February 17, 1939, p. 452; June 2, 1939, p. 158; *NCWC News Service*, April 8, 1938; *Catholic Messenger*, April 28, 1938, p. 10; Hall's quote in *New York Times,* May 22, 1938, p. 8; see also *Catholic World* 147 (July 1938), pp. 492-493; Catholic Daughter's quote in *Catholic World* 151 (September 1940), p. 750; Corrigan quote in *Catholic World* 152 (December 1940), p. 356.

12. *Catholic World* 142 (February 1936), pp. 513-523; ibid., 149 (May 1939), p. 134; *Commonweal*, May 26, 1939, p. 131; *Brooklyn Tablet*,

April 9, 1938, p. 11; *Catholic Transcript*, May 15, 1941, p. 1; *Catholic Herald Citizen*, December 14, 1940, p. 1.

13. James Shenton, "The Coughlin Movement and the New Deal," *Political Science Quarterly* 78 (1958), p. 369; *The Monitor* (San Francisco), April 6, 1940, p. 14; Rev. Ralph L. Harps to Frank Walker, January 1, 1936, General File, 1936, Frank Walker Papers, University of Notre Dame Archives; Charles C. Tansill, "What Price War?" *Catholic Mind* 38 (June 8, 1940), pp. 213-220; *Catholic Herald Citizen,* July 15, 1939, p. 5.

14. Patrick J. O'Shea to John J. O'Connor, June 26, 1939, Neutrality File, John J. O'Connor Mss., Lilly Library, Bloomington, Indiana; *NCWC News Service,* July 24, 1937; the Clerical Reservists of Christ the King to Rev. John A. Ryan, March 27, 1939, John A. Ryan Papers, Catholic University of America Archives; Rev. Edwin Ryan, "Peace in America," *Catholic Mind* 38 (July 8, 1940), pp. 248-253. For a fuller discussion of the origins and substance of Catholic anticommunism, see Chapter 5.

15. J. O. O'Gara, "The Catholic Isolationists," *Catholicism in America: A Series of Articles from the Commonweal*, edited by J. O'Gara (New York, 1954), p. 113; *Boston Pilot*, April 22, 1939, p. 1; *Brooklyn Tablet*, April 29, 1939, p. 2; *Extension Magazine*, June 1936, p. 19.

16. Charles G. Fenwick to Sweeney, December 6, 1936; Schuler to Hierarchy, June 22, 1938; Elizabeth Duncan to Schuler, February 7, 1938; Schuler to Duncan, January 30, 1939, Ser. 5, Box 1 and Ser. 3-a, Box 5, CAIP Mss. The bishops who did reply included the following: Joseph E. Schrembs of Cleveland, Ohio; Karl J. Alter of Toledo, Ohio; Francis C. Kelley of Oklahoma City, Oklahoma; James E. Kearney of Rochester, New York; Peter L. Ireton of Richmond, Virginia; Joseph M. Gilmore of Helena, Montana; James A. Griffin of Springfield, Illinois; Henry Althoff of Belleville, Illinois; John F. Noll of Fort Wayne, Indiana; James H. Ryan of Omaha, Nebraska; McNicholas, official letter, February 23, 1938, CAIP Mss.

17. The following bishops publicly supported Mundelein's statement: Karl Alter of Toledo, Ohio; John G. Murray of St. Paul, Minnesota; Aloysius J. Muench of Fargo, North Dakota; Joseph F. Busch of St. Cloud, Minnesota; Francis M. Kelly of Winona, Minnesota; Vincent Wehrle of Bismarck, North Dakota; John J. Lawler of Rapid City, South Dakota; Alexander McGavick of LaCrosse, Wisconsin; Henry P. Rohlman of Davenport, Iowa; Jules B. Jeanmard of Lafayette, Iowa; Francis C. Kelley of Oklahoma City, Oklahoma; Joseph P. Lynch of Dallas, Texas;

John J. Swint of Wheeling, West Virginia. One notable quality of this list is the presence on it of many leaders of German Catholic areas. *NCWC News Service*, May 22, 1937. Mundelein quoted in Camille Cianfarra, *The Vatican and the War* (New York, 1944), p. 101.

18. *NCWC News Service,* July 17, 1937; *New York Times,* May 29, 1937.

19. Martin H. Carmody to Roosevelt, October 17, 1938, reprinted in *Co umbia* (December 1938), p. 9; Memo from Roosevelt to Sumner Welles, D cember 8, 1938, *Sel. Materials; NCWC News Service:* April 5, 1937; June 1937; August 7, 1937; *Denver Catholic Register,* November 17, 1938, p. 4 Shenton, "The Coughlin Movement and The New Deal," p. 371; *Catholic Action,* January 1939, p. 12; *New York Times,* October 20, 1938.

20. Ready quoted in *NCWC News Service,* February 25, 1941; see also January 27, 1941; April 21, 1941; *Commonweal,* April 29, 1938, p. 2.

21. Chavez quoted in *NCWC News Service,* March 15, 1940; Thorning quoted in ibid., August 25, 1941; *Catholic Action,* November 1940, p.5; *NCWC News Service,* October 29, 1940; Fenwick to Sweeney, January 26, 1935, CAIP Mss., Ser. 3-a, Box 5; for more on this issue see also *NCWC News Service,* March 15, 1940 and Roosevelt to Fenwick, April 28, 1936, in Edgar P. Nixon, editor, *Franklin D. Roosevelt and Foreign Affairs,* 3 vols. (Cambridge, 1969), vol. 3, pp. 283-284.

22. *NCWC News Service,* November 22, 1940.

23. Sumner Welles to Mr. Reed, April 28, 1937, State Department File FW 812.404/1981, National Archives (hereafter cited as SDF); Monsignor Ready to Roosevelt, December 22, 1938, SDF 811.001 Roosevelt, FD/6159; Memo of conversation between Ready, Duggan, and Ray, October 4, 1940, SDF 710 Consultation (2)/688; Ready to Welles, July 30, 1941, SDF 722.2315/2005. During the earlier anticlerical problem in Mexico, Father Parsons had worked with Secretary of State Hull to stop Catholic student demonstrations in the Latin capitals (Hull to Josephus Daniels, May 3, 1937, Box 34, Cordell Hull Manuscript, Library of Congress

24. Rev. Maurice S. Sheehy to Roosevelt, December 3, 1938, *Sel. Material; NCWC News Service,* June 13, 1941.

25. O'Hara to Roosevelt, July 6, 1939; Roosevelt to O'Hara, Official File, 146, Mexico 1933-1940, Box 1, Franklin D. Roosevelt Papers, Hyde Park, New York.

26. Laurence Duggan to Sumner Welles, August 27, 1941, SDF 811.404/270; *NCWC News Service,* September 1, 1941.

27. Taylor to Roosevelt, March 15, 1940, SDF 500.A21/154.

28. The Neutrality Acts which were passed and amended in 1935, 1936, and 1937 contained the following principles:

The First Neutrality Act (August 31, 1935) authorized the president to proclaim a state of war existed, to prohibit export of arms and munitions to all belligerents, and to forbid United States citizens to travel in belligerent ships except at their own risk.

The Second Neutrality Act (February 27, 1936) extended the first, adding an embargo on loans to belligerents and permitting the president to decide when a state of war existed.

The Third Neutrality Act (May 1, 1937) went into effect when the president proclaimed a state of war; it prohibited export of arms and munitions and loans to belligerents but gave the president power to put export of other goods on a cash-and-carry basis—hard currency and provide your own transportation.

29. For a similar interpretation, see the following: Robert A. Divine, *The Reluctant Belligerent: American Entry into World War II* (New York, 1965); William L. Langer and S. Everett Gleason, *The Challenge to Isolation* (New York, 1952); William L. Langer and S. Everett Gleason, *The Undeclared War, 1940-1941* (New York, 1953); Robert A. Divine, *Roosevelt and World War II* (Baltimore, 1969).

30. Robert A. Divine, *The Illusion of Neutrality* (Chicago, 1962), p. 119; *Extension Magazine,* March 1937, p. 19; *Boston Pilot,* January 7, 1939, p. 4; *Commonweal:* September 6, 1937, p. 435; January 17, 1936, p. 310; March 3, 1939, p. 505; *Columbia,* November 1937, p. 526; *Brooklyn Tablet,* May 14, 1938, p. 1; *Monitor,* January 11, 1936, p. 12.

31. William G. Downey, "American Neutrality, Past and Present," *Catholic World* 145 (May 1937), p. 147.

32. David O'Brien, "American Catholic Social Thought in the 1930s," (Ph.D. thesis, University of Rochester, 1965), p. 123; *Catholic Herald Citizen,* October 16, 1937, p. 9; *Catholic Action,* November 1937, p. 18; *NCWC News Service,* April 2, 1938.

33. Bishop Robert F. Lucey to Schuler, February 28, 1938, Ser. 5, Box 1, CAIP Mss.; *NCWC News Service*: October 4, 1937; October 24, 1937; *Commonweal*: March 19, 1937, p. 583; January 7, 1938, p. 281; *America,* September 14, 1935, p. 529; *Davenport Catholic Messenger,* November 26, 1936, p. 4.

34. Memo on Neutrality Act by C. G. Fenwick, September 8, 1937, CAIP Mss.

35. *Boston Pilot*, October 16, 1937, p. 4; *Extension Magazine*, December 1937, p. 18; *NCWC News Service,* October 11, 1937. For the drafting of this speech and reactions to it, see especially Dorothy Borg, "Notes on Roosevelt's 'Quarantine' Speech," *Political Science Quarterly* 72 (September 1957), pp. 405-433.

36. *Commonweal,* October 14, 1937, p. 577; Fenwick to Roosevelt, November 1, 1937, CAIP Mss.

37. *NCWC News Service*, October 5, 1937; Mundelein to Cicognani, October 6, 1937, Roosevelt Papers; Mundelein to Roosevelt, October 6, 1937, SDF 711.00.

38. Cordell Hull to Ambassador Phillips, November 1, 1938, Phillips to Hull, November 4, 1938, Memo by Phillips, November 10, 1938, in SDF 032 Mundelein, Cardinal/14. William Phillips, *Ventures in Diplomacy* (Boston, 1952), p. 222, later explained the reception as a demonstration, for Germany and Italy, of American regard for religion.

39. *Catholic Worker* and *Brooklyn Tablet* were the two most outspoken opponents of defense spending at this time. See *Commonweal*: January 20, 1939, p. 356; January 27, 1939, p. 381; *Brooklyn Tablet*, July 23, 1938, p. 8.

40. Oscar Handlin, *Al Smith and His America* (Boston, 1958), p. 184.

41. Divine, *The Illusion of Neutrality*, p. 253; *Commonweal*, July 14, 1939, p. 299; for symposium see *Commonweal*, February 17, 1939, p. 454; also June 23, 1939, p. 228; June 30, 1939, p. 246; Herbert Wright, "The Bloom 'Neutrality' Bill," *Commonweal*, July 7, 1939, pp. 268-270; *Boston Pilot*: June 24, 1939, p. 4; July 15, 1939; *Brooklyn Tablet*, July 29, 1939, in *Sel. Material; Catholic Transcript,* April 6, 1939, p. 4; for Noll's comments see *Brooklyn Tablet,* April 1, 1939, p. 3.

42. Raphael M. Huber, editor, *Our Bishops Speak: National Pastorals and Annual Statements of the Hierarchy of the United States, 1919-1951* (Milwaukee, 1952), p. 322; John A. Ryan to Honorable Joseph A. Conry, April 23, 1939, Ryan Papers; *Commonweal*: May 26, 1939, p. 131; June 23, 1939, p. 237; William E. Leuchtenburg, *Franklin D. Roosevelt and the New Deal, 1932-1940* (New York, 1963), p. 289; *Sign*, May 1939, pp. 580-581; *Catholic Herald Citizen*, April 22, 1939, p. 7; *Brooklyn Tablet*, April 22, 1939, p. 11.

2

THE SPANISH
CIVIL WAR

General Francisco Franco launched his revolt against the republican government of Spain on July 17, 1936. Rooted in Spanish history, in complex factors reflecting both Spanish character and religious culture, and in recent actions of the government, the revolt led to a bloody war and the eventual triumph of Franco's forces in 1939. By then it had become a symbol and myth for Americans and Europeans alike. Some saw the struggle as the first test between democracy and fascism. To others, it represented a duel between the anti-God forces of communism and the forces of Christian Europe. In the United States, the war became a rallying point for both liberals and Roman Catholics. The American intellectual, disillusioned by World War I, had washed his hands of the dirty power politics of Europe, but now found a new commitment to foreign affairs through an ideological interpretation of the Spanish conflict. Roman Catholics also saw the war in an ideological cast, although they viewed it in different terms from those of the average liberal. Simultaneously, the Roosevelt administration faced the practical task of formulating a foreign policy satisfying to most

Americans, who had little interest in what was taking place in Spain, or Europe, for that matter. As Roosevelt's policy was being implemented, the Spanish Civil War affected how American Catholics viewed the role of the United States in the world and added to the president's problem of erecting a consistent international policy.

1

The Roosevelt administration had no way of foreseeing how the civil war would appeal to Americans. In 1936 Hull and Roosevelt tried to respond to a crisis in international affairs which had dangerous potential for an already tottering European equilibrium. England and France soon took the lead in the formation of a Non-Intervention Committee to prevent the spread of the Spanish insanity. In subsequent months, Hull made every effort to cooperate unofficially with the Non-Intervention Committee. The administration informed Ambassador Claude Bowers in Madrid in August 1936 that the United States would follow its "well-established policy of non-interference with internal affairs in other countries either in time of peace or in the event of civil strife. This government will . . . scrupulously refrain from any interference whatsoever in the unfortunate Spanish situation." Undoubtedly, the message continued, American citizens would support this policy.[1] When Uruguay asked the Department of State to join in a Pan-American effort to conciliate the factions in Spain, Acting Secretary of State Williams Phillips replied that "this country is committed to the principle of non-interference in the internal affairs of other countries."[2]

President Roosevelt knew that such a policy of non-interference displeased some Americans. But he refused to be dragged into the debate over the fascism of Franco or the communism of the republic. Privately, in a September 1936 letter to Ambassador Claude Bowers, he dismissed as a distortion attempts to portray the Madrid government as infested with communists. Publicly, on December 23, 1936, the United States signed the Declaration of Buenos Aires, promising never to intervene in the affairs of other American nations. Roosevelt and Hull both attended the Argentine conference, and the declaration reflected a mood of isolation or commitment to domestic priorities which dominated American foreign policy all during the 1930s. Their reaction to the Spanish affair fit neatly into the general course of New Deal diplomacy.[3]

Despite these noble intentions to remain disengaged from Spain, by the end of the year the war forced a decision upon the administration. The existing neutrality law of the United States prohibited the export of arms to belligerents, but it made no mention of a civil war. American arms manufacturers, eager to turn a profit, correctly assumed that no legal barrier existed to supplying the conflicting forces in Spain. Roosevelt and Hull attempted to overcome this legal oversight by adopting a policy greatly favored by American diplomats moral suasion. Such a procedure had been tried earlier during the Italo-Ethiopian conflict, with mixed results. As Roosevelt explained to reporters on December 29, 1936, the State Department was requesting that American businesses attempting to send munitions to belligerents in Spain refrain from doing so because "it was contrary to the Government policy, and because it was endangering . . . our desire to be neutral in this unfortunate happening."[4] The president's hand of moral platitudes was already being called. The day before, an American businessman, Robert Cuse, had rejected the moral embargo, requested a license to send aircraft parts to the Loyalists, and was now loading his ship in New York. Roosevelt emphasized to reporters that this capricious action by one citizen pointed out the need for more executive authority in the implementation of the neutrality acts.[5]

Hoping to forestall Cuse's intent, the administration requested a joint resolution from Congress making it "unlawful to export arms, ammunition, or implements of war from any place in the United States . . . to Spain or to any foreign country for transshipment to Spain." Congress stood ready and anxious to patch up its earlier work. Isolationist and noninterventionist sentiment quickly fell in line behind Senator Key Pittman, chairman of the Foreign Relations Committee, who introduced the appropriate resolution on January 6. When someone objected that such a step seemed to put Franco on a par with the Loyalists, Pittman patiently explained that there were two groups fighting in Spain and that the rebels controlled as many ports as the Loyalists. He emphasized that his colleagues should "not . . . think of either of the opposing forces in Spain but think of our peace and our own country." To Pittman, both sides in Spain represented "foreign theories of government."[6] The vote demonstrated that the enthusiasm for isolationism which had produced two earlier neutrality acts remained strong. Seldom has a congressional action received such unanimous support. In the House, the embargo was approved by a vote of 406 to 1; in the Senate, by a vote of 81 to 0. Ironically, the act had no effect on Cuse's shipment, which sailed early out of New York harbor and eventually fell into the hands of Franco. No matter. The measure had revealed the sentiments of the administration toward Spain and the vote had indicated that these notions were fully endorsed by Congress.

Later the same year, when Congress and the administration embarked upon a general revision of the 1936 neutrality act, they made sure to include civil wars. The new law, passed on May 1, 1937, retained the president's power to proclaim the existence of a state of war. The proclamation of war would forbid Americans from exporting arms and munitions to a belligerent, from loaning money to a belligerent, and from traveling on a ship that was under the flag of a belligerent. Another clause in the act permitted the president to allow the sale of material other than munitions on a cash-and-carry basis. Without a moment's delay, Roosevelt applied the new law to the Spanish Civil War. In his proclamation, the president stated that "a state of civil strife unhappily exists in Spain and that such civil strife is of a magnitude and is being conducted under such conditions that the export of arms . . . from the United States . . . would threaten and endanger the peace of the United States." He admonished all Americans "to abstain from every violation of the provisions of the joint resolution of Congress." The unofficial administration embargo, inaugurated in August 1936, had grown into federal law in 1937.[7]

The president was being consistent in his foreign policy. As Secretary of State Hull explained, the United States would stay out of Spain, support the European policy of nonintervention, and avoid being dragged into any war.[8] Roosevelt was pleased with this Spanish policy. In July 1937 he boasted that the United States has "honestly maintained not only the letter but the spirit of neutrality," yet is always ready to "render any service to which both sides can agree, looking toward an end of the armed conflict." Obviously, the United States deplored all violations of world peace, but [we] "cannot at this time see [our] way clear to offer mediation because of the certainty that it would be rejected."[9]

This course of nonintervention had wide approval in Congress and seemed best tailored to the public's and Roosevelt's mutual desire to deal with domestic problems rather than become involved in European intrigues.

As the weeks went by, however, an articulate number of Americans began to disagree with this policy. The Spanish Civil War began to change American minds. As German and Italian guns, tanks, and men poured into Spain to aid Franco's rebellion, the conflict assumed the character of an ideological struggle to many liberals. By 1937 the brutal nature of Nazi rule in Germany stood naked to the world. Hitler's ambitions in Europe were more apparent. Liberals recalled that the Spanish Republic had tried to bring democracy to that autocratic, church-dominated nation. True, it was difficult to determine what most Spaniards wanted in the form of a government because of their multiparty system and widespread electoral corruption. But the Popular Front forces of the Left had won control of the government before Franco's rebellion. His uprising seemed to represent another attempt by fascist thugs to crush the voice of the people. Roosevelt soon sensed dissatisfaction with his embargo policy. In Madrid, Ambassador Claude Bowers, an old Jeffersonian liberal, interpreted the war according to American political categories and now argued for the lifting of the embargo. Members of the president's cabinet, especially Secretary of the Interior Harold Ickes, felt the same way. American volunteers to fight for the Loyalists increased in number.[10]

At the same time, the president also learned that American Catholics had a different commitment in the civil war. Pro-Franco sympathy among American Catholics manifested itself on so many occasions that observers assumed the church had blessed the revolt. As Reverend George B. Ford, the liberal and widely respected Catholic chaplain at Columbia University, expressed it, "The official Catholic Mind in this country during the Civil War was pro-Franco."[11] In using the phrase "official Catholic Mind," Reverend Ford no doubt was referring to the 82 members of the American hierarchy who met in Washington in late November 1937. The bishops sent a letter to the Spanish hierarchy, expressing sympathy and admiration. They carefully included in their statement a pledge of loyalty to the democratic principles of the United States, but readers had no problem deciding where these bishops stood. In the first few months after the rebellion, Catholic news sources headlined atrocities by the Loyalists. The news service of the National Catholic Welfare Conference devoted page after page of copy to the raping of nuns, the shooting of bishops, and the burning of churches. Because the NCWC was the major source of international news for many diocesan weeklies, a decidedly anti-Loyalist point of view became established in many Catholic households.[12]

Even the *Commonweal*, which would later adopt neutrality, could print that while peace for Spain was a noble objective, "the victory of the Nationalists' cause is a prerequisite." The *NCWC News Service, America,* and the *Commonweal* agreed that secular reports from Spain were untrustworthy; American Catholics should believe only what they read in Catholic sources. Organizations such as the National Catholic Alumni Federation, the National Council of Catholic Women, and the National Council of Catholic Men never tired of passing resolutions at their annual conventions commending the Nationalists' cause. Reverend Joseph Thorning of Mount Saint Mary's College in Maryland became so enthusiastic a supporter of Franco that he was later decorated by the Spanish government. Michael Williams of the *Commonweal* was scarcely less zealous in his support. Reverend Ford was right. Opinion-makers in the church were definitely pro-Nationalists.[13] But all American Catholics did not agree about Spain, at least not in December 1938. A Gallup Poll appeared which revealed that some 42 percent of American Catholics favored the Loyalist side and 58 percent supported Franco. The same poll indicated that 83 percent of American Protestants were pro-Loyalists with only 17 percent for Franco.[14]

No division existed, however, as to how the United States should react to the war in Spain. Catholic bishops, journals, and organizations were virtually unanimous in their opinion that the United States should stay out. During 1938 and 1939, a few Catholic sources, such as the *Common weal* and the *Catholic Worker*, challenged the pro-Franco bias of many fellow Catholics, but even these liberals disapproved of any involvement by the United States. They took issue over the virtues of Franco and his cause, not over the official neutrality adopted by the United States govern ment. Regarding this policy, American Catholic spokesmen stood united with the mass of their coreligionists. As the editor of the *Commonweal* wrote in January 1937, it was imperative to stop American participation in the Spanish war because of the grave consequences it might provoke.

The *Brooklyn Tablet* approved of this decision of "a plague on both houses" in Spain.[15] In this sense, Catholics shared the general desire for noninvolvement which characterized the 1930s.

2

Despite their desire to keep the United States uninvolved, American Catholics could not avoid feeling strongly about events in Spain. The war had a personal meaning to many Catholics. Any rapid social and political change in Spain had to involve the church. Religion in Spain was not isolated from the arena of public debate, but rather intrinsic to every serious question of national destiny. When Spanish republicans (Loyalists) attempted to change the direction of the nation's development, to modernize Spain, they could not avoid the religious question—what was the role of the church in society and education? Similarly, when mere debate proved inadequate to solve the nation's problems, religious leaders in Spain inevitably became both targets and heroes in the ensuing battle. Spanish anticlericalism was almost endemic. But few American Catholics were prepared for the ferocity of blood-letting that came before and after the Franco uprising. The actual number of clerical victims during the war has been estimated at 8,291 (12 bishops, 283 nuns, 5,255 priests, 2,492 monks, and 249 novices).[16] Whatever the final number or justification, such alleged brutality shocked American Catholics.

Not unnaturally, they reacted to anticlericalism in Spain in terms of their religious experience in the United States. In a perverse sort of way, American Catholics were overly sensitive about anticlericalism because of the relative lack of such persecution and religious politicization in this country. In Spain, leaders on both sides recognized that the church could not remain neutral in the conflict and therefore they expected anticlericalism. Indeed, the Spanish hierarchy soon came openly into the Franco (Nationalist) camp. But American Catholics were different. Many of them apparently wanted both sides in Spain to respect the position guaranteed the church by the First Amendment of the American constitution. As the national officers of the Catholic Daughters of America put it in a telegram to Secretary of State Hull, the United States should officially protest against religious persecution in Spain: "It is man's inalienable right to worship God in any manner he may choose and we feel that Catholics should not be oppressed because of their religious practice. They should be extended the same religious freedom that we in our country grant to all denominations."[17]

Seen in this perspective, American Catholic protest over clerical persec tion in Spain was not only normal but in keeping with the liberal tradition of religious freedom. When reports arrived about the cold-blooded murde of Florentiono Asensio, a Spanish bishop of Aragon, Catholics in America were appalled. Not expecting a blood bath, they could not understand wh so many priests and nuns, who had the character of noncombatants, shou also be killed. This dimension of the war shaped the American Catholic response. They found statements by American writers in opposition to Franco filled with abstract cliches about democracy and fascism but containing not a word of the priests and nuns killed. Liberal Catholics such a Father John Ryan emphasized the killing of religious when explaining wh they were either neutral or supporters of Franco.[18]

The apparent insensitivity to the killing of religious made American Catholics bitter about Protestant reaction to the Spanish Civil War. In August 1937 the Spanish hierarchy addressed a pastoral letter to the worl on why the rebellion against the republic had been necessary. Reprinted i the *New York Times*, the document drew a rejoinder on October 4 from 150 leaders of the Protestant churches in the United States who disputed the hierarchy's attempts to justify revolution against a legal government. Although justification of revolution had an honored place in Catholic political theory and most prominently in the writings of the Spanish Jesu Francisco Suarez, American Catholics did not bother to debate the idea. Rather, Monsignor Michael J. Ready of the NCWC accused the Protestant ministers of attacking a straw man. The Catholic rebuttal came one week later, bearing the signatures of 175 prominent American priests and laym who pointedly asked whether their Protestant brethren really supported a government which made a practice of persecuting Christians.[19] Some scholars later wrote that the number of religious who were murdered was exaggerated and that the church in Spain was a political institution, but this reasoning rang hollow next to the grim story of a raped nun. America Catholics could not comprehend sympathy for such a crowd of thugs.

Furthermore, Catholics associated clerical persecution with the advance of international communism. Since communists were members of the Republican government and Soviet aid soon flowed into Spain

in an attempt to match the aid Franco received from Hitler and Mussolini, it became simple for American Catholics to view the conflict in
terms of a "Red menace." Archbishop McNicholas told an annual convention of the Knights of Columbus that the killing of 300,000 men and
women in Spain for their religious faith made neutrality impossible for
American Catholics. To Archbishop McNicholas, to Bishop John F. Noll,
to Monsignor Ready, to Father Edward L. Curran, and others, these
killings were deliberate plans of atheistic communists. Those who called
for neutrality toward Spain, such as the recently reshuffled editorial
staff of the *Commonweal,* were playing into the hands of the Reds.[20]

The pieces of the puzzle fell together conveniently for American
Catholics. Communist designs for world conquest were well-known.
Equally well-known was the pagan hatred of religion within the Red
camp. Now, in Spain, Marxist imperialism was manifesting itself by
attacking the religious heart of the Spanish people. Father John Ryan
wrote that the coming struggle for mastery of the world would be between communism and democracy. If Catholic Spain fell, warned Monsignor Martin Gillet, master general of the Dominicans, it would become
a pivot for communism. From cardinal to priest, the issue of communism
became entangled with that of clerical persecution as the focus for
Catholic interpretations of the war.[21] No longer was the civil war a political struggle between two traditional factions in Spanish history. It had
become, in the eyes of American Catholics, a clash between militant
atheists and Christians. As Archbishop McNicholas said in his Easter sermon in April 1938, the issue in Spain was "God or anti-God." Hillaire
Belloc, noted English author, told a Fordham University audience in
March 1937 that the battle in Spain was for the "life or death of Christianity." His sentiments were echoed by Father Robert Gannon, president of the university.[22]

The trouble with this Catholic interpretation was that it put Franco
on the side of God and Christianity. Some priests, such as Wilfrid Parsons and F. A. Talbot, thought the Caudillo fit such a role. One monsignor even felt that a victorious Franco would help Catholic missions.
Archbishop Joseph Schrembs of Cleveland saw Franco as another George
Washington.[23] A close reading of these pro-Franco comments supports
the observation of critics that American Catholics did not really know
much about Franco or his movement. But neither did other Americans

or Europeans. Franco's fight against the killers of priests and nuns was enough endorsement for most American Catholics. Others, such as Father Ryan and Father Gannon, admitted the sordidness of Franco's fight but still supported him as the lesser of two evils. To Ryan, fascism was not so serious a danger to democracy as communism. For America's sake he would support a fascist Franco over a Red Spain.[24]

American Catholic statements on the civil war reveal only a very vague notion of Spanish history and of the events leading up to the revolution in the 1930s. Furthermore, the amount of literature which emphasized the communist threat in Spain seems out of proportion to the actual presence of communists in the republican government. Indeed, Catholic concern with the advance of atheistic communism at times bordered on the neurotic. This concern could only distort the chances for a rational interpretation of what was happening in Spain. It led inevitably to a simplistic world view in which the forces of justice were ranged against the forces of evil. In endorsing Franco, American Catholics were deluding themselves into believing that his victory would benefit the United States by preventing communist encroachment.[25]

But despite these problems, Catholic reaction to the civil war does not appear so unreasonable when examined within its historical context. American Catholics were certainly not alone in their ignorance of Spanish history. One could argue that supporters of an immediate disestablishment of the Spanish church, which was attempted by the republican government, were manifesting an antihistorical bias. All Americans, including defenders of the Spanish republic, were ignorant of Spanish history. Attitudes toward the conflict were seldom decided by a study of history. Reductionism appeared on both sides. Was the Catholic vision of Loyalist-communist (i.e., atheist) versus nationalist-Christian any more naive than the simplistic categories of Loyalist-democratic versus nationalist-fascist established by American journalists? Surely too much was made of communist penetration into Spain. But perhaps too little was made of clerical persecutions. Liberals were equally naive about communism both in Spain and in Russia during the 1930s. The purge trials and the German pact with Russia were yet to come. All sides in America had simple views of the war. Deeply committed to a cause for subjective reasons, every side painted its enemies with a broad brush and neglected distinctions. Finally, the Catholic endorsement of Franco in ignorance of his nature and objectives was really a commentary on their Americanism. Unable to fathom what the Spanish generals were about but needing some sort of rationale to protest anticlericalism and communism, American Catholics eventually fell back on the simple equation that if Franco was for religious freedom (which he was not), and against communism (which he was), he must be a good American.

3

With cloudy reasoning and confused motives, American Catholics during 1937 and 1938 became increasingly active on a whole range of issues dealing with Spain. Gradually, this activism involved them in the political problem of United States neutrality. Many Catholics at first became interested in Spain for nonpolitical, humanitarian reasons. In early 1937 Bishop John Molloy of Brooklyn announced the formation of the Spanish Relief Fund. This organization was to collect contributions to help the injured and impoverished in Spain. Money collected by the *Brooklyn Tablet* would be sent to the Spanish hierarchy for distribution. Within two weeks only $11,000 had been collected. As more and more Catholic leaders joined in endorsing the Spanish fund, it climbed to almost $40,000, still a disappointing total. A mass meeting was called for May 19, 1937, to reorganize the entire effort on a broader basis. The resulting American Committee for Spanish Relief (ACSR) launched a new collection campaign. The ACSR held a mass meeting in Madison Square Garden and heard such speakers as E. Allison Peers, Michael Williams, and Father Edward L. Curran explain the need for assistance to Spain. By 1938 the Relief Fund was on a national basis with affiliates in some 30 dioceses. Funds collected were sent to Cardinal Goma y Tomas, primate of Spain. Although aid for all victims of the conflict remained the purpose, critics complained that Cardinal Tomas looked upon Franco as the defender of Christian civilization.[26]

Humanitarianism became the pawn of ideology. The shift was discernable in American Catholic reaction to a proposal to send some 2,000 Basque children, refugees of the Spanish fighting, to the United States for care. During the vicious fighting in the Basque provinces the children had been evacuated to various countries, including England and France. In the United States a Board of Guardians was formed and supported by

Mrs. Eleanor Roosevelt. The White House soon learned, however, of
serious Catholic opposition to bringing the children into the United
States. Cardinal O'Connell of Boston suspected that innocent children
might be used for communist propaganda purposes and to arouse sentiment for one side in the war. After all, the Basques were Catholics who
fought violently against Franco's forces. Cardinal O'Connell felt that the
children could be better cared for in areas where the culture was similar,
particularly the Basque provinces of southern France. A formidable
array of political muscle from the Bay State, including Senators David
Walsh and Henry Cabot Lodge and Representative John McCormack,
supported the cardinal's position. When other leaders of Catholic opinion
also opposed admittance of the children, Roosevelt found himself in
something of a quandary.

In June 1937 Roosevelt sought escape from his dilemma by suggesting
to the Board of Guardians that they use the services of a Catholic welfare
society to bring the children to the United States. Since this was an unlikely development, he was no doubt relieved to have an official opinion
from Sumner Welles in the Department of State that immigration laws
prohibited entrance to the children. In Welles's opinion, which Eleanor
Roosevelt shared, it would be best for the Basques to stay closer to their
original home so that they could be reunited with their families as soon
as the war ended. The subject faded from the news, but it served to remind
the president of the special sensitivity of Catholics to events in Spain.[27]

An even more impressive display of Catholic sensitivity and political
power occurred on January 30, 1938. Some sixty members of Congress
issued a statement which carried their greetings to and expressed their
sympathy for the Spanish *Cortez* (Legislature) as a stirring example to
the world in its fight to preserve democratic institutions. The statement
was a routine petition of the sort which constantly floods congressional
halls. This time, an enterprising group of liberals succeeded in garnering
the signatures of their colleagues for what appeared to be an innocuous
greeting from one legislative body to another. To Catholics, however, it
seemed that Congress had taken sides in the civil war, despite the official
neutrality of the administration. They rose in protest.

The next day, January 31, Monsignor Ready of the NCWC issued a
press statement. He was amazed that "a government which had absolutely
proscribed the exercise of religion" could be praised as an inspiration by

American congressmen. Bishop James E. Walsh denounced this novel description of a government responsible for the massacre of nuns and priests. The National Catholic Alumni Federation deplored the association of America with such forces of destruction. Across the country Catholic spokesmen wrote congressmen and senators. Some hinted that names in the initial statement had been forged. Others reminded their senators of the Logan Act, which prohibited private interference with foreign policy. Senator David Walsh of Massachusetts issued a public statement on February 2, 1938, explaining the "unfortunate affair" as the result of congressional ignorance and carelessness. What really worried Walsh was that congressmen were so insensitive to domestic Catholic opinion that they could sign such statements. As he put it, "Is it that the Catholic group in this country is believed to be so divided, unorganized and indifferent that they are incapable of recognizing an insult or resenting vigorously attacks upon their coreligionists?" Any politician with such a notion was soon disabused of it. Before a week was out, three senators had retracted their signatures and over thirty had issued clarifying statements which revoked their sympathy for the Loyalists. A few, such as Representative Fred Hildebrandt of South Dakota, declared that the statement had been revised after he signed it. Altogether, the incident gave noteworthy demonstration of the vitality of domestic Catholic sentiment. Senator Walsh should have been satisfied.[28] Protest literature was even finding its way to the White House. Someone complained about permitting the use of national parks to groups trying to raise money for the Spanish republic. Spain had become a factor in American politics. When newly elected Congressman Stephen Bolles of Wisconsin explained his victory in November 1938, he emphasized that "I had the guts enough to protest publicly . . . the Red Spain attitude of our congressional delegation." Bolles thought this protest explained why he received 90 percent of the Irish vote in his race.[29]

Increased European tensions, heightened political sensitivity by Catholics, and liberal attachment to the Spanish republic challenged the administration policy of neutrality. In April and May 1938, the Spanish embargo left the area of consensus diplomacy and entered politics. Senator Nye, a leading isolationist and supporter of the initial embargo resolution, now had second thoughts. He had convinced himself that the liberal argument, which insisted that an impartial embargo actually aided Franco, was sound. The impartial embargo failed to distinguish between a legitimate government and a rebel. This same argument had been made in 1937, but the administration's rebuttal, that keeping the United States out of war was the most important consideration, had carried the day. Reconsideration of the embargo reflected a new view of the direction of European politics. Hitler had occupied Austria and was putting pressure on Czechoslovakia. The right-wing rebellion in Spain appeared to many liberals to be part of an international conspiracy. Now Nye introduced in the Senate a resolution calling for the end of the embargo on arms to Spain; Representative Jerry O'Connell of Montana did the same in the House. A number of liberal journalists, such as Max Lerner, immediately supported the proposal, and a stream of letters reached the Senate, the House, the Department of State, and the White House, encouraging embargo revision as a means of stopping the spread of fascism.[30] Among those close to the president, Secretary of the Interior Harold Ickes and Eleanor Roosevelt led a group in favor of aid to the Spanish republic.[31]

The campaign failed. On May 13 the Senate Foreign Relations Committee under the leadership of Key Pittman rejected the Nye Resolution by a vote of 17 to 1. In the House Foreign Affairs Committee, Chairman Sam D. McReynolds had earlier led a unanimous vote not to hold hearings on revising the embargo. He denounced those favoring revision as trying to drag the United States into war. What happened? President Roosevelt had not changed his mind about the Spanish embargo by May 1938 and neither had the American public. A public opinion poll at the time found over 66 percent of those polled to be indifferent about Spain.[32] When Nye first offered his resolution to lift the embargo, Senator Pittman asked for directions from the administration. Hull drafted a reply for Roosevelt's signature. The letter stated: "In view of the continued danger of international conflict arising from the circumstances of the struggle, any proposal which contemplates a reversal of our policy of strict non-interference . . . would offer a real possibility of complications. The proposed legislation would, in my opinion, be unwise." On April 23, 1938, Roosevelt told a group of newspaper editors that he was fully satisfied with how the embargo was working. As he had argued earlier, Roosevelt insisted that a removal of the embargo would help Franco as well as the Spanish republic. He told Ickes the same thing when the secretary made his appeal.[33] By July 1938 Franco controlled over two-thirds of Spain, including such ports as Cadiz and Malaga, but the Loyalists still held Barcelona and other Mediterranean ports. On May 6 Secretary of State Hull publicly opposed American arms shipments to Spain because such a step would repudiate attempts by England and France to contain the affair. Two days before the vote in the Senate Foreign Relations Committee, Roosevelt referred questions about the embargo to the Department of State. One day after the vote, he approved Hull's statement to the press which defended retention of the embargo.[34]

Clearly, both Roosevelt and Hull wanted the embargo retained. Roosevelt could have remained silent about the Nye Resolution, but instead went on record to keep the embargo. His actions have been explained in many different ways. One of the most popular stories has been that American Catholic pressure forced Roosevelt to keep an embargo that he personally disliked. No one can deny that Catholics were sensitive about Spain or that Roosevelt was well aware of this sensitivity. When Norman Thomas left a private interview with the president in 1937, he concluded that "the major thing in Roosevelt's mind was not so much foreign policy but a belief that in his whole policy, domestic and foreign, it was necessary to carry along the Catholic Church."[35] New Deal politicians repeatedly testified to the political dynamite tied to the embargo. Senator Pittman mentioned this in explaining why he was reluctant to discuss revision. Jay Pierpont Moffat, chief of the Division of European Affairs in the State Department, called the bitterness between Catholics and liberals over Spain more heated than "anything I have seen for years." Secretary of the Interior Ickes recorded an interview with Roosevelt on May 14, 1938, at which the president admitted that lifting the embargo would "mean the loss of every Catholic vote next fall and . . . the Democratic members of Congress were jittery about it." What Ickes called the "mangiest, scabbiest cat ever" (Catholic political pressure) was also mentioned by Rexford Tugwell, former advisor to Roosevelt, and by Sumner Welles.[36]

4

Such testimony appears imposing and seems to confirm the conclusion that Catholic pressure was decisive in forcing Roosevelt to reject embargo revision. Yet a study of what Catholics did during this period does not sustain such a conclusion without important qualifications. The relationship between American Catholics and Roosevelt's policy toward Spain can be better understood by distinguishing between general attitudes and the formation of a specific lobby. Obviously, by 1938 Catholic feelings toward the Spanish Civil War were clearly established as part of a general climate of opinion. Catholics did respond when Nye in the Senate and O'Connell in the House offered their bills to revise the embargo. Generally however, the response was disorganized. When Catholics discussed the benefits of the embargo in the spring of 1938, they justified it in terms of American neutralism. As did many other Americans, Catholics thought the measure would prevent United States involvement and so prevent a repetition of World War I. As Reverend Joseph Thorning wrote in praise of the decision of Representative McReynolds not to hold hearings on the O'Connell resolution, "If neutrality was good enough for 20 months . . . it is good policy now." Dr. Herbert Wright of Catholic University, an authority on international law, explained in the *New York Times* that it was not America's fault that Franco got more aid than did the Loyalists. Should the United States set a precedent of aiding the side which needed arms most? Rather, Wright thought we should continue the present neutrality, which was legally sound. Revision of the neutrality laws might be needed, but the *Boston Pilot* saw no reason to alter the concept of remaining neutral and not selling arms to either side in Spain.[37]

Naturally, a few Catholics insisted on invoking the specter of communism. The *Commonweal* deplored attempts by the American Friends of Spanish Democracy to lift the embargo and help the "Red Tyranny." The individuals who sponsored embargo revision were denounced as communist agents, internationalists, munition makers, and antireligious zealots. One editor repeated the same point Representative McReynolds had made—that the sponsors of revision were all leftists from New York City. But it remained for Reverend Dr. Joseph B. Code of Catholic University to draw the most extreme conclusion about the revisionists. Code felt that they were "anti-Catholic," since it was impossible to support "Red" Spain and still be a friend of the church.[38] When Edward J. Heffron, executive secretary of the National Council of Catholic Men, issued a statement opposing embargo revision and urging Catholics to write to their congressmen, he seemed to be indulging in the type of political pressure which impressed Ickes and Tugwell. The trouble with this conclusion, however, is that Heffron issued his call only after the House Foreign Affairs Committee had cancelled hearings on the O'Connell bill. Not surprisingly, few bishops responded to Heffron's call. The first attempt at revising the Spanish embargo failed before a formal Catholic lobby could be mobilized.[39]

But the drive to revise the embargo did not end with the defeat of these May 1938 resolutions. Before the year was out, the issue appeared again in Congress. Members of the Roosevelt administration, led by Secretary of the Interior Ickes, remained undiscouraged by the rejection of Nye's proposal. Liberal journals continued to write in support of embargo revision. After Ickes pressed the subject again in late November 1938, Roosevelt wrote Attorney General Homer Cummings requesting a legal opinion on how the Neutrality Proclamation of May 1937 affected the status of the joint resolution of January 8, 1937, which placed an embargo on arms to Spain. As Roosevelt explained to Cummings, there was a disagreement within the cabinet. The Department of State now argued that if the president revoked his embargo proclamation of May 1, the January 8 congressional resolution, instituting a similar restriction, would remain in force. Ickes, however, felt that the May proclamation canceled out the January resolution and that the Spanish embargo remained in force due to presidential rather than congressional authority. Ickes argued that Roosevelt did not have to go through Congress to lift the embargo. The president concluded his letter to Cummings: "I think there is some merit to this conclusion."[40]

Why was Roosevelt pursuing the matter after his earlier endorsement of the embargo? Most observers argue that Roosevelt was finally awakening to the dangers of fascism in Europe and wanted to remove the unjust embargo restrictions. Admittedly, by late 1938 the president was seeking more control over the conduct of foreign relations. But it seems difficult to believe that if he really wanted to remove the embargo he would have been frustrated by an adverse opinion from the attorney general or from Secretary of State Hull. In fact, even Ickes was still not sure of where Roosevelt stood at the end of the year. As late as December 18, 1938, he wrote that Roosevelt had still not frankly and openly endorsed a change in policy toward Spain. Not until January 29, 1939, when the civil war was drawing to a close, did Ickes again debate the embargo with Roosevelt. This time, the president excused his lack of action, not by pointing to Catholic opposition as he had in May 1938, but by referring to the adverse opinions of Hull, Sumner Welles, and Cummings.[41] Welles had written Roosevelt in January 1939 that the unanimity of congressional action on the joint resolution of early 1937 made it appropriate for the legislature to take the initiative in any revision of the embargo. Similarly, Pittman wrote Hull that the embargo was "too hot a spot to sit with ease," but made no mention of Catholic pressure in particular. He reported that his Foreign Relations Committee received some 35,000 letters on the embargo in one week. The letters came from many different groups.[42]

Roosevelt sought to avoid the Spanish Civil War issue because he had a larger objective. He desired to revise the neutrality laws across the board to allow for more executive discretion. This quest related to the dangers from Hitler rather than to the Spanish Civil War, now virtually finished. He had every reason to keep these two problems separate and distinct. His modest inquiries to Hull and Cummings have the character of a mere gesture to his liberal supporters rather than a serious attempt to erect a new Spanish policy. Indeed, the advice he received from the attorney general was so filled with qualifications that Roosevelt could have used it for any purpose he desired.[43] He knew, however, that to become involved with Spain at this point would only confuse the main question of neutrality revision.

Ickes's explanation of Roosevelt's actions as being the result of Catholic pressure did have substance, but only indirectly. Everyone in the administration knew of Catholic concern over Spain. Hull recalled the protest which followed his expression of horror at the aerial attack on Barcelona by Franco's forces in April. Catholics did not defend the bombing of civilians, but they did take exception to Hull's partiality in denouncing only the terrorism of the Nationalists while ignoring the persecution of the clergy by the Loyalists. Monsignor Ready of the NCWC released a press statement deploring "an inconsistency not to be expected from a leading cabinet officer of our government."[44] More direct was Congressman John W. McCormack, who consistently lobbied against revision of the embargo because it amounted to aiding communists and kept the NCWC informed of the disposition of Congress.[45] He complained to the Department of State about allowing United States citizens to volunteer for the Spanish Civil War, and also objected to a campaign forcing government employees to contribute to the North American Committee to Aid Spanish Democracy.[46] All of these protests convinced Roosevelt of the importance of not confusing executive control of neutrality with the issue of Spain.

5

Despite Roosevelt's efforts, the Spanish embargo question reappeared as a public issue in January 1939. The president's liberal supporters succeeded in tying the issue of Spain to problems of European diplomacy in general, a connection Roosevelt had every reason to avoid. Although the Loyalist cause seemed hopeless by the end of 1938, a new campaign was launched to pressure Congress into embargo revision. This second campaign stirred a vigorous Catholic reaction and helped Catholics to accept isolationist arguments.[47] On December 30, 1938, Louis Kenedy, president of the National Council of Catholic Men, announced the organization of the "Keep the Spanish Embargo Committee." This group petitioned Congress to keep the present neutrality legislation. Taking sides in Spain, which Kenedy thought implicit in any neutrality revision, would endanger the United States. Swiftly, the major spokesmen of American Catholicism fell into line. Charter members of the "Keep the Spanish Embargo Committee" included the archbishop of Baltimore, Michael J. Curley, the general secretary of the NCWC, Monsignor Michael J. Ready, Father John Ryan, Monsignor Fulton Sheen, Father F. A. Talbot, and Martin H. Carmody of the Knights of Columbus. On January 3, 1939, Curley and a few other bishops had letters read to the members of their dioceses at every Mass. The faithful were introduced to the Embargo Committee and asked to attend a rally in Washington on January 9.[48] Those attending this meeting heard Reverend Sheen condemn the Loyalists. Edward J. Heffron of the National Council of Catholic Men and Reverend Joseph F. Thorning also spoke and blamed the communists for attempts to lift the embargo.

Meanwhile, Dennis Cardinal Dougherty instructed his parishioners to petition Congress to keep the embargo. Within two weeks, 10,000 telegrams arrived on Capitol Hill from Philadelphia. A similar response accompanied appeals by Father Coughlin. Behind the scenes William Montavon of the NCWC staff lobbied among small groups of congressmen and senators. He argued the advantages of continuing the established policy of noninvolvement. No wonder Pittman thought the Spanish embargo a hot issue.[50]

Roosevelt's attempt to pave the way for general neutrality revision became confused with Catholic desires to prevent a communist take-over in Spain. The letter that former Congressman John J. O'Connor wrote to the *Commonweal* in January 1939 reflected this confusion. As a successfully purged anti-New Deal congressman, O'Connor had no love for Roosevelt. He insisted that any change in the neutrality laws would only "help the murderous reds of Spain" and praised the work of the Catholic lobby to keep the embargo. Such critics as O'Connor ignored the general European situation and did not consider how neutrality revision would affect America's role in that larger area. The appeals of Cardinal Dougherty and Archbishop Curley and the many telegrams sent to senators and congressmen revealed a similarly narrow focus, with heavy emphasis on communism.[51]

Catholics now associated lifting the arms embargo with getting the United States into war. The *Commonweal* editorialized that amending the present law would be a dangerous extension of executive power. The editors called instead for laws prohibiting the shipment of arms and products "which clearly will go into armament to any foreign country." Senator Joseph C. O'Mahoney of Wyoming received numerous letters from his constituents and from local religious organizations urging him to "fight any attempt to lift the Spanish arms embargo, preserve neutrality and keep us out of war." Edward Heffron of the National Council of Catholic Men argued that lifting the embargo would be "dangerous to the peace and security of the United States." Another editor warned that "if we don't want to be messed up in European conflicts, the thing for us to do is to keep our neutrality laws as is." The Knights of Columbus resolved on January 15, 1939, that the embargo be kept because revision "would contradict principles upon which the United States is founded." Most participants in a neutrality symposium sponsored by the *Commonweal* agreed with this conclusion. *Catholic Action* and Cardinal Dougherty agreed that revision would lead the United States into war.[52]

The Catholic argument against embargo revision had become an argument for isolationism and general noninvolvement. Roosevelt's call in January 1939 for neutrality revision was lost in the shuffle. Not surprisingly, Senator Pittman again decided it would be best to postpone consideration of neutrality revision. Heffron promised that his organization would "not relax [its] vigilance" because of this decision. Ironically, Roosevelt's attempts to revise the neutrality law were frustrated by an issue he always considered incidental, one virtually moot by now, an issue that the president had tried to avoid. If the Spanish Civil War issue had not been around, American Catholics probably would not have responded to the idea of neutrality revision in such a negative way.[53] This fact seems more important than the question of whether or not American Catholics actually dictated administration policy toward the Spanish Civil War. An organized Catholic lobby did exist in January 1939. It did put pressure on public officials. Thousands of telegrams were sent to Congress on the appeal of Father Coughlin, and we may even accept Ickes's testimony that Catholic pressure forced Frank Murphy to change his position on the civil war.[54] But are these facts more important than the general impact of the Spanish question on America's European diplomacy?

6

Historians have argued that Catholic pressure was a key factor which influenced the president's reluctance to lift the embargo. Using the testimony of Ickes and Tugwell, they have emphasized fear of Catholic political retaliation as a moving force within the administration. Since these same scholars are also convinced that American failure to frustrate Franco helped bring about World War II, Roosevelt's indecisiveness here is considered especially unfortunate. To make the tragedy complete, these scholars lament that the president really misread Catholic opinion about Spain; he reacted to a straw man. They quote a Gallup Poll showing that only 39 percent of American Catholics favored Franco, with 30 percent supporting the republic and 31 percent neutral. Apparently, Roosevelt read only the opinions of Catholic leaders. He made a mistake few politicians can afford—confusing leadership rhetoric with popular support.[55]

This criticism of Roosevelt appears unwarranted. Were Catholics divided about Spain? Was Roosevelt confused? A close look at Catholic opinion reveals that many members of this minority, like most of their fellow citizens, were probably indifferent about Spain. A smaller num-

ber were publicly neutral. Rare indeed was pro-Loyalist sentiment among
Catholics. Carlton J. H. Hayes and a few other professors in the New York
City area were rumored to favor the republic, but the only outspoken
Catholic supporter of the Loyalists was Frank P. Walsh, a prominent New
York attorney, pro-New Dealer, and a power in the local Democratic
party. In the late 1930s he found himself in the anomalous position of
being simultaneously a trustee of St. Patrick's Cathedral and heading
the Lawyers' Committee for Loyalist Spain. At a rally in Washington on
November 20, 1938, he urged the lifting of the Spanish embargo on legal
and humanitarian grounds. In retrospect, what appears most interesting
about Walsh's stand is its uniqueness and secular character. He later refused to act as counsel for the Spanish ambassador for "professional
and personal reasons." When the *New York Herald Tribune* reported his
November 20 speech in a way which implied that he was appealing to
"liberty loving Catholics," Walsh quickly wrote a rebuttal denying he
had ever used the words "Catholic or Catholic Church." As he wrote to
a friend, "The idea that I should speak as a 'Catholic layman' or attempt
to advise Catholics upon any matter or even to address them as such
upon a public matter, is as abhorrent to me as it is to you."[56] How different this attitude was from that of the American bishops.

Walsh was virtually the only Catholic figure to support the Loyalists
publicly. Yet he rejected the idea of speaking as a Catholic. No other
important Catholic figure was pro-Loyalist, but a few did adopt an
anti-Franco position. This group included George Schuster, editor at
Commonweal, Professor Harry McNeill of Fordham, Professor Hayes
of Columbia, and Kathleen Norris, the novelist.[57] Dorothy Day of the
Catholic Worker was dedicated to Christian pacifism, not to a revision
of the embargo. Her idealistic position merited condemnation by a
few Catholic bishops.[58] The *Commonweal,* after a decidedly pro-Franco
editorial position under Michael Williams, underwent an internal revolution. After the ouster of Williams, the new editors announced a position
of impartiality on June 24, 1938. Their main motive was concern over
the division the Spanish issue was creating in the United States. The duty
of all Americans, in the editors' view, should be the same—to pray for
all in Spain. Yet neutralism could be expensive. Within a few months the
sales of the magazine dropped by 25 percent as bishops such as John T.
McNicholas of Cincinnati and others banned the distribution of the publication. Other Catholic journals condemned this neutralism.[59]

Dissent from American Catholic leadership opinion about Spain appears to have been incredibly rare. Public opinion polls showed that only four out of ten American Catholics supported Franco. But this did not indicate that many American Catholics were in favor of lifting the embargo on arms to Spain.[60] There is no evidence of a significant minority of American Catholics who opposed the official line of the church. The most notable exception to acceptance of the church's position was the neutralism which led to serious economic consequences for the two journals which adopted it. Under such circumstances, President Roosevelt would have been a very gifted man indeed if he could have seen a split in Catholic sentiment about Spain. How could an abstract statistical sample stand against the pastoral letters and press releases of important Catholic leaders? And other polls demonstrated general American support for neutrality. To fight over the Spanish embargo would only provide additional motives for isolationism.

Furthermore, even when Roosevelt's awareness of Catholic opinion is admitted, it does not follow that such pressure caused him to keep the embargo or that retaining the embargo was a mistake. Criticism of Roosevelt in this area appears just as ill-founded. In June 1940, long after Franco controlled Spain, Roosevelt admitted his supposed mistake about the embargo but explained his actions in terms of pressure from England, France, and the Low Countries, which felt that nonintervention would prevent the spread of a war for which they were ill-prepared.[61] Some confusion about the impact of American Catholics on Roosevelt's decision can be cleared up if we ask whether the president ever really wanted to lift the embargo. That Catholic pressure played a role in the president's evaluation of the embargo seems clear, but it does not prove that he ever wanted to lift it. We should keep in mind that the decision to institute an embargo on arms to Spain was made by the Department of State with Roosevelt's full support.[62] Instead of asking why Roosevelt did not revise his policy, it would be more profitable to ask why he should have wanted to change it. What factors intervened between the time of his initial decision and 1939 which might have called for a revision? The impulse for embargo revision in December 1938 came from outside the White House. American Catholic pressure became fully organized in January 1939, when the Spanish Civil War was virtually over and at a time when Roosevelt had every reason to keep the emotional embargo issue distinct from his European diplomacy. A more reasonable hypothesis would explain Roosevelt's actions as in keeping with his general European strategy and in tune with his desire to separate Spanish affairs from the Nazi threat.

Historians have assumed that revision of the neutrality act became important when the dangers of fascism became apparent to Roosevelt. Yet in January 1939 the dangers of fascism had not convinced England and France of the wisdom of taking a stand in Spain. If Roosevelt's policy at this time was to support the diplomacy of England and France, he had every reason to keep the embargo. If the embargo was originally instituted because the United States wanted to avoid European entanglements, a conclusion supported by the entire course of neutrality legislation, the subsequent developments in the civil war in Spain would have little bearing on whether or not to revoke such a policy. Even if Roosevelt had changed his mind about the virutes of noninvolvement in Europe by early 1939 (a disputed point), he had no reason to become involved in Spain.[63]

Distinguishing between the American public's attitude toward the war in Spain and its attitude about the role the United States government should play in Spain and in Europe as a whole helps to clarify the picture. In fact, Catholic sentiment about keeping the embargo coincided with the neutral posture long favored by the public and the administration. This congruence of opinion, however, does not mean that American Catholics caused the administration's attitude or lack of action. The statements and actions of President Roosevelt and Secretary of State Hull were consistent throughout the period of the Spanish Civil War. Given the sentiments of the American public and the attitudes of France and England, this policy would have been the same even if most prominent American Catholics had been as silent as Trappist monks on the issue.

7

Such a conclusion does not mean that the Spanish Civil War had no consequences for American history. Rather it means that the affair was more important for its impact on American Catholicism than for Catholics' influence on Roosevelt. Ironically, the episode endowed American Catholicism with a reputation for political power that it did not deserve. Despite the many secular motives for Roosevelt's actions, many liberals,

including Ickes and Tugwell, came away from the affair convinced that
American bishops had called the tune. The church received credit for
consummating a policy which the Roosevelt administration conceived.
Politicians, ever respectful of power over voters, could only give increased
attention to the public positions taken by American Catholic spokesmen.[64]

Indirectly, this image of Catholic political power also helped to generate
Protestant bitterness and contributed to the collapse of whatever ecumenism existed between the faiths during the 1930s. Such prominent Protestants as Reinhold Neibuhr accepted the malevolent vision of Catholic
intrigues. Letters to the president warned him that playing up to Catholics
would only lose him esteem among Protestants. "Since when do we need
the permission of the Catholic Church" to change our foreign policy,
asked one disgruntled voter? Others thought Catholics had taken advantage
of Protestant liberalism to wax strong the last few years and were now
trying to influence the government along fascist lines.[65]

The damage to Catholic-Protestant relations was only part of a larger
dissolution of intergroup harmony and of a temporary alliance between
Catholics and liberal Americans. Having experienced the trauma of
religious bigotry during the 1928 election—a campaign which raised
serious questions about the compatibility of Catholicism and American
democracy—Catholics had been reassured by the attention paid them
by Roosevelt and by their initial impression that the New Deal was
similar to papal social teaching. For a brief, exciting period in the early
1930s, American Catholics could stride side by side with American
liberals in denouncing predatory capitalism. Despite the difficulties
over Roosevelt's neutrality toward anticlericalism in Mexico, the 1936
election confirmed that Catholics were firmly entrenched in the liberal
majority supporting the president. Now the Spanish Civil War had
erupted with all of its antireligious violence. Leaders of American Catholicism found themselves battling liberals.

Some liberals were intelligent enough to see the danger in driving
Catholics further into their ghetto for the sake of a war in Spain. Alfred
Bingham wrote, "Let American Progressives beware how they drive
twenty million American Catholics, whose need for fundamental change
is as great as any, into the arms of a Coughlin or . . . a Franco." Catholics
had a tradition of social justice, which earlier had contributed to the
Roosevelt consensus. Now they were forced by anticlerical news, by

fears of spreading communism, and by desire to avoid European entanglements to reject intervention in Spain. This desire to remain uninvolved
with Spain did not differentiate them from either Roosevelt or most
Americans. Indeed, the real radical element was a liberal minority with
an idealistic vision of America's role in the world.[66] Yet to the degree
that Catholics felt the need to support Franco, rather than merely advocate neutrality, they seemed to be endorsing an alien form of government.

Liberals now charged that the American Catholic church was profascist. Had not Monsignor Frank A. Hall, chancellor of the Cincinnati archdiocese, attacked the Committee to Aid Spain with the words: "As liber-
ty-loving Americans we want nothing of either fascism or communism in
our country; but if we must make a choice, we unhesitatingly should
choose fascism as the lesser of two evils"? Did not Professor Edward Fen-
lon of Brooklyn College argue that because fascism had no fixed set of
offensive principles, it was not as dangerous as atheistic communism?
The similar attitude of Father Coughlin was well known. He combined
extreme nationalism, fervent anticommunism, and a fear of international
Jewry into an isolationist outlook. The Italian character of the papacy,
the anti-Semitism of Coughlin, and now the support for Franco all
seemed to fit a pattern. Historically, the church had proved compatible
with just about every type of regime from monarchy to democracy. So
popular did this argument of Catholic fascism become that a group of
journalists and scholars finally counterattacked by publishing "13 Pages
of Straight Talk About the Catholic Church and the Fascist Question"
in the liberal newspaper *P.M.* during May 1941. Catholic journalists such
as Theodore Maynard and George Shuster argued that the pope had condemned both the general notion of totalitarianism and National Socialism
in his encyclicals, that European Catholics were leading the opposition to
Franco, and that support for the Spanish Nationalists was to be explained
by the issue of clerical persecution under the Spanish republic. Yet the
lingering suspicion that Catholic authoritarianism could never be completely reconciled with democracy continued up to World War II. It made
American Catholic leaders especially sensitive to charges of being opposed
to the diplomacy of President Roosevelt.[67]

For the time being, however, the struggle over the Spanish embargo
confirmed and strengthened many Catholics in their commitment to
isolationism. The entire affair led to the frustration of Roosevelt's

attempts to gain more discretion in foreign policy. The episode also helped to delay the time when American Catholics would appreciate the virtue of an active foreign policy by the United States. It hardly prepared them to revise their attitudes toward Europe at a time when the expansion of Hitler made revision a virtue.[68] Indirectly, the affair also delayed general neutrality revision. Senator Pittman was frightened away from the question for some time. After revision failed again in mid-1939, it took the outbreak of a general European war before the administration could break the neutrality blockade.

These problems developed without the redirection of Roosevelt's foreign policy by American Catholics. Confusion over the role of the Catholic lobby comes from the refusal to admit that noninvolvement in Spain represented all that seemed best in historic American diplomacy. One of the results of such misunderstanding has been the myth of Roosevelt and the internationalists giving in to an embargo only because of the political pressure of American Catholics. The Catholic position was in line with traditional American isolationism. The embargo becomes reactionary only if we see it through the ideological mirror of historians who view Franco as a harbinger of World War II and American neutrality as a cause of that conflict.

NOTES

1. Quoted in Samuel I. Rosenman, *The Public Papers and Addresses of Franklin D. Roosevelt,* 13 vols. (New York, 1938-1950), vol. 6, p. 191.

2. *New York Times,* August 21, 1936.

3. F. Jay Taylor, *The United States and the Spanish Civil War* (New York, 1956), p. 123.

4. Robert A. Divine, *The Reluctant Belligerent: American Entry into World War II* (New York, 1965), pp. 25-26; Press Conference, December 29, 1936, in Rosenman, *Public Papers,* vol. 5, pp. 621-622.

5. Press Conference, December 29, 1936, in Rosenman, *Public Papers,* vol. 5, p. 621; Allen Guttman, *The Wound in the Heart: America and the Spanish Civil War* (New York, 1962), pp. 88-90; Fred L. Israel, *Nevada's Key Pittman* (Lincoln, Nebr., 1963), p. 149.

6. *Congressional Record,* 75th Cong., 1st Sess., pp. 73-75; Pittman quoted in Israel, *Nevada's Key Pittman,* p. 149.

7. Proclamation No. 2236, May 1, 1937, in Rosenman, *Public Papers*, vol. 6, pp. 185-187.

8. Cordell Hull, *The Memoirs of Cordell Hull*, 2 vols. (New York, 1948), vol. 1, p. 514.

9. Roosevelt to Undersecretary of State Welles, July 3, 1937, OF 422-C, Box 2, Franklin D. Roosevelt Papers, Hyde Park, New York.

10. Bowers to Roosevelt, August 11, 1937, PSF, Box 16, Spain, Roosevelt Papers; Guttmann, *The Wound in the Heart*, p. 117.

11. Rev. George B. Ford, "Interview," Columbia Oral History Project, Columbia University, p. 108.

12. *Catholic World* 146 (January 1938), p. 487; *Commonweal*: December 3, 1937, p. 143; July 30, 1937, p. 334; Michael Williams, "The Truth about Spain," *Commonweal,* June 25, 1937, p. 231; *Commonweal:* October 15, 1937, p. 578; November 12, 1937, p. 77; Taylor, *The United States,* pp. 113n, 122.

13. *Commonweal*, July 30, 1937, p. 334; J. David Valaik, "American Catholics and the Second Spanish Republic, 1911-1936," *Journal of Church and State* 10 (Winter 1968), pp. 17-19; see also the *NCWC News Service* for March, June, and July 1937 for numerous reports of Loyalists' atrocities.

14. Clipping from the *Washington Post*, December 30, 1938, in OF, 422-C, Box 2, Roosevelt Papers. See Hugh Thomas, *The Spanish Civil War* (New York, 1961), for a balanced analysis of the complexities of the civil war.

15. *Commonweal*, January 8, 1937, p. 287; *Brooklyn Tablet*, January 16, 1937, p. 9.

16. See Thomas, *The Spanish Civil War,* pp. 46-47, 171-176, and appendix II for casualties; the most provocative part of the liberal constitution was the outlawing of all religious education.

17. Quoted in the *New York Times*, February 27, 1939.

18. *NCWC News Service*, March 22, 1937; *Commonweal,* March 12, 1937, p. 537; Donald F. Crosby, "Boston's Catholics and the Spanish Civil War, 1936-1939," *New England Quarterly* 44 (March 1971), p. 100; Ryan to Carl D. Thompson, October 28, 1937, John A. Ryan Papers, Catholic University of America, Washington, D.C.

19. *Catholic World* 146 (November 1937), p. 238; *New York Times*: September 3, 1937; October 4, 1937; October 6, 1937; October 14, 1937.

20. David J. Valaik, "American Catholic Dissenters and the Spanish Civil War," *Catholic Historical Review* 53 (January 1968), p. 553; see also Roger Van Allen, *"The Commonweal" and American Catholicism* (Philadelphia, 1974), pp. 61-66, 70-73.

21. Guttmann, *The Wound in the Heart*, p. 202, mentions *America, Catholic Action, Catholic Mind, Catholic Digest, Catholic World, Columbia,* and *Sign*; see also R. M. Darrow, "Catholic Political Power: A Study of the Activities of the American Catholic Church on Behalf of Franco during the Spanish Civil War, 1936-1939" (Ph.D. thesis, Columbia University, 1953), p. 59; Divine, *The Reluctant Belligerent*, p. 32; Crosby, "Boston's Catholics," p. 100.

22. *NCWC News Service*: March 19, 1937; April 23, 1938.

23. Ibid.: April 12, 1937; April 16, 1938; Valaik, "American Catholic Dissenters," pp. 537-538; Guttmann, *The Wound in the Heart*, p. 37.

24. Frederick L. Broderick, *The Right Reverend New Dealer: John A. Ryan* (New York, 1963), pp. 233-234.

25. This might be called the traditional view of Catholic reaction. It is shared by Valaik, Taylor, and Guttmann.

26. *NCWC News Service*: October 2, 1937; April 2, 1938; June 26, 1938; *Commonweal*: February 5, 1937, p. 397; February 19, 1937, p. 456; May 7, 1937, p. 29; May 14, 1937, p. 57; May 28, 1937, p. 129; June 4, 1937, p. 141; February 11, 1938, p. 423.

27. Darrow, "Catholic Political Power," p. 86; Taylor, *The United States*, pp. 158-159; McCormack to Roosevelt, June 10, 1937, OF 422-B, Box 2, Roosevelt Papers; *Boston Pilot*, June 5, 1937, p. 1; *NCWC News Service*, June 1, 1937. See Joseph Lash, *Eleanor and Franklin* (New York, 1971), pp. 567-570, for Eleanor Roosevelt's involvement and attempts to prod the president into lifting the embargo.

28. *New York Times*, February 1, 1938, and February 4, 1938; *Commonweal*: February 11, 1938, p. 423; February 18, 1938, p. 451; David I. Walsh, press release, February 2, 1938, David I. Walsh Mss., Holy Cross Library, Worcester, Mass.; Horace O'Connor to Roosevelt, February 12, 1938, OF 422-C, Box 2, Roosevelt Papers; *Boston Pilot*, February 12, 1938, p. 4; Taylor, *The United States*, p. 156.

29. William F. Gorman, Ancient Order of Hibernians, to Roosevelt, June 9, 1938, OF 422-B, Box 2, Roosevelt Papers; William F. Montavon

of NCWC to McIntyre, July 7, 1938, OF 422-B, Box 2, Roosevelt Papers; Stephen Bolles to John J. O'Connor, November 22, 1938, Congress, 1939 file, John J. O'Connor Mss., Lilly Library, Bloomington, Ind.; *New York Times,* February 12, 1938.

30. Darrow, "Catholic Political Power," pp. 140-145.

31. Harold L. Ickes, *The Secret Diary of Harold L. Ickes,* 3 vols. (New York, 1953-1954), vol. 2, pp. 389-390; Lash, *Eleanor and Franklin,* p. 569.

32. A resume of public opinion on the Spanish Civil War is included in note 60; Israel, *Nevada's Key Pittman,* p. 156.

33. Roosevelt to Pittman (n.d.), OF 422-C, Box 2, Roosevelt Papers; Ickes, *Diary,* vol. 2, p. 389.

34. Darrow, "Catholic Political Power," pp. 146-150; see also Robert Divine, *The Illusion of Neutrality* (Chicago, 1962), p. 225; William Leuchtenburg, *Franklin D. Roosevelt and the New Deal* (New York, 1963), p. 223; Lash, *Eleanor and Franklin,* p. 569; *NCWC News Service,* April 12, 1938.

35. Norman Thomas, "Interview," Columbia University Oral History Project.

36. Israel, *Nevada's Key Pittman,* p. 157; Julius W. Pratt, *Cordell Hull,* 2 vols. (New York, 1964), vol. 1, pp. 215, 226; Ickes, *Diary,* vol. 2, pp. 389-390; Guttmann, *The Wound in the Heart,* p. 119. A number of historians have found this testimony conclusive proof that Roosevelt did act under Catholic pressure. Guttmann, Divine, and Taylor all accept the role of Catholic pressure but qualify it by pointing to other forces, such as a desire to cooperate with England and France. Unfortunately, except for the testimony of Ickes and a general statement by Rexford Tugwell, we have no firm evidence of Catholic influence. Taylor writes that "reported" appeals were made to Roosevelt by Catholic leaders; that James Farley "may have" advised Roosevelt of Catholic political dangers; that "perhaps big city bosses regarded Spain as too hot" (Taylor, *The United States,* pp. 173-174, 186). Claude Bowers, 2,500 miles away, also testified to the influence of Catholic pressure on Roosevelt (ibid., p. 185).

37. *NCWC News Service:* April 12, 1938; April 11, 1938; *Boston Pilot:* April 2, 1938, p. 4; May 14, 1938, p. 4; Taylor, *The United States,* p. 85.

38. *Commonweal,* February 25, 1938, p. 479; *Boston Pilot,* May 21, 1938, p. 4; *Brooklyn Tablet,* May 14, 1938, p. 1; Code quoted in *NCWC News Service,* April 8, 1938.

39. *NCWC News Service*, April 2, 1938.

40. Memo from Roosevelt to Attorney General Homer Cummings, November 28, 1938, OF, 422-C, Box 2, Roosevelt Papers; Ickes, *Diary*, vol. 2, p. 470.

41. Ickes, *Diary*, vol. 2, pp. 528, 566.

42. Donald F. Drummond, *The Passing of American Neutrality, 1937-1941* (Ann Arbor, Mich., 1955), p. 91n; Israel, *Nevada's Key Pittman,* p. 157.

43. Richard P. Traina, *American Diplomacy and the Spanish Civil War* (Bloomington, Ind., 1968), pp. 214-216.

44. Darrow, "Catholic Political Power," p. 120. Ready, quoted in *Catholic Action*, April 1938, p. 4.

45. *Boston Pilot,* June 24, 1938, p. 12; *Catholic Herald Citizen,* August 28, 1937, p. 3; Crosby, "Boston's Catholics," pp. 90-94.

46. McCormack to Roosevelt, October 4, 1938; and Roosevelt to McCormack, October 10, 1938, OF 422-B, Box 2, Roosevelt Papers.

47. Divine, *The Illusion of Neutrality*, p. 237; Traina, *American Diplomacy*, pp. 207-208.

48. A partial list of the sponsors of the rally includes the following names: Frank H. Biel of the Knights of St. John; Mrs. Minerva C. Boyd of the Daughters of Isabella; Mrs. George H. Bradford of the International Federation of Catholic Alumnae; Thomas H. Cannon of the Catholic Order of Foresters; Colonel Thomas F. Carlin of the Knights of Columbus; Martin H. Carmody, national leader of the Knights of Columbus; Leo J. Dohn of the Catholic Youth Organization; Marcy C. Durry of the Catholic Daughters of America; John Eibeck of the Catholic Knights of St. George; John E. Fenton of the Ancient Order of Hibernians; Mrs. Mary Filzer Lohr of the National Catholic Women's Union. See the *New York Times,* December 31, 1938; Archbishop M. J. Curley to Priests and People of Washington and Vicinity, January 3, 1939, in Box 145, Frank P. Walsh Papers, New York City Public Library; Traina, *American Diplomacy*, pp. 210-211.

49. *New York Times,* January 10, 1939.

50. Traina, *American Diplomacy*, pp. 210-212.

51. *Commonweal,* January 20, 1939, p. 344; *Boston Pilot,* January 14, 1939, p. 1; January 28, 1939, p. 1, carried headlines that pressure to lift the embargo was communist directed.

52. *Commonweal,* January 27, 1939, p. 366; Mrs. Fred Russold to

O'Mahoney, January 18, 1939, and the entire file on the embargo, Box 45, O'Mahoney Papers, University of Wyoming; Heffron quoted in *Catholic Action,* February 1939, p. 3; *Columbia,* February 1939, p. 24; Michael F. Doyle to McIntyre, January 15, 1939, OF 422-C, Box 2, and PPF 1771, Roosevelt Papers; *Commonweal,* February 17, 1939, p. 455 for symposium; this same thesis found support in the pages of *Catholic Herald Citizen,* January 7, 1939, p. 7; *Catholic Transcript,* January 5, 1939, p. 4; *Boston Pilot,* June 11, 1938, p. 4. Not surprisingly, the "Keep the Spanish Embargo Committee" and the NCWC listed the same Washington address.

53. Traina, *American Diplomacy,* pp. 218, 220; *Boston Pilot,* January 28, 1939, p. 1.

54. Thomas Bailey, *The Man in the Street* (New York, 1948), p. 208, says 100,000 messages were sent to Congress due to Catholic pressure; Ickes, *Diary,* vol. 2, pp. 604-605.

55. For this point of view, see especially the following: Guttmann, *The Wound in the Heart,* pp. 116, 203, and "An Indictment of American Policy," in Guttmann, editor, *American Neutrality* (Boston, 1963), pp. 96, 99. Taylor, *The United States,* p. 152; J. David Valaik, "Catholics, Neutrality, and the Spanish Embargo, 1937-1939," *Journal of American History* 54 (June 1967), pp. 73-85; Traina, *American Diplomacy,* p. 204.

56. Crosby, "Boston Catholics," p. 82, found few dissenters in that city. Roger Baldwin, "Interview," Columbia University Oral History Project, p. 132; Valaik, "American Catholic Dissenters," p. 554; Memo by Walsh, February 8, 1937, Box 145, Frank P. Walsh Papers; clipping from the *New York Herald Tribune,* November 22, 1938, and for quote see Walsh to editor of *New York Herald Tribune,* November 25, 1938, Box 145, Frank P. Walsh Papers; Frank Walsh to Pat J. Dean, November 29, 1938, Frank P. Walsh Papers.

57. Leuchtenburg, *Roosevelt,* p. 224. Valaik, "American Catholic Dissenters," pp. 546 and 554, concludes that "among Catholic intellectuals there was considerable anti-Franco sentiment but not necessarily much sympathy for the Spanish Loyalists." Valaik admits, however, that most clerics refused to dissent from the bishops' line.

58. Dorothy Day, *The Long Loneliness* (New York, 1952), p. 218; Valaik, "American Catholic Dissenters," pp. 541-542.

59. Valaik, "American Catholic Dissenters," pp. 540, 549, 551;

Commonweal, June 24, 1938, pp. 229-230; Roger Van Allen, *"Common-weal,"* pp. 61-66.

60. Public opinion polls support the conclusion that most Americans remained indifferent about the Spanish Civil War and overwhelmingly opposed to American intervention:

1. On January 11, 1937, Americans were asked: "In the present war . . . are your sympathies with the Loyalists . . . or are they with the Rebels, or with neither side?" In a national poll some 66 percent refused to take sides. On May 10, 1937 some 79 percent refused to take sides.

2. On December 16, 1938, a sample was asked: "Do you think the ban, as provided by the Neutrality Act, prohibiting our country from selling war materials to either side in the Spanish Civil War, should be removed?" 76 percent said no; 24 percent said yes.

3. On January 7, 1939, the public was asked: "Should Congress change the Neutrality Act to permit the shipment of arms to the Loyalists?" 79 percent said no; 21 percent said yes. Even on the question of merely sending food to the Loyalists, 52 percent said no.

4. On February 2, 1939, 40 percent of those polled indicated they had not been following the Spanish Civil War. Of the 59 percent who were following it, some 29 percent opposed permitting Loyalists to buy arms in the United States. See Hadley Cantril, editor, *Public Opinion, 1935-1946* (Princeton, N.J., 1951), pp. 807-808.

61. Ickes, *Diary,* vol. 3, p. 217.

62. Traina, *American Diplomacy,* pp. 47-53, 224.

63. For a similar argument, see John G. Gagliardo, "A Defense of American Policy," in Guttmann, editor, *American Neutrality,* pp. 102-103. Divine, *The Reluctant Belligerent,* p. 79, suggests that the Spanish embargo imbroglio led Roosevelt to hesitate in calling for general neutrality revision.

64. Ickes, *Diary,* vol. 2, p. 611; Darrow, "Catholic Political Power," pp. 150, 214.

65. Guttmann, *The Wound in the Heart,* p. 72; Norman S. Burdett to Roosevelt, January 15, 1939 and quotation from Horace W. O'Connor to Roosevelt, February 12, 1938, OF 422-C, Box 2, Roosevelt Papers.

66. Alfred Bingham, "War Mongering on the Left," *Common Sense* 6 (July 1937), pp. 11-15; Guttmann, *The Wound in the Heart,* pp. 46,

209; Traina, *American Diplomacy*, pp. 124-125, distinguishes between realists and a messianic school within the Department of State.

67. Hall quoted in *NCWC News Service*, May 15, 1937; Valaik, "American Catholic Dissenters," p. 547; John J. Carrigg, "American Catholic Press Opinion with Reference to America's Intervention in the Second World War" (M.A. thesis, Georgetown University, 1947), p. 134; Theodore Maynard, "Catholics and the Nazis," *American Mercury* 53 (October 1941), p. 391; David O'Brien, *American Catholics and Social Reform* (New York, 1968), p. 87; Guttmann, *The Wound in the Heart*, pp. 10-20; Patricia McNeal, "Origins of the Catholic Peace Movements," *Review of Politics* 35 (July 1973), p. 363.

68. Darrow, "Catholic Political Power," p. 211.

3

DEBATE AND ENTANGLEMENT

As Hitler prepared to annex Poland in September 1939, American Catholics, like most of their fellow citizens, feared the prospects of involvement. Earlier in the year, members of the Catholic press had strongly opposed attempts to revise the neutrality legislation by a bill proposed in June; they objected to such revision because it would involve us in war. Still, as late as August 30, 1939, 60 percent of all citizens polled fatalistically concluded that the United States could not avoid getting into another general European war if one came.[1] On September 1, German tanks rumbled across the Polish plain; war was here. Would American Catholics support the new attempt by the administration to revise neutrality, an attempt presented by Roosevelt as the best means of keeping the nation at peace and also avoiding the ultimate danger of a Nazi-dominated Europe? Would Catholics be moved by events in Europe to accept increasing United States intervention in the conflict? Public opinion was a dynamic force in the formation of American foreign policy from 1939 to 1941. What Catholics and other Americans thought about the war helped shape the character and pace of

Roosevelt's decisions. In a sense, the president sought a mandate for action from the American public. In response, a great public debate took place which touched upon the basic issues of America's role in the world. National policy took shape in this cauldron of opinion.

During the period from September 1939 to Pearl Harbor in December 1941, two questions struggled for answers in American opinion: should the United States support all-out aid for the Allies, even if it meant war, or should the nation stay aloof? The "America First" movement symbolized the anti-involvement proposition. Those favoring intervention gravitated toward the Committee to Defend America by Aiding the Allies. American Catholics played a vigorous role in this debate. Both interventionists and noninvolvement factions recognized that American Catholics represented an important segment of the population, one to be proselytized with profit. Liberal Catholics might argue that there was no "Catholic" position toward intervention, but as long as high-ranking clerics made public statements about foreign policy questions, and as long as these men influenced the members of their church to support either aid to the Allies or isolationism, the church was a factor. Neither Roosevelt nor other groups could ignore the influence of the church leaders in determining public opinion and influencing Congress, which in turn could dictate foreign policy.

After the Spanish embargo debate, American Catholicism had become more isolationist and had endorsed neutrality legislation. Although a few men, such as George Cardinal Mundelein, supported an aggressive foreign policy, most leading prelates appeared to be isolationists. When war came to Europe on September 1, 1939, the Catholic press and Catholic leaders pledged themselves to support the president in this crisis. Their support, however, was influenced by the belief that Roosevelt would keep us out of war. He was a nationalist first and not, as Reverend James Gillis, editor of the *Catholic World*, called Wilson, an anglophile "with a crazed ambition to shape the destinies of the world." On November 11, 1939, a poll of Catholic college students found 96.5 percent opposed to United States entry into the war. Even as Polish soldiers fled before the German blitzkrieg, the Catholic Press Association of the United States resolved that it "deprecates any tendency to embroil the United States of America in the present war." Cardinal O'Connell of Boston expressed fervent thanks that the administration was firmly committed to staying out of the European war. Bishop Thomas K. Gorman of Reno joined a local club dedicated to preventing United States involvement in any "European or occidental conflict."[2] Such sentiments were repeated frequently during the next year all across the country by bishops, priests, and laymen.

1

In asserting their opposition to United States involvement, American Catholics fell back on a few general ideas, almost cliches, which they carefully refined in articles and speeches. One popular argument for isolationism took the form of a theologically determined view of history. This idea assumed that the war had been caused by man's corrupt nature. Monsignor Fulton Sheen frequently pointed out on his radio program that the war was "a judgment of God." Reverend Dr. Joseph B. Code of Catholic University explained that the conflict emerged from the "exclusion of Christ from public life" which began with the Reformation. Father Robert I. Gannon of Fordham explained that nothing but war could come to a people who forgot God.[3] This sort of reasoning made noninvolvement not only logical but necessary. How could anyone tamper with the working out of divine vengeance?

Sinful man had made the war, but American Catholics also believed that European man was more sinful than most. Earlier suspicions had been confirmed by the attack on Poland. Catholics, despite cultural ties with Europe, accepted the notion of America's moral superiority. Europe was now paying for its centuries of atheism and neopaganism. Archbishop Joseph Schrembs of Cleveland, Archbishop John J. Mitty of San Francisco, Reverend James Gillis, and others emphasized this aspect of the war. As Monsignor Martin C. Keating phrased it, anyone who believes Europe "can be reformed by force of arms is a maniac." Such a broad view of events explains the equanimity expressed by Father Gannon who, while admitting the terror of the war, asserted that at most it meant "the end of an epoch, and many other epochs have been ended in history."[4] The conclusion seemed obvious: there was no just side in the present conflict. Archbishop John T. McNicholas of Cincinnati explained that with the confused motives of the different allies, it was impossible to "consider this 'funny war' a Holy Crusade"; there could be no moral justification for entering it.[5]

American Catholics placed little credence in the image of a demonic Hitler bent upon world conquest in late 1939 and 1940. Such a vision arose out of later American involvement in the fighting. Now some Catholic leaders de-emphasized the war's moral dimension. It was just another round in the long series of imperialistic struggles, "an international war based on greed, a struggle to the death between two irreconcilable systems of economy." as Archbishop Francis J. L. Beckman wrote. Why should the United States worry "if Hitler and Mussolini simply want some of England's colonies," asked Edward J. Heffron, executive secretary of the National Council of Catholic Men. England had acquired its colonies by the same ruthless means. Reverend Edward L. Curran, president of the International Catholic Truth Society, campaigned to prevent old country ties and affections from blinding Catholics to the "materialistic wars of Europe." Bishop Joseph M. Corrigan, rector of Catholic University, put it this way: "Economic losses to be apprehended because of changes of sovereignty . . . on the continents of Europe, Asia, and Africa do not and cannot constitute a compelling reason or a justification for sending thousands and thousands of our citizens to mutilation and death on foreign shores or in foreign seas." Corrigan, Gillis, Gannon, and Father Coughlin hammered away on the moral sterility of the European war. To Gillis it was merely an attempt to rearrange the British empire, an "impossible organization" to begin with. To Coughlin, Beckman, and other the war was the outer manifestation of an economic revolution. After all, wrote Gannon, Germany had a right to "its economic existence," which had been ignored by the Treaty of Versailles. The United States had no role to play in such a dirty little affair. These Catholics meant to insure neutrality even if it required active politicizing in their diocesan newspapers to counter propaganda in the secular press.[6]

Reminding people of the errors of the earlier crusade and world war proved a popular means of promoting neutrality. Some men, such as Bishop John M. Gannon of Erie, Pennsylvania, might recommend that the church totally ignore the war in Europe as the "handiwork of civil governments" and plead that the Catholic press refrain from writing about the conflict. But other prelates, such as Archbishop Michael J. Curley of Baltimore, feared that to ignore the war would allow the United States to drift into the conflict and repeat the absurdity of 1917. Curley and Gillis both recalled that the United States had gone to war to save democracy and "produced a crop of dictators." They begged for no more quixotic attempts to enforce justice in Europe. The Catholic press prayed that America would "not allow herself to be used by the allies as she was the last time"—to bankrupt us and "sacrifice the flower of our youth." Even Archbishop Francis Spellman, who had been appointed to the New York See in 1939 and was generally sympathic to the administration, could not resist preaching to the national convention of the American Legion in September 1940 that, while our idealism of 1917 had been genuine, our democratic system was not transportable. Martin Carmody, a leader of the Knights of Columbus, urged his colleagues not to repeat the mistake of 1917 since Europe was filled with only "hate and greed." The next day the Knights passed a resolution affirming their belief in nonintervention and deploring the current policy of the administration. Bishop William A. Griffin of Trenton feared that the entire sordid process by which we were tricked into World War I might easily be repeated in 1941.[7]

Visions of the future as well as the past forced Catholic leaders to oppose a strong foreign policy. Many argued in favor of noninvolvement on the grounds that another crusade would promote revolution in the United States or, at a minimum, would postpone social reforms. "Our first front is at home, our first duty is to our neighbor, our first obligation to our country," wrote Bishop Charles H. Leblond of St. Joseph, Missouri. While we run around "trying to put out our neighbor's fire," said Cardinal O'Connell of Boston, "we may well come home to find our own burned down in our absence." Archbishop Curley warned that America's "economic structure will collapse" along with its social arrangement if it entered the war. "Capitalism will dig its own grave by moving toward war," warned Archbishop McNicholas in a Christmas sermon of 1940. Such Catholic leaders as Archbishop Spellman, Monsignor Sheen, Reverend LaFarge, Mrs. Vincent L. Greene, president of the League of Catholic Women, George Johnson, director of the Educational Department of the NCWC, and Dr. Robert Pollock of Fordham, all insisted that we had plenty of problems to solve at home without going abroad.[8] Unstated but present within these fears of domestic dislocation were Catholic apprehensions over the advances which communism might make in such circumstances, especially if the United States should end up being allied with Russia.[9]

Catholics looked to Europe and saw a morally obscure conflict, the prospect of Soviet intervention, and the possibility of American participation destroying domestic institutions. No wonder they concluded that the best course of action for the United States was to remain aloof while building its strength. Such a course would guarantee that America would be "the real strong man at the next peace conference table." Our opportunity would come when peace appeared, said McNicholas, O'Connell, and others. The Reverend Dr. Edwin Ryan of the Institute of Ibero-American Studies at Catholic University gave a lofty expression to this theory of disengagement. We would stand as the great sanctuary of Western civilization during the crisis. After the war we would restore culture to the world. As Archbishop Beckman phrased it, the United States had "a sublime mission in a world almost totally at war."[10] Regardless of how it was phrased, in lofty or mean terms, the message spelled trouble for Roosevelt's diplomacy.

2

Catholic isolationism manifested itself in attacks on Roosevelt's revised foreign policy program. Difficulties appeared soon after England and France declared war on Germany. The Catholic press had unanimously praised the official neutrality of the United States. But when Germany and Russia proceeded to divide up Poland, the president again tried to revise the existing neutrality legislation to permit the sale of military equipment as well as strategic material under the cash-and-carry formula. Despite some talk of reasserting traditional international law for neutrals, Roosevelt's real motive was to help the Allies who controlled the seas. Unfortunately, public opposition to neutrality revision remained so strong that the president had to equivocate and argue that a new law would help America stay out of the war. At no time did the administration satisfactorily explain how an extension of the cash-and-carry principle to military equipment would keep America at peace. Roosevelt's disingenuous argument converted few men in Congress or out. Isolationists protested vigorously during the debate over passage of the Fourth Neutrality Act. After spending much time and effort creating three previous measures, all designed to keep the United States out of war, Congress could not supinely accept an attempt to turn the country into an arsenal for democracy. Such a step would resemble closely the trade arrangements which existed during World War I and helped to push America into that earlier struggle.[11]

The American hierarchy finally became officially aware of the war and spoke out on the world situation at their annual meeting in Washington in November 1939. Their statement overflowed with banalities and general sentiments of gratitude that the United States was working for peace.[12] But such generalities had a way of becoming more specific when conveyed through less official channels, such as the editorials of diocesan newspapers, press releases by individual bishops and clergymen of distinction, and the writings of leading Catholic journalists. Here was the front line of Catholic resistance to Roosevelt's attempts at neutrality revision.

Naturally, some antagonism to neutrality revision grew out of Irish-American hatred for England. The proposed neutrality act would be un-neutral because most of the benefits would go to England and other nations which had refused to pay their earlier war debts. But the ethnic variable, intermingled with memories of World War I, often expressed itself through religious channels. Both Jim Farley and Senator Francis T. Maloney of Connecticut warned Roosevelt that there might be strong Catholic opposition to neutrality revision.[13] Senator David Walsh, Irish and Catholic, opposed revision of the neutrality law by sending a form letter to every priest (non-Irish included) in the United States. The letter included a recent speech by Walsh against revision and requested that the clerics keep in touch on how they might cooperate to avoid American involvement in the European war. Similarly, ex-Congressman John J. O'Connor, another Irish Catholic, campaigned against revision of the Third Neutrality Act on the ground that it was another attempt by Roosevelt to usurp congressional power. He also enlisted the support of isolationist priests.[14]

Father Coughlin, working with O'Connor, went on the air to argue that cash-and-carry of arms would lead inexorably to war. Patrick Scanlan, editor of the *Brooklyn Tablet*, associated those in favor of neutrality revision with those favoring the triumph of communism in Spain. The Catholic folk hero, Al Smith, had taken to the airwaves to argue the virtues of Roosevelt's policy but was denounced by both Coughlin and Scanlan, and even falsely accused of having a personal stake in the sale of arms. Reverend James Gillis of the *Catholic World* argued that Roosevelt and others were being hypocritical in urging passage of the Fourth Neutrality Act under the guise of nonintervention when what they really wanted was to aid England and France. Roosevelt would have earned more respect from Gillis if he had at least openly admitted his plan. Why repeat the stupidity of 1917? Gillis asked. Again England would be painted as an innocent lamb, despite her long tradition of imperialism. Other leading Catholic publicists who joined in denouncing neutrality revision included Reverend Dr. Edward L. Curran, president of the International Catholic Truth Society, Archbishop Francis J. L. Beckman, and Judge Edward Matthews. These men, and the editors of most diocesan papers, argued that neutrality revision would involve the United States in war and benefit no one but the communists. The editor of the *Commonweal* argued that repeal of the embargo would end chances of the United States playing the role of peacemaker. If we stayed uninvolved we might be in a better position to play a decisive role in ending the war.[15]

Roosevelt anticipated some clerical and lay Catholic opposition to his policies, but he also counted on some friendly churchmen to support neutrality revision. He took steps to insure such support. A campaign to blunt criticism and guarantee Catholic support soon involved the cooperation of Al Smith, George Cardinal Mundelein, and Father John Ryan. Smith finally accepted the argument advanced by William Allen White, later chairman of the Committee to Defend America by Aiding the Allies and a zealous supporter of Roosevelt's policy, that some appeal to Catholics should be made in light of the widespread anti-British prejudice among the Irish. On October 1, 1939, Smith was introduced to a national radio audience as a "prominent Catholic layman" and gave what Harold Ickes called "a good speech, delivered with the old Al Smith spirit," endorsing the president's amendment to the neutrality law and objecting to the attempt by certain Catholics to make a religious issue out of foreign policy. Roosevelt applauded White's work in enlisting Smith for the cause, even though the ex-governor declined to speak in Boston on the same topic.[16]

Father John Ryan also rushed into the breach to promote Roosevelt's plan. A professor at Catholic University and a leading social thinker, Ryan readily accepted White's call to join the National Non-Partisan Committee for Peace through Revision of the Neutrality Laws, a precursor to the

Committee to Defend America. On October 5, 1939, he wrote Clark M.
Eichelberger, a leader in the pro-Allied lobby, that the existing embargo
favored Germany when the United States should be helping England and
France. "If Hitler is victorious," predicted Father John Ryan, "not only
religion but the whole of Christian civilization in Europe will be gravely
endangered." After Coughlin's radio attack on the administration's revision plans, the National Non-Partisan Committee convinced Ryan to
join Charles Fenwick of the CAIP in a rebuttal over a national network.
Catholics returning from Mass on Sunday, October 24, heard Ryan
announce that the United States "is morally obliged to do all that it
reasonably can to defeat Hitler and destroy Hitlerism." While not advocating immediate entry into the war, Ryan did argue that cash-and-carry
aid to the Allies might be a way to keep America out of the war. Fenwick
limited his remarks to pointing out that the existing neutrality act actually gave aid to Germany by denying England the advantages of its naval
power.[17] The arguments of 1916 and 1917 were reappearing.

Ryan knew the dangers of engaging Catholic isolationists such as
Coughlin and Father Edward L. Curran in a public debate. He had already
declined such a debate with Curran on the arms embargo for fear of giving scandal to the faithful by having two clerics fighting in public. Ryan
and Coughlin had tangled earlier in the 1936 election campaign. Now,
once again, hundreds of scurrilous letters from Coughlin's supporters
flooded Ryan's office. Their accusations against Ryan ranged from
war-mongering, splitting the Catholic vote, and being an Anglican to
being a puppet, with Roosevelt pulling the strings. Such vehemence
convinced Ryan that, should the bishops publicly attack Coughlin, it
would merely mean that thousands of his followers would immediately
quit the church. Most of these letter-writers saw little difference between Germany and England. Most felt that aid to either side would
merely play into the hands of the Russians. The keys to Catholic
isolationism appeared to be anticommunism and a general dislike of
Europe.[18]

George Cardinal Mundelein's support of neutrality revision was an
extension of his general endorsement of Roosevelt and the New Deal.
His diocesan newspaper, the *New World*, thought the issue clear—if
Hitlerism triumphed, Western civilization was finished. Furthermore,
aid to England would keep the United States from being dragged into

war. So eager was the Cardinal to refute Catholic isolationists that on
October 1 he worked with White House aide Tom Corcoran on a pro-
Roosevelt speech to be delivered over the facilities of the National
Broadcasting Company. The next day he was dead at 67, victim of a
sudden coronary attack. Despite the untimely event, the cardinal's
auxiliary bishop, Bernard J. Sheil, who was even more committed to
Roosevelt's diplomacy, went ahead with the speech. Most listeners
identified Sheil's remarks with Mundelein, but few knew that Corcoran
had played a role in drafting the speech. Sheil thanked God that "in
these critical revolutionary years in Europe we have had the matchless
political leadership in foreign affairs of President Roosevelt." In essence,
Sheil called upon Catholics, with the words of Cardinal Mundelein, to
support Roosevelt's recommendation to revise the neutrality laws. The
best thing for Catholics to do in memory of the cardinal was simply to
trust in the president and permit him to use his expert knowledge to
direct our foreign policy.[19]

Sheil's endorsement of the administration drew considerable attention. The talk seemed to be both a eulogy of Cardinal Mundelein and
his last will and testament. When the Vatican newspaper, *Osservatore
Romano*, quoted passages in the speech, the *New York Times* concluded
that the pope approved neutrality revision. Roosevelt certainly approved
and announced himself delighted with Sheil's "grand" effort. He wined
and dined the bishop at the White House; Tom Corcoran also attended.
Roosevelt hoped the speech by Sheil and the work by Al Smith and
Father John Ryan would help to overcome Irish and Italian opposition
to neutrality revision and rally American Catholics behind aid to
England.[20] He expressed his concern over Catholic opposition to neutrality revision to Archbishop Francis Spellman of New York, who had been
trying to promote the idea of an American ambassador to the Vatican.
Spellman worriedly read a memo from Roosevelt on the efforts by
American Catholics to defeat neutrality revision. Why should the president appoint an ambassador to the Vatican if Catholics worked against
his program? The Reverend Maurice Sheehy, head of religious education
at Catholic University, shared Spellman's dismay at such criticism of
Roosevelt and publicly predicted that the failure of neutrality revision
would be "the most tragic bit of stupidity in our history." In Sheehy's
mind, the existing neutrality laws merely aided Germany and Russia.[21]

Commentators might insist that neutrality was neither Catholic nor religious in character. Yet Catholics *qua* Catholics were being asked either to support the revision or reject it. Coughlin appealed to Catholics. Roosevelt and William Allen White acknowledged a religious dimension by appealing to Al Smith, Father John Ryan, Cardinal Mundelein, and Archbishop Spellman for support. The outcome of their debate was mixed. The discussion probably helped prevent the growth of a univocal Catholic posture toward neutrality revision, or at least the image of such a posture in the minds of non-Catholics. Isolationist and revisionist Catholics canceled themselves out and the religious dimension was neutralized, permitting other variables, such as party affiliation, to work more effectively. In the House of Representatives, forty-one Catholics voted to revise the neutrality act, but twenty-three voted against the administration. In the Senate, seven of the eleven Catholic members supported Roosevelt. The split was primarily along party lines. The eventual passage of the Fourth Neutrality Act on November 4, 1939, must be attributed more to general congressional sympathy for the Allies than to the clever strategy of the executive department. But the final act also made explicit the establishment of European combat zones into which American ships were forbidden to proceed. Sympathy for the Allies did not mean that the United States wanted to get into the war.[22]

3

The next serious clash between Catholics and Roosevelt arose from attempts to pass a military draft bill. If Catholic leaders could become active on neutrality revision, a religiously neutral issue, the Burke-Wadsworth Universal Selective Service Bill, a measure which touched home, could be expected to provoke even more interest. Before passage, the bill stimulated an impressive display of Catholic clerical unity. The selective service proposal involved no grave matter of conscience. But the American church did take what amounted to an official position against the draft. Indeed, few Roosevelt measures met with such clerical opposition. In early July 1940 the administration announced plans for the first peacetime draft in American history. The Catholic press experienced a moment of unity as, from the *Boston Pilot* to the *Inland Catholic* of Spokane and from the *True Voice* of Omaha to the *Sign* of Union City,

New Jersey, editorials rang with the same tone of denunciation. Similarly the bishops of the country, John T. McNicholas of Cincinnati, Joseph Schrembs of Cleveland, and Michael J. Curley of Baltimore, condemned the idea of a peacetime draft as totalitarianism. Liberals at the *Commonweal* found themselves on the same side of a public issue as Archbishop Francis J. L. Beckman and other Catholic isolationists. Beckman, Curley, and Patrick Scanlan of the *Brooklyn Tablet* warned that the bill represented a concerted effort to work the public into a war psychosis. It was just another part of the propaganda plot to get the United States into war on the side of England. As Senator Walsh of Massachusetts told the annual convention of the Knights of Columbus, a peacetime draft would only lead to precipitous action at a time when we should be trying to "avoid all wars originating in Europe, Asia and Africa."[23]

McNicholas, Schrembs, and others, although not extreme isolationists, criticized and exaggerated the bill's tendency to regiment and militarize the country. Like the editors of the *Commonweal*, these men were unwilling to accept such a step until voluntary techniques had been exhausted and unless there was imminent danger of invasion. McNicholas and Monsignor Ready of the NCWC agreed that the government should not try a compulsory draft until it had attempted to raise volunteers for one year of service. Both men were confident that millions would flock to the colors in defense of the nation. Significantly, all Catholic commentators spoke of a conscripted army as a means of self-defense. Few raised the possibility that such troops might be used to fight in Europe.[24]

Catholics also argued that provisions of the conscription bill attacked religion in the United States, violating the principles of separation of church and state. Many clerics honestly believed the Burke-Wadsworth bill threatened the existence of the Roman Catholic church. A number of leading bishops expressed such a fear after studying the initial draft of legislation presented to Congress in July 1940 and finding its provisions for clerical exemption totally inadequate. Dennis Cardinal Dougherty joined Beckman, McNicholas, and Bishop John F. Noll in urging Catholics to write to their congressmen to request an amendment exempting clergymen. Father Robert I. Gannon of Fordham warned that "irreligious intellectuals" must not be permitted to determine who should be drafted. The original bill would have permitted the president to "disorganize the Catholic Church, to abolish its long established customs, to disrupt its centuries old practices," in the opinion of the editor of *Extension Magazine*. He and others expressed concern that Roosevelt would be able to draft the entire Catholic clergy.[25]

Indignation and consternation arose because the bill failed to provide for the exemption of seminarians and brothers from military duty and called for a deferment of priests only. Deferment, of course, was not automatic, as was exemption. In fact, some senators, such as Morris Sheppard of Texas and Josh Lee of Oklahoma, opposed any specific exemption of ministers of religion. Such a bill surprised Catholics, who had expected a reinstitution of the 1917 exemption of clergy from the draft. On July 4, 1940, the bishops of the administrative board of the NCWC issued a public statement on the problem. Unlike extreme isolationists such as Beckman and Father Coughlin, these men were willing to admit that the "tragic circumstances of the present" required certain defensive measures by the government, including "the training of large numbers of our citizens in the arts of warfare." Self-protection dictated these steps, argued the bishops, but the dangers should not be exaggerated. Nor should we simply endorse "programs promoted by any group, be it militarist, isolationist, or interventionist," without subjecting it "to critical appraisal and cool judgment." Furthermore, the statement read, "no plan for the national defense should do unnecessary violence" to America's religious heritage.[26]

On July 11, 1940, Monsignor Ready of the NCWC passed these objections on to the president. Roosevelt replied by promising that the bishops' point of view would be given every consideration. To insure such consideration, Catholics immediately launched a lobby for revision of the bill in Congress. They sought to have the bill specifically exempt priests, seminarians, and brothers. Out in Wyoming, Catholic Senator Joseph C. O'Mahoney received letters from Bishop P. A. McGovern of Cheyenne and Reverend Robert M. Kelley, president of Regis College of Denver, asking for revision of the draft bill. McGovern argued that Catholics repudiated pacifism but felt that military service was "incompatible with the clerical and religious state." The government had recognized such a status in 1917. The new policy could only weaken the "free operation of . . . spiritual forces" essential for democracy. McGovern estimated that exemptions would affect about 34,000 priests of all ages, 14,000 students, and 5,000 brothers. Kelley insisted on the exemption of Jesuit novices, scholastics, and brothers who could better serve the nation in a spiritual capacity. Senator O'Mahoney politely

replied to both men that he expected a broader exemption policy to
be incorporated into the final bill.[27] Other politicians shared this conviction, especially after such groups as the Catholic Central Verein of
America, the Catholic Women's Union, the National Conference of
Catholic Men, and various bishops, priests, and editors urged their
friends and associates to write to senators and congressmen calling
for an exemption amendment. Archbishop Beckman tried to capitalize
on the exemption problem, using it to attack the very notion of a draft.
He sent a telegram to Senator Walsh, informing him that the "overwhelming majority of Catholic people in the Midwest are vigorously
opposed to compulsory peacetime draft legislation." Bishop Christian
H. Windelmann of Wichita addressed a letter to Congress in which he
requested exemption for priests, religious, and seminarians. Form
letters to this effect left the National Council of Catholic Men's offices
for Congress on July 24.[28]

A high point of the campaign came when Monsignor Ready, as he
predicted in his letter to Roosevelt, appeared in black suit and Roman
collar before committees of both houses of Congress to argue the Catholic bishops' disapproval of the original bill. On July 11, 1940, Ready had
asked the Senate Committee on Military Affairs that deferment status
be changed to exemption status for priests, seminarians, and brothers.
He delivered the same message to the House Committee on Military
Affairs on July 30, 1940. Ready even seemed to reflect the extreme
isolationist position of Beckman and Coughlin by hinting that the original language of the bill was a product of military thinking, arguing that
no such draft was needed at this time and strongly urging that a voluntary enlistment be attempted first. If a bill had to be passed, however,
Ready insisted that immunity rather than deferment should be the
normal right of every clergyman. Catholic leaders reassured the nation,
however, that no one should interpret their opposition or Ready's
testimony as a threat to resist the draft. Time and time again they
explained that, while they opposed the bill, if it was made law, an
individual, if called, must serve unless it conflicted with his conscience.
Even in a case of conflict, the citizen should give the government all
benefit of doubt.[29]

Ready's testimony and the Catholic lobby produced results in both
houses of Congress. On July 30, 1940, Representative John McCormack
supported an amendment to exempt seminarians, priests, and brothers.

In the Senate on August 16, Edwin C. Johnson, a Colorado Democrat, introduced a similar amendment covering priests and students in preparation for the ministry. Other senators supporting such a move included Francis T. Maloney of Connecticut, Joseph F. Guffey of Pennsylvania, W. Warren Barbour of New Jersey, Allen J. Ellender of Louisiana, Theodore F. Green of Rhode Island, A. B. Chandler of Kentucky, David I. Walsh of Massachusetts, James M. Mead of New York, Arthur Vandenburg of Michigan, and many others. Even Brigadier General William E. Shedd, army assistant chief of staff, offered testimony in August that the War Department wanted deferment of divinity students included in the bill.[30]

The Catholic campaign was so effective that it generated a reaction. Drew Pearson and Robert S. Allen wrote in their *Washington Merry-Go-Round* column that honest and sincere Catholics such as Ready were being used, "at least in part, by a group of pro-Nazi bundite-isolationists to serve their own interests." Ready dismissed such charges as nonsense. Isolationism was a weak cause indeed if it could derive satisfaction from the final form of the Burke-Wadsworth bill. By the end of August, both the Senate and the House had adopted a bill which exempted from service "regular or duly ordained ministers of religion and students who are preparing for the ministry in theological or divinity schools recognized as such for more than one year prior to the date of enactment" of the bill. The clergy would still have to register, but they were now exempt from service. By January 1941, the Selective Service System had established a rule exempting lay brothers of the Catholic church from the draft on the basis of certification by Archbishop Edward Mooney of Detroit that in canon law they were regular ministers of religion. The director of selective service also noted in his decision the statements made by Chairman Andrew J. May of the House Military Affairs Committee and Joseph F. Guffey of the Senate, which indicated that brothers were covered by the original exemption. The church would function during the war with little disturbance from the draft.[31] The entire episode reveals the degree of unity achievable by American Catholics on a nontheological problem, the deep distrust of most clerics for militarism and foreign adventure, and the effectiveness of Catholic pressure on Congress.

On the eve of the first drawing of selective service numbers in late October 1941, the president joined Archbishop Spellman at a review of the Reserve Officers Training Corps at Fordham University. On the next

day, as he drew the first draft number, the president read a statement
from representatives of the "three faiths." The Catholic portion came
from a month-old speech by Spellman, a copy of which he had sent to
Marguerite LeHand with the notation: "Hope the enclosed is along our
president's line of thought." Roosevelt quoted the cardinal as saying,
"I do believe it is better to have protection and not need it than to need
protection and not have it." Spellman insisted that the United States
wanted peace but must prepare for war because of what happened to
peace-loving nations which did not prepare. "We really cannot longer
afford to be moles who cannot see, or ostriches who will not see. . . .
We Americans want peace and we shall prepare for a peace, but not a
peace whose definition is slavery or death." This was the type of endorsement that Roosevelt wanted from Catholics in support of his policies.[32]

4

   Once the draft bill had been passed, an increasing number of Catholic
leaders threw their support behind the more popular cause of general
preparedness. Such a consensus was grounded in a firm belief that military appropriations were for self-defense. Earlier, in 1938 and 1939,
some Catholic writers had lamented that an increase in military spending
invariably led to foreign adventures. A few social thinkers, such as Reverend John F. Cronin of St. Mary's Seminary of Baltimore, had expressed
concern over the prospects that domestic reform would be sidetracked
by defense mobilization. But by late 1940, as the administration's program
became more and more elaborate and as the rapid collapse of France demonstrated German power, leaders of American Catholicism generally endorsed preparedness. The administrative board of the NCWC offered no
objections and in November 1940 pledged its cooperation in defense
work.[33]
   Many different motives prompted Catholic support of preparedness.
Men such as Bishop James H. Ryan of Omaha urged Catholic support
for military spending because events in Europe had proved that only
force made any impression on some foreign leaders. Bishop Joseph F.
Rummel of New Orleans considered support of defense spending a requirement of citizenship; Bishop Francis P. Keough of Providence,
Rhode Island, agreed. Bishop John M. Gannon of Erie bluntly denounced

those who would oppose "the decisions of lawfully constituted authority."
Gannon told the Catholic Daughters of America that "wheresoever our
flag goes, there we go." In the words of Archbishop Edward P. Mooney,
national defense was "only common sense in a bully's world." No one
would have reason to question the loyalty or patriotism of American
Catholics on the issue of national defense. Few voices were now raised
about the dangers of such preparation leading to war. Forgotten was the
analogy of military preparedness having propelled the United States into
World War I. Even the most violent opponents of Woodrow Wilson's
crusade, such as Reverend James Gillis, had to fall in line behind Roosevelt's preparedness campaign.[34]

But would Irish Catholics support outright aid for England? Preparedness and self-defense might be acceptable, but American aid to one of
the belligerents could only be interpreted as direct intervention in the
war. By mid-1940 Roosevelt's commitment to the cause of England had
been made clear. Despite the proximity of a presidential election campaign, he authorized the exchange of fifty over-age destroyers for nine-
ty-nine year leases to certain British bases covering approaches to the
Western Hemisphere. In consummating this exchange with the aid of
Admiral Harold Stark, Roosevelt upset Senator David Walsh of Massachusetts, who had authored an act in June 1940 providing that American
equipment could be released only if the navy certified that it was useless
for defense. Walsh wrote Roosevelt that the exchange with England
would hurt the Democrats politically because it was a warlike act and
most Americans wanted peace. Roosevelt replied by emphasizing the
strategic advantage gained by the acquisition of the island bases.
"Honestly, Dave," wrote the president, "these islands are of the utmost
importance to our national defense as naval and air operating bases."[35]

Walsh and other Catholics remained unconvinced. A contributor to
the *Catholic World*, John V. Connorton, wrote that the exchange was
another step in the mounting campaign to get the United States into war
on the side of England. He warned Catholics that their opposition to aid
for England would lead liberals to make charges of clerical fascism. But
Connorton considered himself a liberal and saw no reason "why the great
social reforms of the New Deal should be exposed to the uncertain future
of a great international war." He and the liberal editors of the *Commonweal* urged the strengthening of the United States rather than the strip-

ping of our defenses for England. They deplored the passive way most
Americans accepted Roosevelt's swap.[36]

Similarly, when Roosevelt moved to a more expansive program of
aid to England, the Lend-Lease bill of early 1941, Catholic publicists
loudly complained. Reverend John LaFarge wrote that the Lend-Lease
act signaled the end of popular sovereignty and the beginning of dictatorship in the United States. He personally felt that the best hope for a renewal of justice in the world was to keep America out of any European
conflict. Reverend Joseph Thorning went so far as to insist that Roosevelt demand that the British stop persecuting Ireland before granting
Lend-Lease aid to England. Reverend Edmund A. Walsh of Georgetown
University, a noted author on diplomatic topics and head of Georgetown'
foreign service school, deplored any attempt to save England by risking
United States involvement. One editor called Lend-Lease the formal end
of our foreign policy and a repudiation of the ideas of George Washington
another agreed that the passage of Lend-Lease would make "it virtually
certain that the United States will be involved in the war within a few
months at most."[37] The bill even led to a temporary rapprochement
between Father Coughlin and the NCWC. Still, this Catholic opposition
does not appear very much different from the disapproval expressed by
millions of other Americans.[38] Administration stalwarts such as Senator
Joseph C. O'Mahoney were bombarded with letters protesting the bill.[39]

Catholic wariness of Lend-Lease centered on fears Catholics shared
with fellow citizens rather than on a unique Irish-Catholic anglophobia.
They suspected that the act would give the president too much power
and that it would lead the United States into war. But it was precisely
the connection between such measures as Lend-Lease and eventual
American participation in the war that most supporters of the administration refused to admit. American public opinion polls from 1939
through 1941 reflected this attitude. From a position of disinterest in
Europe in early 1939, public opinion moved steadily toward the idea of
supporting England, but always with the stipulation that America stay
out of war. More and more Catholic leaders were beginning to share this
sense of limited involvement, provided it did not mean that American
boys would fight in Europe. Even Reverend James Gillis, no friend of the
British, was eventually willing to at least extend to them most-favored-na-
tion status in our trade. But he wanted it understood that no American bc

should get into "this new European catastrophe, the latest in an unending series caused by the vicious and dangerous tactics of European politicians." In November 1940, sixty prominent Catholic priests and laymen signed a public statement urging unlimited aid to England on the understanding that if Americans did not act, they would be "left to face the dictators . . . alone." Bishop Robert E. Lucey of Amarillo and Bishop Edwin V. O'Hara of Kansas City were the most prominent of the signers. In the next month, forty-four men from this same group opposed a plan by Herbert Hoover to send food to the people under Nazi occupation on the grounds that it would defeat the British blockade, make food available to the German army, and be "contrary to the best interests of Christianity," which apparently was represented by the British navy. This statement directly challenged an earlier endorsement of the Hoover plan by Cardinal O'Connell of Boston. Perhaps it was this conflict that explains the absence of any clerical names from the second list, which included such supporters as Francis E. McMahon, Carlton J. H. Hayes, Harry J. Carmen, and William M. Agar.[40]

This same circle worked with The Century Group, an association of eastern anglophiles, to promote Catholic interventionism in 1940 and 1941. Seeking an early American entry into the war to aid England, they established the Fight For Freedom Committee to promote their cause. Since American Catholics represented "the strongest and steadiest force for appeasement in the country," according to William Agar, the group's Catholic expert, it is not surprising that much work went toward reeducating this segment of the population. Agar, Hayes, Ross Hoffman, and Chancellor James Byrne of New York University collected and distributed pro-intervention statements by leading Catholics in the United States and England. Archbishop Joseph Schrembs, Bishop Robert E. Lucey, and Edwin O'Hara proved cooperative.[41]

At the same time, priests such as Reverend Maurice Sheehy and Father John Ryan, while working for aid to England, did not go as far as Agar and The Century Group. Ryan expressed the thinking of an increasing number of Catholics by writing that he did "not want to see our country get into the war in the sense of sending soldiers to Europe and I am sure that there is no danger that that will happen." Time and time again, elements of the Catholic press in early 1941 reluctantly admitted the need for aid to England but simultaneously urged Roosevelt to keep the United

States out of the war. In 1941 Archbishop Spellman of New York joined
Al Smith, Carlton Hayes, and others to lead a pontifical mass in prayer
for the suffering people of Great Britain. Archbishop Edward A. Mooney
of Detroit coordinated the Catholic Relief Service to help England. But
these same men vehemently objected to suggestions of sending American
troops abroad or of declaring war.[42]

Of course, such thoughts were far from Roosevelt's mind at this time.
In fact, he argued that Lend-Lease would help to keep the United States
out of war. Moving cautiously with the bill, after a great deal of contact
with congressional leaders such as John McCormack and Sam Rayburn,
Roosevelt eventually acceded to demands by the House for periodic reports on shipments abroad and for a time limit on the powers of Lend-
Lease. These concessions helped push the bill through despite unfriendly
testimony before the Senate Foreign Relations Committee by such men
as Joseph P. Kennedy, who had recently resigned as ambassador to England, and Professor Herbert Wright of the Catholic University. Their
negative testimony did not offset the endorsement of Lend-Lease by
Michael Williams, editor of the *Commonweal*. Williams also emphasized
that the well-known opposition to Lend-Lease by Father Edward L.
Curran and Cardinal O'Connell of Boston did not mean that the church
opposed the bill. Despite some congressional dismay, confusion, and
debate over the possibility of aid going to Russia, Roosevelt finally
signed the measure on March 11, 1941.[43]

5

The president had a victory but he also had every reason to be upset
at what appeared to be continued Catholic opposition to his foreign
policy. First, Catholics opposed neutrality revision; then, selective service; now, Lend-Lease. They were even flirting with the America First
Committee. This organization, begun in September 1940 through the
efforts of R. Douglas Stuart and General Robert E. Wood, advocated
the following goals: to erect an impregnable home defense system; to
convince the public that democracy's preservation depended upon keeping out of war; to defeat Roosevelt's foreign policy, which was leading
the country into war.[44] Even a dull mind could see how this organization
might effectively appeal to a considerable segment of the American

Catholic population. Indeed, the America First Committee network in the eastern United States had strict instructions not to criticize Father Coughlin because of the support his followers were giving the cause. In appointing a national committee for publicity, Wood and Stuart saw to it that at least three Catholics served as members. A zealous "America Firster" in Brooklyn went even further by sponsoring a national poll of the Catholic clergy, the results of which indicated widespread identity of interest between the club and the Catholic priesthood. In May 1941 pamphlets issued by the America First Committee quoted from the statements made by the bishops of the administrative board of the NCWC only a month earlier. Monsignor Ready of the NCWC protested the use of statements out of their context, but despite his indignation a common enthusiasm for staying clear of the European conflict un-doubtedly existed. No one could have been more sympathetic than Archbishop Beckman of Dubuque, who happily joined Senator Burton K. Wheeler on June 21 at a large America First Committee rally and spoke over nationwide radio in behalf of the cause.[45]

This flirtation by Catholics with the America First Committee had dangerous potential for the administration. Even more dangerous, however, was the prospect of an alliance between the followers of Father Coughlin and the pro-German faction in the United States. The president was disturbed enough about such a prospect to write worriedly to Ed Flynn, political boss of the Bronx, of some rumors which had reached the White House. The pro-German publisher Verne Marshall of Iowa had approached Democratic leaders in New York City for sup-port. Even worse, "in one of the Brooklyn districts the Marshall crowd and Father Coughlin's crowd have come together."[46]

Fortunately, the president had at his disposal means by which to redirect such Catholic attitudes. Many church leaders seemed less sure of their isolationism. He had been encouraged by the support given Lend-Lease by men such as Father John Ryan, Archbishop Spellman, and Reverend Maurice Sheehy. The problem seemed to be one of providing encouragement for this interventionist faction while not appearing to meddle in church matters. Roosevelt did not hesitate to become involved because he was convinced of the importance of religious opinion and of the effectiveness of prelates in controlling such opinion. His displeasure with Catholic opposition to Lend-Lease and support of the America First Committee was conveyed directly to Ameleto Cicognani the apostolic delegate, by Myron Taylor, special representative to the Vatican, who was then visiting the United States. This episode marked the beginning of Roosevelt's ultimately successful campaign to force American Catholics into his foreign policy consensus. At the president's direction, Taylor complained bitterly to Cicognani about how the America First Committee had distributed in May some 25,000 leaflets in which official Catholic sanction for nonintervention by the United States was implied. Cicognani explained the actions already taken by Monsignor Ready to correct this deceit and insisted that the original statement was not inimical to the administration's policy. Simultaneously, Taylor's assistant in Rome, Harold Tittmann, Jr., passed on the same protests at what he called the pro-Axis stand of American churchmen in conversation with the Vatican secretary of state. Monsignor Montini of the Vatican, who later became Pope Paul VI, wasted little time in presenting a detailed rebuttal to such charges. He insisted that not one of the 116 American bishops supported Hitler, that the NCWC Board of Bishops had issued statements in favor of the preparedness program, that only two high-ranking prelates had opposed Roosevelt's program (Tittmann guessed that this referred to Cardinal O'Connell of Boston and Archbishop John T. McNicholas), and that, to the best of the Vatican's knowledge, very few of the 34,000 Catholic priests in the United States were sympathetic to the Nazis.[47]

Neither Cicognani nor Montini understood Roosevelt's need for more support in the conduct of his foreign policy because they did not understand how American political leadership functioned. That the clergy were unsympathetic to the Nazis was not enough; they might also be unsympathetic to Roosevelt's policies. Even so, the president could hardly accept Montini's generalizations about the attitude of the American clergy. From Philadelphia he had just received word from Michael F. Doyle, an enthusiastic supporter and ardent Catholic, that the antiadministration philippics of Archbishop Beckman represented the thinking of a group of Catholic prelates of German ancestry, most of whom resided in the West.[48]

Doyle promised to work against such influences within the church. He was joined by Reverend Maurice Sheehy of Catholic University, who had earlier written Roosevelt of a plan to sponsor a series of talks by leading Catholics, including Bishop James H. Ryan of Omaha and Cardinal Arthur Hinsley of England, both of whom would praise the administration's program. In early 1941 Sheehy wrote the president's secretary, Missy LeHand, promising to give a nationwide address condemning "fence-sitters" and calling for support of the "chief," even if it meant the loss of his post at Catholic University. Later the same year he suggested to Vice-President Henry Wallace that liaison be established between Cardinal O'Connell of Boston, an increasingly bitter critic of the administration, and the president. According to Sheehy, O'Connell was approaching senility and simply wanted to be in on what was going on.[49] Roosevelt made no attempt to direct these efforts but certainly welcomed them.

Harold Ickes, secretary of the interior, also worked on the Catholics to bring them in line. He had been after Roosevelt for months in 1939 to put pressure on the Vatican to appoint Bishop Sheil, who was pro-administration, to the politically sensitive episcopal chair in Chicago, which was vacant. When Bishop Samuel A. Stritch of Milwaukee was eventually transferred to Chicago, Ickes could only pout about Roosevelt's timidity and talk with Frank Murphy about how the American hierarchy was giving aid to fascism by its neurotic anticommunism. He felt that the president would have to exert pressure to get them in line.[50]

Actually, American Catholics were already moving into Roosevelt's consensus, even before his pressure on the church became noticeable. The Vatican's estimate of the attitude of the American church may have been more accurate than Roosevelt could perceive. Bishop Robert Lucey of Texas and Father John Ryan were both charter members of the Committee to Defend America by Aiding the Allies. Lucey, especially active in 1940 and 1941, kept insisting on the need for the nation to take a stand against unjust aggression. He felt that neutrality in the face of German attacks in Europe was tantamount to criminal negligence. Those citizens who thought it possible to isolate the United States from the trouble and to maintain democracy in a world of totalitarianism were speaking nonsense, in his judgment. Lucey argued that the future of the United States was "bound up with the security of the world."[51] Father John Ryan gave speeches equating Hitler with Attila the Hun and warned of the destruction of religion which would follow a Nazi triumph. Unequivocally, Ryan announced that "the United States is morally bound to do all that it reasonably can to defeat Hitler, and destroy Hitlerism." In

1940 Ryan had urged American support of a compromise peace which
would not leave Europe open to Soviet penetration. But by June 1941
he had lost any sense of timidity about urging United States intervention
and thoughts of a compromise peace were far from his mind.[52]

Other Catholic leaders were also joining the parade to Roosevelt's
interventionist coalition. Francis P. Matthews, leader of the Knights of
Columbus, publicly denounced the notion that the United States could be
indifferent to what was happening in Europe. By 1941 the editorial staff
of the *NCWC News Service* agreed with Edward Heffron of their education
department that Hitlerism had to be stopped and that isolationism would
only prevent the United States from playing a mediating role at the peace
conference. As Postmaster General Frank Walker expressed it to the National Conference of Catholic Charities in 1941, "we cannot have char-
ity in our hearts and insist that this war which has involved three-fourths
of the earth's surface is no concern of ours." Walker predicted that a German victory would mean the end of spiritual freedom in the United States.

The Department of State worked consistently to bolster the efforts
of Catholic internationalists. Undersecretary of State Sumner Welles
personally supplied information to the pro-Roosevelt bishop of St.
Augustine, Florida, Joseph P. Hurley. The bishop requested assistance
in June 1941 in composing a speech which, he predicted, "will go far
towards refuting the claim of some Catholic publicists that they have
papal support for their attitudes [of isolationism]." As Welles wrote his
assistant, Hurley "is . . . one of the two or three outstanding members
of the Catholic hierarchy in this country and is wholly and completely
cooperative in the field of foreign policy." Welles erred about Hurley's
ranking in the American hierarchy but was right about his support of
Roosevelt. A copy of Welles's speech, explaining American attitudes
toward the recent invasion of Russia, quickly reached Hurley in Florida.[54]

Bishop Hurley had earned his reputation of being a friend of the administration by his consistent praise of the president. The praise began
on the very day Hurley was transferred from the Vatican to his new post
at St. Augustine in November 1940. He lauded Roosevelt for reacting to
the war in a way which would localize it and would protect American
interest. Such an approach made more sense to the bishop than the silly
game of "simulated" neutrality. In a number of public addresses in May
1941, the bishop berated those who insisted that communism was Ameri-

ca's number one enemy when in fact "today the first enemy of our humanity—the killers of our priests, the despoilers of our temples, the foe of all we love both as Americans and Catholics—is the Nazi." Hurley attacked the enemies of the administration who had sought to defeat neutrality revision, the draft bill, and Lend-Lease. The next month, on nationwide radio, he referred to Roosevelt's critics as men from the "crank school of economics, the tirade school of journalism, and the ostrich school of strategy."[55] Needless to say, such an endorsement of Roosevelt's policy by a Catholic bishop recently returned from a tour of duty at the Vatican provoked considerable attention in the United States.

Hurley's speeches upset both Cicognani, the apostolic delegate, and Archbishop Spellman of New York. Everyone expected Father Coughlin and Archbishop Beckman to resent these pro-Roosevelt statements, but, in addition, many American bishops disapproved of an eccesiastical call for war at a time when the pope was calling for peace. Cicognani himself was at a loss to explain why Hurley saw fit to give such a strong endorsement of Roosevelt's foreign policy after having just returned from a Vatican assignment and having been only recently invested with the miter. Spellman and Cicognani were most concerned over the grave public dissension which Hurley's speech prompted among American Catholics. The ecclesiastical leaders of Boston, Cincinnati, Baltimore, and Dubuque had been calling for nonintervention. Now the bishop of St. Augustine had come out for full American participation in the conflict. Those Americans favoring intervention quickly adopted Hurley's speeches as a sign that the Catholic church endorsed Roosevelt's policy, much as the America First Committee was using other Catholic statements to defend isolationism. The NCWC requested that Hurley disassociate himself from any official standing as a spokesman for the church on foreign policy.[56]

In addition, both Cicognani and Spellman complained to the Vatican about Hurley's performance. These men would have preferred more clerical silence on such a sensitive topic, a subject upon which American Catholics disagreed. According to Cicognani and Spellman, most Catholics favored giving aid to England but were against getting into a war. Most Catholics opposed Hitler, but they also opposed Russia. Most American bishops agreed that the United States should try to promote

a settlement in the war. Of course, there were a few bishops who were
stronger in their views on nonintervention. Hurley's boosting of Roosevelt merely gave these Catholic isolationists an opportunity to shout
back. Beckman, Curley, Shaughnessy, and McNicholas jumped at the
chance, as did such publications as the *Brooklyn Tablet*, the *Catholic
Review* of Baltimore, the *Tidings* of Los Angeles, and the *Witness* of
Dubuque. Beckman even went on national radio on July 27, 1941, to
denounce Hurley (without naming him), and to emphasize that the
United States had no stake in the war being fought over "the sordid
motive of economic imperialism." Archbishop Curley of Baltimore
complained privately about Hurley's endorsement of Roosevelt.[57]

Such discord in American Catholicism embarrassed Cicognani and
Spellman. The latter wrung his hands over stories appearing in the
secular press about clerical brothers fighting in public. But, as
Cicognani wrote to Rome, there was a limit to what one could do.
He admitted considering "the possibility of making Monsignor Beckman
shut up." But upon seeking advice from other bishops, Cicognani was
told to avoid a confrontation since Beckman would not back down
without a public fight.[58] The apostolic delegate and Spellman appeared
primarily concerned over two prelates fighting in public. A sense of
propriety rather than the endorsement or rejection of Roosevelt's policy
seemed most important.

6

Such discord was fast disappearing, however. More Catholics joined
the Roosevelt consensus each day. For example, Cicognani did not
threaten to "shut up" Bishop Robert Lucey, who had been making
similar endorsements of intervention and denouncing isolationism for
months. Father John Ryan, Reverend Maurice Sheehy, and others were
active members of the White Committee, which was virtually an official
lobby for the administration. The Catholic Association for International
Peace had endorsed intervention by April 1941. As Francis McMahon
of Notre Dame told delegates to the fifteenth annual convention of the
CAIP, American isolationists were to blame for the present international
chaos. Spellman might privately regret Hurley's speeches and the blatant
way Attorney General Frank Murphy had gotten himself invited to the

annual meeting of the Knights of Columbus in order to round up support for Roosevelt's policies. But no public attempt was being made to restore some sort of neutrality to the outlook of American Catholics, except for the increasingly hysterical outbursts of Father Coughlin and Archbishop Beckman.[59]

As the United States in the summer of 1941 drew ever closer to active participation in the war, American Catholic opinion appeared to be shifting. A highly articulate interventionist group grew in strength. Despite Roosevelt's worries, the isolationists had not captured American Catholics after all. Arnold Lunn, an English Catholic leader, surveyed the American scene and optimistically concluded that isolationism was not as widespread among his coreligionists as he had feared. The situation seemed much better than it had in 1917. Indeed, German American Catholics were interventionists now, and "a strong minority of U.S. Catholics believe Roosevelt is right and are willing to fight if necessary." George Shuster of the *Commonweal* also observed that most American Catholics were opposed to Hitler and were willing to follow the lead of the president.[60]

Some of these reports represented wish-fulfillment, but Catholic isolationism did appear to be retreating before the preparedness campaign. Significantly, interventionist sentiment among Catholic leaders developed at a pace compatible with general public opinion. Such compatibility can be explained partially as the common reaction of all Americans to the events taking place in Europe. Roosevelt himself seldom moved beyond general consensus politics during this time. Yet the comments of Catholic leaders suggest other reasons for their shift in opinion. Nothing frightened Catholic leaders such as Spellman and Ready more than the danger of being labeled disloyal. Clerical critics of Roosevelt's foreign policy faced the problem of trying to be honest in their opinions and yet not jeopardizing Catholic integration into American life. If interventionism became official government policy, could Catholics risk criticism without promoting alienation? For some the answer was no. Catholics had a taste of alienation as a result of their stand in the Spanish Civil War and found it bitter. An increasing number of Catholics supported the administration as part of the requirements of patriotism, which in turn was identified with good Catholicism. The Catholic Daughters of America heard Representative Mary T. Norton of New Jersey announce that "nowhere in the world has the Catholic viewpoint been more respected and encouraged than in our beloved America." The conclusion followed that cheap criticism of the administration's foreign policy should be avoided. Bishop John M. Gannon of Pennsylvania called for "uncompromising support of the President." Earlier, Dr. Robert H. Connery of Catholic University had encouraged the Catholic press to push Americanism because it was virtually synonymous with Catholicism. Monsignor Michael Ready of the NCWC and Archbishop Spellman were especially sensitive to any suggestion that American Catholics might have a unique or different perspective about events in Europe. To one critic Ready replied that the Catholic clergy had the same attitude toward the war as the American public.[61]

As Roosevelt's pro-British policy of early 1941 became more official and gained public support, Catholic leaders moved either to active endorsement of the administration or to a position of semineutralism which applauded all acts of self-defense and simultaneously mouthed easy platitudes about universal brotherhood. Undoubtedly, the events in Europe helped to change Catholic opinion. Yet it also appeared as though Catholic leaders feared the consequences upon their national identity if they became outright opponents of the president's policies. After the estrangement over the Spanish Civil War, Catholic leaders were desperate to reassert their place in the community. If a national consensus was forming behind Roosevelt, Catholic leaders could scarcely afford to be out of step. Equally important, American Catholics had increasing reason to believe that Roosevelt's foreign policy was in step with the desires of the Holy Father. After the ill-will generated by the Spanish embargo, Catholics sought reassurance. President Roosevelt had taken a big step in providing such comfort earlier on Christmas Day 1939, by appointing a personal representative to the Holy See. By the middle of 1941 this appointment began to bear handsome fruit in winning over American Catholics to the Roosevelt point of view.

NOTES

1. For the various polls on neutrality from 1936 through 1939, see Hadley Cantrill, editor, *Public Opinion, 1935-1946* (Princeton, N.J.,

1951), pp. 966-967; John J. Carrigg, "American Catholic Press Opinion with Reference to America's Intervention in the Second World War" (M.A. thesis, Georgetown University, 1947), p. 4.

2. Carrigg, "American Catholic Press Opinion," pp. 13, 15, 44-45, 47; *Catholic World* 151 (July 1940), p. 493; *NCWC News Service:* December 8, 1940; August 9, 1940.

3. Sheen quoted in *NCWC News Service*: February 3, 1941; June 16, 1940; June 13, 1941.

4. *NCWC News Service*: May 24, 1940; May 27, 1940; December 1, 1941; Keating quoted in August 30, 1940; Gannon quoted in April 26, 1940.

5. *Catholic World* 150 (December 1939), pp. 216, 265.

6. Beckman quoted in *NCWC News Service*: May 31, 1940; Heffron quoted in March 4, 1941; Corrigan quoted in October 27, 1940; Curran quoted in *New York Times,* November 4, 1940; Gillis in *Catholic World* 152 (March 1941), p. 641; Gannon in *Boston Pilot,* September 9, 1939, p. 8; *Davenport Catholic Messenger,* September 28, 1939, p. 1.

7. Gannon quoted in *NCWC News Service*: January 27, 1941; Curley quoted in September 6, 1940 and May 6, 1941; for Spellman comments see September 22, 1940; also September 3, 1940; *Columbia,* October 1939, p. 14; Griffin quoted in *NCWC News Service,* January 13, 1941; see also *Denver Catholic Register,* September 7, 1939, p. 1.

8. Leblond quoted in *NCWC News Service,* January 24, 1941; O'Connell in *Columbia,* July 1941, p. 17; Curley in *NCWC News Service:* May 9, 1941; McNicholas in December 28, 1940; June 16, 1940; March 31, 1941; *Catholic World* 150 (December 1939), p. 317; *NCWC News Service:* April 28, 1940; October 6, 1941; March 26, 1940.

9. See Chapter 5 for Catholic fears of communism.

10. *Catholic World* 152 (October 1940), p. 27; Ryan quoted in *NCWC News Service,* April 15, 1940; Beckman quoted in *Catholic Herald Citizen,* August 2, 1941, p. 3; *Commonweal,* August 22, 1941, p. 411; *NCWC News Service,* November 28, 1941.

11. Robert A. Divine, *The Illusion of Neutrality* (Chicago, 1962), p. 305; William L. Langer and S. Everett Gleason, *The Challenge to Isolation,* 2 vols. (New York, 1952), vol. 1, pp. 225 and 226; William E.

Leuchtenburg, *Franklin D. Roosevelt and the New Deal, 1932-1940* (New York, 1963), p. 294.

12. Raphael M. Huber, editor, *Our Bishops Speak: National Pastorals and Annual Statements of the Hierarchy of the United States, 1919-1951* (Milwaukee, 1952), p. 225.

13. James Farley, *Jim Farley's Story* (New York, 1948), p. 203; Harold L. Ickes, *The Secret Diary of Harold L. Ickes*, 3 vols. (New York, 1953-1954), vol. 3, p. 43; Carrigg, "American Catholic Press Opinion," p. 47.

14. *Brooklyn Tablet*, October 21, 1939, p. 1; John J. O'Connor to *New York Times*, September 6, 1939, Neutrality File, John J. O'Connor Mss., Lilly Library, Bloomington, Ind.

15. *Brooklyn Tablet,* September 16, 1939, p. 1; *Commonweal,* November 10, 1939, p. 77 (where Michael Williams dissented from this opposition and supported revision); *Catholic World* 150 (November 1939), pp. 129-137; Father John Ryan to Rev. F. J. Reiner, November 3, 1939, Ryan Papers, Catholic University, and Rev. Edward L. Curran to Ryan, October 12, 1939, ibid.; *Commonweal,* September 29, 1939, p. 505; clipping from *Catholic Herald Citizen,* October 7, 1939, in *Selected Materials from the Papers of Franklin D. Roosevelt Concerning Roman Catholic Church Matters* (microfilm), Roosevelt Library, Hyde Park, N.Y.

16. Divine, *Illusion of Neutrality*, p. 305; Ickes, *Diary*, vol. 3, p. 28; memo to FDR from E.M.W., October 18, 1939, Box 48, PSF, Franklin D. Roosevelt Papers, Hyde Park, N.Y.

17. William Allen White to Ryan, October 2, 1939, Ryan Papers; Ryan to Clark M. Eichelberger, October 5, 1939, Ryan Papers; copy of "Shall the Embargo be Lifted?" by Ryan, Ryan Papers; *Catholic Herald Citizen*, October 21, 1939, p. 1; F. L. Broderick, *The Right Reverend New Dealer: John A. Ryan* (New York, 1963), p. 255. Some Catholics, such as the editor of the *Catholic Transcript* and Michael Williams of the *Commonweal*, were upset at the public argument between priests like Ryan and Coughlin and at the injection of a Catholic dimension into the debate (see *Catholic Transcript*, October 19, 1939, p. 4; *Commonweal*, November 10, 1939, p. 77).

18. Rev. Edward L. Curran to Ryan, October 12, 1939, Ryan Papers; at least three hundred such letters are collected in the Ryan Papers: see Embargo File, 1939; Ryan to Martha Dalrymple, November 6, 1939; Ryan to Peter W. Harding, October 25, 1939, Ryan Papers.

19. *The New World*: September 23, 1939, p. 4; September 15, 1939, p. 4; Ickes, *Diary*, vol. 3, pp. 28-29; Copy of address of Most Reverend Bernard J. Sheil, D.D., Auxiliary Bishop of Chicago, October 2, 1939, in *Sel. Material; Chicago Tribune*, October 3, 1939.

20. *New York Times*: October 5, 1939; October 3, 1939; Ickes, *Diary*, vol. 3, p. 63; Roosevelt to Frank Knox, October 4, 1939, in Elliott Roosevelt, editor, *F.D.R.: His Personal Letters*, 4 vols. (New York, 1947-1950), vol. 4, p. 933.

21. *Washington Post* [n.d.], clipping in *Sel. Material*.

22. Ryan to Right Rev. Matthew F. Smith, editor of the *Register*, November 4, 1939, Ryan Papers.

The Senate voted 55 yeas, 29 nays and 17 not voting on House Resolution 306 to revise the neutrality act. Prominent Catholic senators favoring the measure included Francis T. Maloney (Conn.), James M. Slattery (Ill.), and James C. O'Mahoney (Wyoming). David Walsh (Mass.), voted against the bill. In the House the Fourth Neutrality Act passed: yeas 243, nays 172, not voting 14. The ethnic vote appeared inoperative. From New York City came endorsement for the bill from J. A. Fay, James A. Fitzpatrick, and L. A. Buckley. A. F. Maciejewski and Leo Kocialkowski of Chicago also approved, as did John McCormack of Boston. Registering negative votes were Lewis Connery of Lynn, Mass., Vincent F. Harrington of Sioux City, Carol O'Day of New York, Martin Sweeney of Cleveland, and Joseph B. Shannon of Kansas City. See *Congressional Record*, 76th Cong., 2nd Sess. (November 3, 1939), pp. 1356, 1389.

23. *NCWC News Service*, August 23, 1940; for press opposition, see the survey run by *NCWC News Service*, August 12, 1940; *Social Justice Review*, October 1940, p. 195; *Commonweal*, July 5, 1940, p. 219; *Boston Pilot*, August 24, 1940, p. 4; Carrigg, "American Catholic Press Opinion," p. 75.

24. *Commonweal*: August 23, 1940, p. 257; July 5, 1940, p. 219; *Social Justice Review*, October 1940, p. 195.

25. *NCWC News Service*: August 5, 1940; August 19, 1940; Gannon quoted in October 14, 1940; *Catholic Herald Citizen*: August 10, 1940, p. 7; August 17, 1940, p. 1; *Extension Magazine*, September 1940, pp. 16-17.

26. Huber, *Our Bishops Speak*, p. 344.

27. Rev. Ready to Roosevelt, July 8, 1940, *Sel. Materials;* McGovern to O'Mahoney, July 24, 1940; Kelley to O'Mahoney, August 9, 1940; O'Mahoney to Kelley, August 13, 1940; all in O'Mahoney Mss., University of Wyoming, Laramie, Wyoming.

28. *Catholic Action,* September 1940, p. 26; *NCWC News Service:* August 3, 1940; August 12, 1940; for Beckman and Winkelmann see *Catholic Herald Citizen*, August 17, 1940, p. 1.

29. Ready's testimony is reproduced in *NCWC News Service*, July 30, 1940; see also *Catholic Action*, August 1940, p. 11 and November 1940, pp. 20-21.

30. *NCWC News Service*: July 30, 1940; August 6, 1940; August 10, 1940; August 13, 16, 20, 30, 1940; January 31, 1941; *Catholic Action*, September 1940, p. 24.

31. *The Washington Post*, August 13, 1940; *NCWC News Service* for August 1940, and January 1941; for provisions of bill see *U.S. Statutes at Large, 1939-1940*, vol. 54, p. 888.

32. Spellman quoted in Robert I. Gannon, *The Cardinal Spellman Story* (New York, 1962), p. 185; Robert E. Sherwood, *Roosevelt and Hopkins*, rev. ed. (New York, 1950), p. 196; *NCWC News Service*, October 29, 1940.

33. *NCWC News Service:* November 14, 1940; January 31, 1941; April 7, 1941; April 26, 1941; August 25, 1941; Thomas T. McAvoy, "American Catholics and the Second World War," *Review of Politics* 6 (April 1944), pp. 134-135; *Boston Pilot*, November 23, 1940, p. 9. The administrative board of the NCWC at this time consisted of the following prelates: Edward Mooney of Detroit, chairman; Francis J. Spellman of New York; John Gregory Murray of St. Paul; John T. McNicholas of Cincinnati; John B. Peterson of Manchester; John A. Duffy of Buffalo; Francis C. Kelley of Oklahoma City and Tulsa; John Mark Gannon of Erie; Hugh C. Boyle of Pittsburgh; Edwin W. O'Hara of Kansas City.

34. *NCWC News Service:* September 22, 1941; July 21 and July 22, 1941; Gannon quoted in July 14, 1941; Mooney quoted in *Catholic Action,* November 1940, p. 12. See also *NCWC News Service:* January 1, 1941; June 6, 1941; May 26, 1941.

35. Leuchtenburg, *Roosevelt*, p. 304; Walsh to Roosevelt, August 19,

1940; Roosevelt to Walsh, August 22, 1940, in David I. Walsh Mss., Holy Cross Library, Worcester, Mass.

36. John J. Connorton, "Will America Go to War?" *Catholic World* 152 (January 1941), pp. 396-402; *Commonweal*, September 13, 1940, p. 417.

37. John LaFarge, S. J., "The Church in the New Order," *Catholic Mind* 39 (April 22, 1941), pp. 22-25; *NCWC News Service*: February 2, 1940; May 9, 1941; *Denver Catholic Register*, March 13, 1941, p. 1.; William V. Shannon, *The American Irish* (New York, 1964), p. 342; *Extension Magazine*, March 1941, p. 18; Carigg, "American Catholic Press Opinion," p. 109.

38. Speaker McCormack to author, December 24, 1968, warns of the oversimplification of pinpointing only Catholic opposition to Lend-Lease, but does not deny such opposition. For McCormack's role, see the detailed study of Lend-Lease by Warren Kimball, *The Most Unsordid Act: Lend-Lease. 1939-1941* (Baltimore, 1969), pp. 151-153.

39. Kimball, *The Most Unsordid Act*, p. 173; *NCWC News Service*, February 17, 1941; *Boston Pilot*, January 20, 1941, p. 4; also, Boxes 57 and 63 of O'Mahoney Mss. are filled with protest letters.

40. *Catholic World* 151 (May 1940), p. 133; *NCWC News Service*: March 22, 1940; November 4, 1940; December 14, 1940.

41. Agar quoted in Mark Chadwin, *The Warhawks: American Interventionists Before Pearl Harbor*, Norton edition (New York, 1968), pp. 61, 70, 94, 146-147.

42. Ryan to Mrs. Friede Z. Bowen, June 26, 1940, Ryan Papers; *NCWC News Service*: January 6, 1941; February 2, 1941; June 4, 1941; *Commonweal*, March 21, 1941, pp. 532-533.

43. John M. Blum, editor, *From the Morgenthau Diaries*, 3 vols. (Boston, 1959, 1965, 1967), vol. 2, pp. 224-225; William L. Langer and S. Everett Gleason, *The Undeclared War, 1940-1941* (New York, 1953), pp. 268, 278-279.

44. Selig Adler, *The Isolationist Impulse: Its 20th Century Reaction* (New York, 1957), pp. 273, 294; for the best history of the movement see Wayne Cole, *America First* (Madison, Wisconsin, 1953).

45. *NCWC News Service*: May 26, 1941; June 27, 1941; Leuchtenburg, *Roosevelt*, p. 311; Cole, *America First*, pp. 21, 76, 136-137; *Catholic*

Action, June 1941, p. 19; see also *Commonweal*, October 31, 1941, pp. 37-38, for a discussion of the validity of the clergy poll. While there was a high rate of agreement on all questions of noninvolvement (91.5 percent) and a wide geographical spread of responses, only 35 percent responded to the poll.

46. Roosevelt to Flynn, January 16, 1941, PSF, Flynn, Roosevelt Papers.

47. Notes of Monsignor Montini of conversation with Harold Tittmann, Jr., June 1941, in Pierre Blet et. al., editors, Secrétairerie D'État de sa Sainteté, *Actes et Documents du Saint Siège Relatifs à La Seconde Guerre Mondiale*, 5 vols. (Citta Del Vaticano: Libreria Editrice Vaticana, 1967-), vol. 4, p. 546 (hereafter cited as *Holy See and War*); Cicognani to Maglione, June 17, 1941, *Holy See and War*, vol. 4, pp. 555-558. Taylor's appointment will be discussed in Chapter 4.

48. M. F. Doyle to Colonel McIntyre, August 2, 1941, *Sel. Material*.

49. Sheehy to Roosevelt, August 10, 1940; Sheehy to Marguerite Le-Hand, February 6, 1941; and Sheehy to Henry Wallace, April 5, 1941, in *Sel. Materials*.

50. Ickes, *Diary*, vol. 3, pp. 110, 114, 228-229.

51. Broderick, *The Right Reverend New Dealer*, p. 256; *NCWC News Service*: May 6, 1940; September 6, 1940; December 6, 1940.

52. *NCWC News Service*: March 25, 1940; Ryan quoted in June 2, 1941; *Catholic Action*, February 1941, p. 17.

53. *Columbia*, November 1939, p. 11; *Catholic Action*: October 1941, p. 23; May 1941, p. 24; *NCWC News Service*: Walker quoted in October 21, 1941; January 6, 1941.

54. Bishop J. P. Hurley to Sumner Welles, June 26, 1941, and Welles to Anterton, June 30, 1941, SDF 860C.00/885.

55. *NCWC News Service*, May 2, 1941; June 17, 1941; July 6, 1941; *Commonweal*, July 18, 1941, p. 303.

56. Spellman to Pope Pius, September 4, 1941, *Holy See and War*, vol. 5, p. 182; Cicognani to Maglione, September 1, 1941, *Holy See and War*, vol. 5, report 57, pp. 175-178.

57. Cicognani to Maglione, September 1, 1941, and Spellman to Pope, September 4, 1941, *Holy See and War*, vol. 5, pp. 175-178, 181-182; Hurley quoted in *Commonweal*, August 8, 1941, pp. 375-376.

58. Cicognani to Maglione, October 28, 1941, *Holy See and War*, vol. 5, pp. 285-288.

59. Walter Johnson, *The Battle Against Isolationism* (Chicago, 1944), pp. 69-70; *NCWC News Service*: October 14, 1941; April 19, 1941; Spellman to Pope Pius, September 4, 1941, *Holy See and War*, vol. 5, p. 182; Ryan to Monsignor Sheen, June 10, 1940, Ryan Papers (in which he urges Sheen, Bishop Sheil, Msgr. Haas, Father Robert I. Gannon, Bishop O'Hara, Al Smith, Colonel W. J. Donovan, and other prominent Catholics to join the White group); see also inside front cover of *Commonweal*, July 25, 1941, for full page ad by "Fight for Freedom, Inc.," calling upon Catholics of America to "wake up" and quoting Bishops Hurley and James H. Ryan about Nazis being the number one enemy of Catholicism and Americanism.

60. Arnold Lunn, "American Catholics and the War," *New Statesman & Nation* 22 (August 23, 1941), p. 180; George Shuster, "Conflict Among Catholics," *American Scholar* 10 (January 1941), pp. 6-9; *Commonweal*, September 26, 1941, p. 543.

61. *NCWC News Service*: July 8, 1941; Norton quoted in July 11, 1941; May 26, 1940; February 28, 1941.

4

THE VATICAN

The problems that developed over the Spanish Civil War and neutrality revision had convinced President Roosevelt of the need for closer contacts with the Catholic church. On December 24, 1939, the White House announced that the president had sent similar Christmas letters to Pope Pius XII, to Dr. George A. Buttrick, president of the Federal Council of Churches of Christ in America, and to Rabbi Cyrus Adler, president of the Jewish Theological Seminary of America. This was hardly earth shattering news, on the face of it. Roosevelt had taken many such ecumenical steps in the past. But more than the usual platitudes were involved this time. He wrote to Buttrick and Adler of the need for cooperation among churches to promote peace, but his message to the pope included a statement of the president's intention to dispatch a personal representative to the Holy See. Myron E. Taylor, head of an American refugee organization and former chairman of the United States Steel Corporation, was suggested as the nominee. This presidential representative would help to promote "our parallel endeavors for peace and the alleviation of suffering."[1]

1

How had this novel decision come about? Rumors of Roosevelt's plan
to extend diplomatic relations to the Vatican had become stale by the
late 1930s. The Vatican itself had long been interested in the resumption
of formal relations.[2] Adding the name of an American ambassador to the
already extensive list of those from European and Latin nations maintaining diplomatic missions would enhance the pope's moral standing. Also
important was the desire to establish a Vatican liaison between the United
States government and the growing population of American Catholics.[3]
Roosevelt, of course, was quite conscious of the Vatican's international
and political muscle.[4] It was only reasonable to expect him, as the leader
of a political coalition containing several million Catholics, to be sensitive
to the Vatican. Yet Protestant votes were more numerous and the idea of
contacts with the pope offended many voters. A rumor in the *New York
Sun* of March 8, 1934, on the subject provoked Reverend Edward W.
Schramm, editor of the *Lutheran Standard*, and Thomas E. Boorde,
director of *Protestant Action,* to write to Roosevelt requesting a formal
denial.[5] Protestants sensed a more friendly attitude toward the Vatican
by Roosevelt, but no public mention was made of a mission. Roosevelt
worked covertly and became serious about it only in late 1939. His
final decision to send Taylor to Rome grew out of a series of encounters
with American church leaders.

George Cardinal Mundelein of Chicago and Archbishop Francis Spellman of New York both fostered United States recognition of the Vatican
as a means of promoting the integration of Catholics into national life.
Both men were capable of translating their desires into effective political
channels. They held spiritual and political leadership in strongholds of
Democratic party membership. Cardinal Mundelein had eagerly cham-
pioned most of the New Deal and supported Roosevelt for reelection in
1936.[6] As tensions in Europe increased with the advent of Hitler,
Mundelein began supporting an internationalist foreign policy.[7]

It was only natural for the cardinal to entertain the president when
he arrived in Chicago on October 5, 1937, to give his "Quarantine"
speech, in which he suggested the need for international cooperation
to contain aggressive nations. Over tea, Roosevelt flattered Mundelein

by asking him whether the Vatican would be interested in collaborating in such a movement. The cardinal encouraged Roosevelt to approach the pope, who would welcome the chance of cooperating for peace. Roosevelt then admitted that he was considering the feasibility of an "unofficial envoy" to the Vatican to represent him. Mundelein responded enthusiastically and personally volunteered to contact the apostolic delegate about the idea. He immediately wrote Ameleto Cicognani, informing him of the president's remarks and advising him to seek guidance from the Vatican. Within a month word came from Rome of the pope's endorsement of such an envoy. Mundelein, when he transmitted this news to Roosevelt, was drafted to work out the details of the project.[8]

The president was in no hurry, however, and the issue surfaced again only in late 1938. When one considers the president's reluctance to turn the rhetoric of his quarantine speech into reality, his procrastination over the Vatican appointment fits a pattern. Now, in 1938, Cardinal Mundelein was on his way to Rome. But he interrupted his trip for an overnight visit to the White House during which he and Roosevelt had ample time to discuss the prospects of establishing direct communications between the White House and the Vatican. Mundelein planned to pursue the question of an American at the Vatican when he arrived in Rome in early November 1938, even though the Department of State denied such rumors.[9] Unfortunately, his mission failed. As an outspoken opponent of Hitler and a close friend of Roosevelt, Mundelein was an excellent target for the barbs of the Nazis. When Ambassador William Phillips met the cardinal at Naples with an elaborate reception by order of the president, German newspapers presented a theory of a conspiracy by which Mundelein planned to announce formal United States recognition of the Vatican as a payoff for having delivered the Catholic vote to the Democrats at the last election.[10] Some Americans might laugh at the suggestion of a Chicago cardinal of German extraction delivering the votes of Boston Irishmen, but there was enough apparent substance to the accusation to cause concern. Clearly Catholics had voted for Roosevelt in large numbers in 1936 and, just as certainly, Mundelein had been an outspoken supporter of the president during the election. If Mundelein should now announce the beginning of United States-Vatican relations, the German press would appear clairvoyant. When interviewed, Mundelein appeared upset by these accusations and hinted that the

Germans had guessed right.[11] Shortly after this incident Pius XI died. The next year Mundelein also died and there was still no representative at the Vatican.

Archbishop Francis Spellman of New York continued to work for the same cause. Although not a senior member of the American hierarchy, he still enjoyed many advantages in securing United States recognition of the Vatican. As a native of Boston, he had enlisted the support of Joseph Kennedy, a prominent Catholic and a major contributor to Roosevelt's campaign chest. Furthermore, Spellman was a close friend of Eugenio Cardinal Pacelli, Vatican secretary of state before his election as Pope Pius XII to suceed Pius XI.[12] During the period from 1933 to 1936 Spellman dropped hints to both Kennedy and James Roosevelt, the president's son, about the wisdom of United States-Vatican relations. Then, in 1936, Roosevelt was approached. The occasion was a visit to the United States by Pacelli, with Spellman as his escort. Pacelli's itinerary included a two-week tour of the country, a stay in New York City as the guest of Myron Taylor, and, finally, a luncheon visit with the recently reelected Roosevelt at Hyde Park on November 5, 1936. Throughout the visit, church officials explained that Pacelli was gathering information on the character of American Catholicism. Spellman, acting as Pacelli's press secretary, issued innocuous bulletins on the cardinal's conversations. After the visit to Hyde Park, the pattern was repeated. Reports of the private conversation between Roosevelt and Pacelli remained speculative. But both friendly and hostile reporters agreed that the two men had discussed recognition of the Vatican.[13]

As a result of the visit, Spellman emerged as an important source of information on Catholicism for the White House. Undoubtedly, the designation of Spellman to replace the deceased Cardinal Hayes as archbishop of New York City, his close ties to Pacelli, and his friendship with Kennedy were important factors in Roosevelt's decision to use him as an intermediary. The spiritual leader of New York Catholics automatically became a political figure of some significance. By September 1937, Spellman could write of his frequent visits to the White House and of converting James Roosevelt to the cause of Vatican recognition. The president, it appears, was also sympathetic but did not think he could muster a congressional majority for an ambassador at this time.[14]

2

A number of problems had to be resolved before a representative from the United States could present his credentials at the Vatican. When Cardinal Pacelli became pope in early 1939, Roosevelt sent a personal note of congratulations. The Catholic press applauded when the president followed up his note by sending Joseph Kennedy, then ambassador to England, to Rome as the special representative of the United States at the papal coronation. This appointment was the fruit of a suggestion made by Cardinal Mundelein and seconded by Ambassador Phillips.[15] But not all Americans shared the pope's joy at seeing Kennedy at the coronation on March 12, 1939. Among the many who heard the proceedings over network radio, the members of the United Lutheran Church in America and the Southern Baptist Convention reacted with strong protest at what they considered a violation of the principles of separation of church and state.[16] Such outbursts insured that Roosevelt would have no illusions about a renewal of Vatican relations meeting public approval. Still, ten days after the coronation, the apostolic delegate wrote the new Vatican secretary of state, Luigi Cardinal Maglione, that prospects for the establishment of relations remained bright. Maglione, in reply, hoped that "the good intentions manifested by the President on this subject can come to a concrete conclusion with a minimum of delay."[17]

In the midst of this aura of good will, Roosevelt experienced at first-hand the concrete problems of diplomatic collaboration with the Vatican. As a peace gesture the president sent telegrams to both Mussolini and Hitler, seeking guarantees that they would refrain from further aggression. Badly timed—they came only one day before Germany swallowed up what was left of Czechoslovakia—the messages were also impolitely worded to isolate Hitler and Mussolini as aggressors. Simultaneously, Roosevelt had Assistant Secretary of State Sumner Welles approach Monsignor Ready of the NCWC to request papal endorsement of the messages. Ready, impressed with the zeal of Welles's presentation, asked Cicognani to seek support from Maglione at the Vatican. The pope had already received similar requests to support the president's messages from France and England.[18]

An embarrassing situation developed. The Vatican found it difficult to supplement Roosevelt's messages to the dictators. Despite pressure from other nations and Pius XII's keen desire to establish closer accord with the United States, Vatican diplomats, led by Maglione, felt, correctly as it turned out, that singling out Hitler and Mussolini for commitments could only infuriate them. Roosevelt's approach might reflect the facts of international life, but it was also unneutral and had little prospect for success. A Vatican endorsement would only alienate Germany and Italy from Catholic influence. Also, the pope had his own peace offensive planned, one he considered more promising than Roosevelt's scheme.[19]

Maglione therefore replied to Cicognani that "present relations between the Holy See and Germany do not make direct intervention with Hitler possible."[20] Of course, neither Welles nor Roosevelt had requested direct intervention by the Vatican; all they wanted was public association with the president's messages, something the American bishops of the NCWC had already done. Welles wondered why the pope could not do as much when he thanked Monsignor Ready for the NCWC support. Welles felt sure that "some public pronouncement by the Pope in support of the peace message would have the most beneficial effect."[21] After this rebuttal, Roosevelt might well have considered the Vatican unresponsive as a diplomatic ally and unworthy of formal recognition by the United States. Granted that an international organization such as the Vatican could not be as nationalistic in its endorsement of Roosevelt's policy as the NCWC, but if the United States and the Holy See could not cooperate on this issue, what prospects were there for the future?

The situation was saved for future American-Vatican comity by a fortuitous event. The Holy See now launched its own peace offensive. This move, coming right after Roosevelt's abortive campaign of April, gave the impression of belated Vatican collaboration with the United States.[22] In fact, the Vatican offensive was entirely independent. During the early part of May, the pope approached five major European powers, deliberately excluding the United States and Russia, about holding a conference to iron out existing international problems. The suggestion of another international conference, coming on the heels of the dismember-ment of Czechoslovakia, met a lukewarm response. After considerable fencing by all nations concerned, Mussolini dropped the curtain on the farce by blandly announcing that the general reduction of international tension in the last few weeks obviated the need for such a parley. Maglione accepted this absurd interpretation of the European climate with an alacrity which makes one suspect the sincerity of the original papal proposal.[23]

An intriguing dimension to this peace offensive was the willingness of the Vatican to exclude the United States. On May 9, Secretary A. S. Rogers of the American Embassy at Rome called at the Vatican to request information on the rumored papal peace conference. Instead of welcoming United States cooperation, Maglione's assistant, Monsignor Joseph Hurley brushed Rogers off. Yet Hurley, when he was later appointed bishop of St. Augustine, Florida, would work eagerly to promote American foreign policy interests. But now he remained aloof, and Rogers became almost obsequious in his assurances that the United States would support a Vatican conference. Could not the Vatican give the United States some information on its plans? Hurley tossed the question aside by denying that the pope had invited the five major European powers to the Vatican.[24] When the State Department persisted in its queries, Maglione finally wrote Cicognani in Washington that the pope assuredly had planned to "request [Roosevelt's] good offices should the idea of a conference have been carried out."[25] Monsignor Howard J. Carroll of the NCWC carried this message to Welles, who replied that Germany had really killed the Vatican's plan. He firmly disagreed with Maglione's assertion that tensions had eased. Nonplussed at this reply, Carroll hinted that perhaps a discreet meeting between Welles and Cicognani could be arranged to discuss the matter. Welles, in contrast, showed little concern to disguise his association with a Vatican official. Even the president encouraged these proceedings. But when the news media inquired about collaboration between the United States and the Vatican, both sources denied such rumors.[26]

Despite denials, a considerable degree of contact existed between the Vatican and the United States long before December 1939. Welles emerged as the chief go-between for Roosevelt and the pope. With the president's encouragement, Welles accepted Carroll's invitation and on June 29, 1939, dined at Cicognani's home in Washington, D.C. The burden of Welles's conversation concerned America's willingness to take part in "a conference of nations to adjust the present cause of world unrest." Roosevelt had been trying to launch such a conference ever since late 1937, only to meet with opposition from Secretary of State Hull and English Prime Minister Neville Chamberlain.[27] Yet the president's own equivocation and the isolationists' strength in Congress made Cicognani skeptical of such plans. For his part, the apostolic delegate explained that the pope had refrained from supporting the president's peace initiative because of his desire to remain uncommitted to any one national faction. As he rose to leave, Welles acknowledged the Vatican problem of neutrality, but felt that the president was correct in identifying the nations most responsible for European unrest. The next day Cicognani was on his way to Rome to report to the Vatican and encourage further meetings.[28]

His arrival in Italy sparked renewed rumors of pending United States recognition of the Vatican. When Cardinal Enrico Gasparri, a Catholic legal expert, returned to the United States with Cicognani in late July, the *New York Times* intimated that his mission was to iron out technicalities for an American mission to the Vatican. Despite these flights of conjecture, a lengthy interview between Cicognani and the pope, and an encouraging note from Roosevelt to Spellman in August 1939, no appointment followed.[29] Indeed, Roosevelt seemed increasingly wary of such a step.

Welles and Hull now became the chief advocates of a Vatican mission. After Ambassador Phillips in Rome approved the idea, Welles wrote Roosevelt that a mission to the Vatican could provide the United States with unique and substantial information on European intrigues. The first attempt at collaboration had failed, but Roosevelt had every reason to believe that the pope shared the American outlook on international developments. For example, *Osservatore Romano,* the semi-official Vatican paper, and Pope Pius himself had been laudatory of Roosevelt's neutrality message after the invasion of Poland in September 1939. Spellman continued to press his campaign and to support preparedness. A large majority of American Catholics could be won over by the appointment. The president remained skeptical. His first step on the road which would end in Myron Taylor's appointment appears surreptitious.[30] On October 2, 1939, one month after the outbreak of hostilities in Poland, he wrote Hull about establishing contact with the Vatican because of the need to care for war refugees. Since there would be many refugees as a result of the war and many of them would be Roman Catholics, the subject should be discussed and liaisons established with the Vatican. What better method of liaison than a "special mission to the Vatican?"[31]

When one considers the already extensive contacts with the Vatican
and the arguments of Hull and Welles, Roosevelt's suggestion of using
the refugee issue looks like a subterfuge. Certainly, neither Hull nor
Welles felt that the care of displaced persons was an adequate reason for
a Vatican mission. But the president was in a predicament, a fact which
he admitted when he called Spellman to the White House on October 24,
1939. Roosevelt justified his two years of procrastination by emphasizing
the importance of proper timing in such an appointment. As Spellman
recalled it, by "timing" Roosevelt meant that he wanted to act when
most Americans would support him. The president's entire approach to
diplomacy reflected this same reluctance to lead public opinion. Now,
with war a reality, the moment seemed proper for parallel peace efforts
by Washington and Rome. Furthermore, the holiday season would be a
good time to make the announcement. Christians would be in a generous
mood and a suspicious and perhaps hostile Congress would not be in
session. It was hoped that a temporary mission, all that Roosevelt dared
venture at this time, would eventually blossom into a permanent one once
Congress and the public saw the advantages of such an arrangement.[32]
Cicognani, informed of this conversation, reported to Rome that recognition was imminent.[33]

3

The Catholic world rejoiced when Roosevelt announced the appointme
of Taylor as personal representative to Pope Pius XII on December 24, 19:
Yet the president's actions left a number of questions unanswered. For
example, if he was so concerned with public support of the project, why
did he wait until Congress was out of town to make the appointment? The
steps leading up to the announcement all support the conclusion that
Roosevelt's motives were a mixture of diplomatic, political, and humanitarian considerations. Hull and Welles had every reason to believe that the
Vatican diplomatic sources on European conditions could well supplemen
the more secular and orthodox channels already available to the Department of State. On Italian affairs, even Ambassador Phillips agreed that
Vatican information would be indispensable.[34]

Only ignorance of the history of the Democratic party and of Roosevelt would allow the belief that domestic political considerations had

been ignored in the decision to send Taylor to Rome. Catholics made up
a substantial segment of the Roosevelt coalition. In 1936 Roosevelt
carried the urban centers of Catholicism by wide margins. The Democratic machines in New York, Boston, and Chicago were all controlled by
Catholics. One does not have to assert crassly that the president sought
the Catholic vote by the appointment or that it was a payoff for past
political support by Mundelein.[35] Roosevelt appreciated the importance
of good relations with the American hierarchy and had a keen awareness
of Catholic political power. Such astuteness appeared in his attempts to
help the Vatican find an appropriate replacement for Mundelein and
personally to pick a politically sound bishop for the newly organized
Washington archdiocese.[36]

Neither can simple idealism be ignored in assessing motives for Roosevelt's decision to appoint Taylor. Both the president and the pope were
working to preserve some semblance of sanity in Europe. What could be
more natural than the convergence of the neutral, supreme spiritual leader
in Europe and the leader of the most powerful unengaged nation in the
world? Certainly this noble motive was most frequently mentioned by
Myron Taylor in his own evaluation of why he was sent to the Vatican.
He considered his task to be one of coordinating the spiritual forces of
the Vatican and the United States to promote peace, a collaboration
designed "to give to the world's moral forces . . . unity of goal and plan,
leadership in concerting their influence, encouragement for their humanitarian services to alleviate suffering."[37]

Idealism aside, Roosevelt knew that some people would raise objections to the mission. This knowledge influenced his decision to select
Taylor and to make the appointment a personal one. Archbishop Spellman
had suggested a number of names, including that of the former ambassador
to Italy, Breckenridge Long. But Roosevelt finally picked Myron Taylor,
who already had considerable experience on the Intergovernmental Committee on Political Refugees, a humanitarian agency with contacts at the
Vatican. Furthermore, Taylor had spent considerable time in Italy at his
villa in Florence and was a personal acquaintance of the pope. As former
chairman of United States Steel Corporation, he was wealthy enough to
finance his own mission, an invaluable asset because of expected congressional resistance to any request for appropriations. Being an Episcopalian,
he met Hull's demand that the appointee be a non-Catholic to blunt

Protestant objections. Finally, word from Spellman and the Vatican indicated that the pope would welcome Taylor.[38]

But would Taylor welcome the appointment? He was just recovering from a serious illness, one which would plague him for months and delay his departure for Rome until February 1940. As Taylor was sixty-five years old, his wife understandably had serious misgivings about the wisdom of his accepting the appointment. Roosevelt sought to reassure her by telephone on December 22, insisting in his most convincing manner that Taylor could easily handle the job and still spend most of his time in Florence. Hull confirmed this rather honorific view of the mission by wiring Ambassador Phillips that "unless problems require his [Taylor's] continuous attendance in Rome, it is assumed that he will be able to spend most of his time at his villa in Florence."[39] Apparently, if an elderly and sick man could do the job while vacationing in Florence, the administration did not conceive the mission as potentially decisive in European diplomacy.

Another unique feature of the appointment emerged in Taylor's unorthodox title of "personal representative." Roosevelt went to great lengths to present Taylor as *sui generis*, on a personal mission from the president rather than involved in a normal diplomatic assignment. As always, Roosevelt's motives were complex, but fear of Protestant protest was obviously a factor. This fear also played a role in the decision to keep the appointment temporary, despite assurances to Spellman that it would eventually become permanent. Cicognani, the apostolic delegate, shared this same impression as he wrote the Vatican that while only Congress could make a permanent appointment, "everybody understands that, after such a decision, *alea iacta est* ["the die is cast"] and the only thing is to hope that the problem will be settled as it deserves."[40]

The president himself deliberately cultivated confusion about what Taylor was to do in Rome. To reporters' queries about Taylor's mission, Roosevelt replied in a flippant and cryptic manner. When one reporter asked the president to describe Taylor's activities, the reply began, "He will get up in the morning, eat his breakfast and go through the normal functions of a human being in a post of that kind."[41] The reporters laughed but the confusion continued. Later, as Protestant opposition to the appointment grew, Roosevelt did explain that he wanted to "mobilize the moral forces of the world," and that it was only through the pope that he could establish effective contact with Roman Catholics. This desire meant sending to Italy "a communicating agent" rather than giving diplomatic recognition to the American apostolic delegate.[42] Taylor was on a personal mission from Franklin Roosevelt to Pope Pius XII. The assignment did not constitute the establishment of diplomatic relations with the Vatican. As Adolf A. Berle, assistant secretary of state, insisted to Spellman at the time of the announcement, Taylor was to be "Ambassador Extraordinary."[43] Secretary of State Hull and his assistant, Breckenridge Long, remained so concerned about the political sensitivity of the appointment that they denied Taylor use of Department of State stationery and suggested that he spend most of his time in Florence.[44]

Not all of these fine distinctions had Taylor's approval. Problems soon emerged. He demanded and was granted ambassadorial rank. It was a question of protocol, Roosevelt explained. Furthermore, once in Rome, Taylor badgered Ambassador Phillips for expense money to cover the shipping cost of his personal effects. Eventually he was given secretarial assistance, and Harold Tittmann, a member of the consular service in Rome, as an aide.[45] All of this proved that Taylor, while perfectly willing to accept his special role, insisted firmly that this uniqueness should not mean less prestige. As he wrote with pride later on, Roosevelt wanted to "distinguish all aspects of my office from those of a diplomatic mission."[46]

The Vatican, aware of the uniqueness of the Taylor mission, agreed with the new ambassador. Cicognani and Maglione both noted certain irregularities in the appointment but were disposed to ignore these aberrations. Cicognani insisted that the crucial fact was the appointment itself, even if Roosevelt had to mask it as a Christmas greeting by sending similar letters to Rabbi Adler and Dr. Buttrick. The difference, of course, was that the pope got a representative while the other gentlemen received only a note. Maglione understood and promised to receive Taylor "with all honor due to the dignity of the important mission entrusted to him." When the ambassador arrived in Rome, the pope received him in the Hall of the Little Throne, a break with diplomatic tradition, but it was still a full-dress affair including Swiss Guards and court chamberlains.[47]

The president had stressed Taylor's role as a personal representative, but Roosevelt could not control how his language was interpreted by

others. In the eyes of the Vatican, Taylor was an ambassador—his power
derived from representing the president of the United States. As such
he would receive all of the normal honors extended to regular missions.[48]
Rome's reasoning had a certain logic even if it did ignore the political
sensibilities Roosevelt faced in the United States. Taylor acted as a
regular diplomat. He had a letter of appointment from the president of
his country. Granted that he was not designated by the United States
Senate and no funds had been appropriated for his mission, did these
internal considerations of American legalism abridge or modify in any
way Taylor's functional situation? Taylor worked in fact as an ambassador and was so understood by the Vatican.[49]

4

Few Americans appreciated Roosevelt's distinctions in the appointment. American Catholics just ignored them and applauded. So exaggerated was their response and so high-pitched their enthusiasm that one
suspects that Vatican recognition became a source of additional security
to Catholics who remained unsure of the compatibility of their national
and religious allegiances. They still worried about how non-Catholics
viewed these two loyalties. The hierarchy, with the exception of Cardinal
O'Connell of Boston, who opposed the appointment because he anticipated Protestant criticism, applauded Roosevelt's action. Archbishop
Spellman led the way with a public pronouncement combining an assertion
of Catholic patriotism with applause for the timeliness of Roosevelt's
move to cooperate for peace with the Supreme Pontiff.[50] Similar endorsements came from Archbishop Joseph Schrembs of Cleveland, Bishop
John M. Gannon of Erie, Pennsylvania, and Bishop James H. Ryan of
Omaha. "Say what you will about some of the domestic policies of President Roosevelt," wrote Ryan, "when it comes to the field of foreign
affairs he is easily the outstanding statesman of the contemporary
world."[51] Monsignor Fulton Sheen wired Roosevelt that Taylor's assignment was "the first concrete recognition any great nation in modern
times has given to the spiritual and moral foundations of peace."[52] Continuing in this hyperbolic vein, the Reverend Wilfred Parsons, S.J., a
long-time critic of Roosevelt's diplomacy, called the decision "the merg-
ing of the spiritual power of the Church with the physical power of the

United States."[53] All elements of the Catholic press echoed these expressions, including the liberal *Commonweal*, the ultra-conservative and anti-New Deal *Brooklyn Tablet*, and the socially conscious *Catholic Action*.[54]

The general public appeared more divided about the appointment. The still imperfect American Institute of Public Opinion investigated the issue in January 1940, by asking a representative sample of citizens if they thought "the United States should send an Ambassador to the Court of Pope Pius in Rome, as it does to foreign countries?" Since this type of regular diplomatic arrangement was precisely what Roosevelt tried to avoid, the respondents' views—Yes, 37 percent; No, 43 percent; No Opinion, 20 percent—were not entirely relevant.[55] At the same time, elements of the secular press supported the mission. Such leading syndicated journalists as Arthur Krock, Raymond Clapper, and Jay Franklin came out strongly in favor of Taylor's assignment.[56]

Protestant leaders deplored the appointment. It may be too facile to speak of a universal Protestant attitude to Taylor's mission, but a significant number of opinion-makers became enraged at the idea. Most vitriolic in their protests were the Baptists, Methodists, and Lutherans, with the Presbyterians and Disciples of Christ not far behind. The Federal Council of Churches of Christ in America, although originally somewhat divided in opinion, eventually joined the call for a withdrawal of Taylor's appointment.[57] Many Protestant groups disliked the appointment but were reluctant to oppose a measure which had been adopted in the interest of world peace. This dilemma led to some equivocation on the part of Presbyterians and the Federal Council of Churches. The argument, however, seemed to be primarily over whether Taylor should be recalled immediately from Rome or not. Few ministers advocated a permanent mission.[58]

All across the United States, groups passed resolutions condemning the appointment and demanding the recall of Taylor. In what appeared to some as a strange alliance, the journal of liberal Protestantism, the *Christian Century*, gave vigorous editorial support to the opinions of many fundamentalist groups. To this faction of Protestantism the issue was clear. As the Reverend Doctor George Truett said in his presidential address to the sixth annual congress of the Baptist World Alliance, the pope "has in fact no better title to receive governmental recognition from the United States than . . . the head of the least of the Baptist associations in the hills of North Carolina."[59]   Presumably, Truett could think of no more humbling comparison.

The grounds for opposition varied from group to group, but some common themes emerged. Certain individuals wrote in the spirit of the Reformation, suggesting that Roosevelt had made an alliance "with the devil at Rome, Pope Pius."[60] Others argued more reasonably that the appointment represented a violation of the First Amendment. Although Roosevelt called it a personal mission, his claim did not disguise the issue to Dr. Louie D. Newton of the Southern Baptist Convention, who asked, "Can the President . . . make an appointment . . . to any . . . group, be it religious, political or what not, without thereby officially representing and involving the people of the United States?" Clearly, the appointment, as the Vatican itself argued, derived sanctions from the presidential office, not the person of Franklin Roosevelt.[61] A small amount of favorable Protestant opinion seemed lost in the chorus of opposition.[62]

The tone of this protest provoked a counterattack by Catholics. As predicted by Dr. Buttrick in a letter to Roosevelt, Taylor's appointment did result in the deterioration of the good relations between the churches. Catholics resented what they thought were Protestant accusations that the Romans sought to subvert the American government.[63] The Catholic hierarchy responded in the same temper to Protestant criticism. Francis Spellman, archbishop of New York, set the belligerent tone. On the occasion of his investiture with the pallium (sacred vestment) on March 12, 1940, Spellman spoke at length on Taylor's appointment, expressing confidence that 21,000,000 American Catholics and most "men of good will" approved of Roosevelt's actions. Spellman was inclined to dismiss ignorant opposition, for surely no honest man would oppose the collaboration of the president and the spiritual leader of 300,000,000 souls in the cause of peace. As for the "shibboleth" of separation of church and state cited by critics, the archbishop pointed to American ambassadors to England and Japan, remarking that the king and emperor were both heads of churches, yet no one questioned the constitutionality of our representations at these courts.[64]

Bishop James H. Ryan of Omaha also addressed himself to the controversy in a lengthy open letter to the *New York Times* on May 12, 1940. Seeking to convince critics of the advantages of Taylor's appointment rather than merely to condemn them, the bishop called for a spirit of "political realism" and listed two main reasons for recognition of the Vatican. First, all Latin American countries were represented there; therefore, the United States could use the Vatican to promote Pan-Americanism. Second, the Vatican was "the listening post of the world" and a good source of diplomatic intelligence. Ryan called for an end to religious emotionalism and more hardheaded realism. Other countries easily avoided the problem of distinguishing between political and religious recognition of the Vatican. Why should the United States, the most pragmatic of nations, be frustrated by this minor theoretical distinction?[65]

In retrospect, it appears that much of the Catholic and secular rebuttal to Protestant criticism missed the point. Opportunities for a serious dialogue were squandered. Admittedly, Protestants invoked concepts such as "religious freedom" and "separation of church and state" carelessly, without bothering to provide a sophisticated constitutional elaboration. This led some Catholics and secular observers to accuse opponents of the appointment of using the constitutional issue as a mere cover for simple anti-Catholic bigotry. While unquestionably there was some fanaticism, it seems too simple to write off the protest in these terms. Many Protestants lacked a background in Constitutional law but instinctively appreciated that the appointment of a presidential envoy to the head of the Roman Catholic church was contrary to tradition. Those defenders of the appointment who cited the precedent of United States relations with the nineteenth-century Papal States missed the point. The Vatican was now clearly a spiritual and religious symbol, while in the nineteenth century it had been a state of some territorial consequence. Although it was difficult to prove how Taylor's trip to the Vatican would interfere with religious freedom in America, many Protestants used the term "religious freedom" to express their resentment at the special recognition of the Roman Catholic church implicit in the appointment. To some Protestants, the designation seemed to help confirm the pope's imperious theological position of uniqueness and supremacy. Allusions by Catholics to figurehead English kings and Japanese emperors hardly satisfied these critics. Appeals for realism and pragmatism might make some converts, but few Protestants accepted the value of a listening post at Rome.[66]

President Roosevelt's realism resembled that of Bishop James H. Ryan, but Roosevelt also realized that such reasoning would not prevent protests. In dealing with this opposition, Roosevelt revealed an evenhandedness and sensitivity which enabled him to defuse a situation of potential explosiveness. His decision to appoint a Protestant, the temporary and personal nature of the mission, and the linkage of the announcement with the Christmas spirit of peace were all designed to keep the expected protest to a minimum. The minimum was considerable.[67] Presidential Secretary Steven Early announced to the press that initial reaction to the appointment as reflected in White House mail was favorable, but he knew better. The Department of State was being bombarded with complaints.[68] On January 9, 1940, representatives of Lutheran, Seventh Day Adventist, and Baptist churches appeared at the White House to discredit Early's optimistic report. After a brief meeting with the president, Reverend J. C. McElhaney of the Seventh Day Adventist church and Dr. Ralph Long of the Lutheran World Convention admitted having protested the appointment without a full appreciation of the temporary nature of the mission.[69] Publicly, Roosevelt remained sanguine about the outcome of the meeting, but privately he wrote Senator Josiah Bailey of North Carolina, himself a leading Baptist layman, that "if some of my good Baptist brethren in Georgia had done a little preaching from the pulpit against the Ku Klux Klan in the 1920s I would have a little more genuine American respect for their Christianity!" Roosevelt concluded by incorrectly predicting that the White House conference was so effective that "we shall hear little or nothing more of [the Taylor issue]."[70]

Little indeed. Buttrick, recovered from an attack of congeniality induced by presidential attention, was soon requesting reassurance from Roosevelt that Taylor's mission would be very temporary. There were unsettling news reports that the Vatican considered Taylor a regular ambassador. Roosevelt quickly allayed Buttrick's fears with a personal note dated March 14, 1940, restating the old arguments: the appointment did not constitute formal relations; the ambassadorial rank was for social purposes; the motive for the appointment was the advancement of world peace. The president concluded that he was sure that "all men of good will must sympathize with this purpose" and that he found it hard to accept the fear of a union of church and state as a serious objection.[71] After a few more reassuring letters to strategically placed individuals, Roosevelt moved on to other matters, and the issue faded from public view because of apprehension over renewed German advances in Europe. But no one was reconciled and Protestants continued to protest until President Harry Truman ended the connection with the Vatican.

Perhaps Roosevelt would have met less opposition if he had been more
bold in leading public opinion. But he had equivocated and had explained
his intention in an obfuscating way. He himself always had clear-cut ideas
about the Vatican appointment but he kept them to himself. He was sure
that the mission would make American Catholics happy and pay political
dividends in November. The pope was a force for peace in Europe and
association with him would enhance chances for a settlement. While there
was no guarantee that the Vatican would share its diplomatic secrets with
Taylor, at least he would be in a position to take advantage of assistance
if it was offered. Finally, there was the hope, held fondly for some time,
that collaboration might prove fruitful in keeping Italy out of the war.[72]
Roosevelt also realized the unavoidably negative aspects of the appointment and this made him delay and obscure his plans. His problems with
Protestant opposition came as a result of the particular religious organization of Roman Catholicism. Taylor went to the Vatican because it was the
head of a worldwide monolithic religious community. The uniqueness of
the mission resulted from the unique centralization of Catholicism and not
from a deliberate attempt by Roosevelt to discriminate. He would have
made similar appointments to the leaders of international Protestant
churches if they had existed and he had contemplated a mission to the
head of the Eastern Orthodox Church. Hull later dissuaded him by warning of the political difficulties in such a course.[73]

5

Considering the uproar surrounding his appointment, Taylor's actual
achievements in his post were rather modest. This was not entirely his
fault. When he arrived in Rome in early 1940, the objectives of his mission remained somewhat obscure. True, his letter of appointment spoke
of collaboration between the president and the pope for world peace. Yet
chances of peace at this time were remarkably dim. In fact, Taylor's first
issue did not concern international peace. As his automobile drew up
before the Vatican for the first working meeting with the pope and Cardinal Maglione, the ambassador recalled a final briefing from the president.
In Roosevelt's words, Taylor "might express the thought that there is a
great deal of anti-Jewish feeling in the dioceses of Brooklyn, Baltimore,
and Detroit, and that this feeling is said to be encouraged by the church."
The president knew that these same areas were controlled by Catholic

leaders who preached a strong isolationist line.[74] Taylor told Maglione
on February 27, 1940, that such anti-Jewish action by men like Father
Coughlin could lead to an anti-Catholic reaction. Maglione listened sym-
pathetically. He expressed incredulity at the idea that anti-Semitism
could be preached by good Catholics after the vigorous stand taken by
Pius XI in defense of the Jews. He would willingly examine a formal
protest if Taylor wanted to submit one. Both the ambassador and the
president, however, preferred to keep the question casual and avoid
publicity. Consequently, the Vatican let the matter drop.[75]

The entire tenor of Taylor's mission was revealed in this first encounter. Roosevelt had a vital interest in the attitudes of American
Catholic leaders and desired to use the papacy as a means of controlling such opinion. This desire loomed larger than vague hopes for collaboration for peace. The president's intentions became obvious when
Taylor approached the Vatican about the appointment of a liberal
bishop to the recently created archdiocese of Washington. At the time,
Archbishop Michael J. Curley was holding down both the Baltimore
and Washington posts. Curley's vigorous isolationism and criticism of
the administration hardly endeared him to Roosevelt. In the president's
mind, the best solution would be for the church to appoint Bishop
Bernard Sheil to the Washington diocese. In fact, the president had been
promoting Sheil since the death of George Cardinal Mundelein in 1939.
At that time, he had used Frank Walker to approach Archbishop Spellman
of New York, with the idea that Sheil would make a good replacement
for Mundelein in Chicago. Unfortunately, Bishop Samuel A. Stritch of
Milwaukee had already been selected by the Vatican for the Chicago
position. This decision did not sit well with either Walker or Roosevelt.
But Spellman assured the president that Stritch was a progressive man
who supported the administration and even had Stritch write a lengthy
letter explaining his attitude toward the president. Stritch described
Roosevelt's leadership as "courageous and enlightening" and also denied
having opposed revision of the neutrality laws in October 1939. Spellman
forwarded all of this information on to Roosevelt.[76]

The president appeared stalemated in his promotion of Sheil for
Chicago. But encouraged by Secretary of the Interior Harold Ickes and
Frank Murphy, he now suggested to both Spellman and the Vatican that
Sheil receive proper recognition for his splendid work as aide to

Mundelein. What could be more appropriate than appointing Sheil to Washington? Taylor explained to Cardinal Maglione that Curley's vigorous isolationism and criticism of the administration compared unfavorably with Sheil's attitude. Sheil would be *persona grata* in administration circles. Maglione adroitly side-stepped this attempted politicization of the appointment of bishops, a historical thorn in the church's side, by insisting that the Sacred Consistorial Congregation must handle such assignments. Curley continued to control the Washington post.[77]

Undaunted by these setbacks, the president finally got around to seeking Vatican collaboration to promote international peace. Both Roosevelt and Pope Pius XII felt it important to keep Italy out of the war which began with the German invasion of Poland on September 1, 1939. Each man had different motives. Roosevelt had earlier told his ambassador to Italy, William Phillips, that he had no brief against dictators so long as they did not attack their neighbors. The president was quite willing to come to some understanding with Mussolini because he felt it imperative to keep Italy out of the German camp. Pius XII, in contrast, felt that war would only reap the whirlwind for Italy. The Vatican consistently opposed Italian adventurism.[78] The scene appeared set for a collaboration. Surely Mussolini would take notice of pressure from both the Vatican and the United States. Earlier, Roosevelt had sent messages to Mussolini suggesting that he play the role of European peacemaker. The Duce had been formal and negative in his replies. Now war was under way and apprehension grew daily that Italy would join Germany in attacking France. Taylor expressed this urgency in his attempts to promote Vatican peace initiatives. He was surprised to learn, however, that the Vatican had very poor communications with the Duce. Mussolini already knew the pope's attitude about war and saw no need to encourage such a critic. The pope did inform Taylor that informal contacts reported that Mussolini was still undecided about his future course. The Italian people, repeated the pontiff, were assuredly opposed to war.[79]

After this encouraging conversation, Taylor decided to ask Roosevelt to put pressure again on Mussolini to stay out of the war. On meeting with Cardinal Maglione on March 15, 1940, Taylor emphasized that Roosevelt wanted to know if he could expect papal cooperation in trying to keep Italy neutral. Maglione agreed to raise the question with the pope.

In the meantime, on March 18, 1940, Assistant Secretary of State Sumner Welles arrived for an interview with the pontiff. Welles had just concluded a fast fact-finding trip to European capitals to ascertain prospects for peace. In his conversation with the pope, Welles found support for his own pessimistic estimate of the situation. Maglione, Welles, and the pontiff all agreed that none of the belligerents was interested in a peace proposal at this time and that an abortive attempt could only weaken general opportunities for a later settlement. Welles also inquired about Italy's position vis-à-vis the war. Maglione told him that the Italian people did not want war but that Mussolini was the key and, with Taylor's suggestion fresh in his mind, he hinted that the Allies could keep Mussolini out of the war by generous diplomacy. Welles and Taylor both became enthusiastic for such collaboration. Maglione probably had something more tangible in mind originally, such as recognition of Italian claims in the Mediterranean, but since association with the most powerful neutral in the world could only enhance the moral standing of the papacy, he agreed to a joint endeavor despite past evidence of Mussolini's intransigence.[80]

It took Taylor some time, however, to convince Washington of the wisdom of another appeal to Mussolini. Secretary of State Hull recalled the fruitlessness of earlier attempts. While awaiting the president's decision during April, Taylor found additional encouragement in conversations with Maglione and Monsignor Joseph Hurley, Maglione's assistant. Both men now felt that an appeal from Roosevelt to Mussolini was worthwhile. France was on the verge of collapse and Mussolini was tempted to join Hitler in victory. After Francois-Poncet, the French ambassador to the Vatican, hinted that his country was eager to come to terms with Italy, Taylor once again wired Roosevelt to urge him to make an appeal to the dictator. Taylor guaranteed Vatican support.[81]

On April 24, 1940, Taylor's mission bore first fruit. Both Roosevelt and Pope Pius wrote Mussolini. The pope congratulated the Duce on keeping the peace and prayed that Italy would be spared the ravages of war. Roosevelt made much the same points and hinted that the United States would plead Italian security needs to the Allies. Unfortunately, Mussolini sent a polite but negative reply to Roosevelt. Taylor remained undaunted. He continued to think that the United States could keep Italy out of the war. Maglione knew better. The pope's letter to Mussolini merely resulted in the suggestion of the Italian ambassador to the Vatican that Pope Pius not meddle in such affairs. By May 17, 1940, Taylor reluctantly admitted to Roosevelt that there was no chance of any further "parallel action at this time." On May 23, Pius told Taylor that Mussolini would go to war in two or three weeks and nothing the Vatican did would affect this decision. Throughout this attempt at collaboration, Taylor had "a higher opinion of the Holy Father's authority" than was justified. Moral suasion could no longer force an emperor to travel to Canossa.[82]

On June 10, 1940, Italy entered the war as an ally of Germany. Attempts at collective pressure by Roosevelt and Pope Pius to turn Mussolini from his course were unavailing. He was bound as an ally of Germany and had ambitions which could not be satisfied by sitting on the sidelines. Despite their failure, however, the campaign at least demonstrated that the Vatican and the United States could work together. The pope continued to call for peace without success. Roosevelt continued to distinguish Italian efforts from those of Germany. In his opinion, the Italian alliance with Hitler was unnatural. As Roosevelt told Cicognani, the apostolic delegate, in January 1941, Italy could make a separate peace. Furthermore, he expressed understanding for the Italian need to expand and have some influence over the Suez Canal. A diplomatic failure had served to enhance the mutual respect of the Vatican and the United States for each other.[83]

In the forthcoming months Roosevelt continued to seek Vatican support for his foreign policy. He desired to promote a pro-allied outlook at the Vatican and to use papal influence to blunt American Catholic isolationism and obstructionism. Taylor himself soon fell ill and had to return to the United States for extended medical treatment. His assistant, Harold Tittmann, continued the mission. During subsequent months Tittmann met frequently with Vatican officials and made clear the commitment of Roosevelt to the Allied cause. In April 1941, when Maglione asked for an explanation of current United States policy toward the war, Tittmann said his country would "never allow Hitler to win this war no matter how long it might last." From Washington, Secretary of State Hull urged Tittmann to convince the Vatican that the United States would not "stand on the sidelines," but would help resist aggression.[84]

Obviously, the pope and his staff could not really believe that the United States would become directly involved in another European war. Had not the United States rejected membership in the League of Nations and passed neutrality legislation during the 1930s? The Vatican also believed that most Americans, including Catholics, were isolationists. The pope even suggested that England might be defeated before the United States could become involved. To all of this Tittmann replied that the United States would fight on alone if necessary because compromise with Hitler was impossible. He also told the pope that isolationist influence in the United States "could be discounted."[85]

But, less than a month after Tittmann's assessment, the United States complained to the pope about the isolationism of American Catholics. This strange turn of events resulted from the Department of State's desire to convince the pope of Roosevelt's opposition to Hitler and to enlist both the Vatican and American Catholics in the crusade against the Nazis. In May 1941 Tittmann cabled Hull that a number of sources in the Vatican, including the Father General of the Jesuits, Vladimir Ledakousky, shared Roosevelt's opinion that the American hierarchy did not understand the real threat to the Catholic Church from Hitlerism. Cardinal O'Connell of Boston and Archbishop McNicholas of Cincinnati were singled out as representatives of this confusion. These Vatican sources urged Tittmann to approach the pope directly and ask him to inform American clerics of the danger to the church. Tittmann was pessimistic about the pope's playing such a role, but he was willing to try if Washington thought it advisable.[86]

This information from Tittmann offered Roosevelt and Hull, who were both dissatisfied with the current attitude of the American clergy toward United States diplomacy, an opportunity to exert some pressure from the top. Perhaps the pope could bring American Catholics into the Roosevelt consensus. Yet, after discussing Tittmann's suggestion with Myron Taylor, the administration thought it best to approach the problem from within the United States. As we have seen, Taylor went to see Cicognani in June 1941 and explained that American Catholics were not adequately supporting the president. Cicognani replied with an elaborate defense of the American clergy, documenting an overwhelming dislike for Hitler and emphasizing the impossibility of unanimity among 34,000 clerics. Taylor turned this information over to Hull who in turn cabled Tittmann that reliable sources indicated that American Catholics were fully behind the president. Using the data Cicognani had supplied Taylor, Hull informed Tittmann that all of the 116 dioceses in the United States

were aware of the Nazi threat to the church. "With the possible exception of two well-known prelates . . . who have opposed American entry
into the war," wrote Hull, "no other church dignitary of any rank has
spoken adversely on the subject." Hull's statement was used to scuttle
Tittmann's idea of approaching the pope. Ironically, the information for
the statement came from the apostolic delegate, an agent of the pontiff.[87]

Despite Hull's decision, Tittmann still faced the problem of convincing the Vatican that the United States was committed to the defeat of
Hitler. In a conversation in May 1941 with Monsignor Montini, Vatican
Undersecretary for Ordinary Affairs, the American bluntly announced
that the Vatican was being nearsighted by not seeing that "its only chance
was victory by the Anglo-Americans." Personally, Tittmann thought Vatican neutralism was a result of the conviction that German domination of
Europe was inevitable. To correct his view, Assistant Secretary of State
Sumner Welles directed that Tittmann be sent weekly summaries of the
progress of rearmament in the United States and copies of remarks by
American clergymen supporting the Roosevelt program. This information
was to be used to reassure the Vatican.[88]

What Tittmann and Welles failed to appreciate was the sincere desire
of the pope to promote a settlement of the war. He was disappointed that
the United States was forsaking the role of peacemaker to assume a
semibelligerent status. The Americans were wrong to think that the
Vatican wanted to enter the Allied camp but were afraid of the Germans.
This view failed to appreciate the Vatican's desire for neutrality. In contrast to Tittmann's view of papal fears of Germany was the view of the
German ambassador to the Vatican, who reported that the pontiff was
bitterly disappointed about the semibelligerency of the United States.
Tittmann continued to show the pope the information sent him by
Welles on American rearmament. The pope was impressed but also upset
at the loss of an ally for peace.[89]

In June 1941 the Vatican position toward the war became further
complicated by Hitler's decision to invade the Soviet Union. Declaring
himself defender of Western civilization against Bolshevism, Hitler
expected Vatican encouragement. In the United States, Roosevelt and
Hull struggled to erect a new policy toward Russia, aware that the
specter of communism could easily lead both the Vatican and American
Catholics to oppose United States intervention on the side of the USSR.

6

To complete the consideration of Taylor's appointment as a representative to the Vatican, a short diversion into the domestic political arena is
necessary. Indeed, the entire episode reveals how acutely Roosevelt
appreciated the interrelationship of diplomatic and domestic affairs. The
president had every reason to consider the domestic political dividends
which could be reaped by the Vatican appointment. Catholics constituted
an important part of his coalition, a coalition that was showing signs of
combat fatigue by 1940. In the 1938 congressional elections the Republicans had made their first significant gains since 1928. The election of 1940
would be extremely critical for both the Democratic party and for Roosevelt's foreign policy.

The president was too realistic a politician, too old a veteran of New
York politics, to ignore the Catholic church in any political equation.
His approach to the religious factor in politics resembled his approach to
other problems: he would play the honest broker of different interests.
As he told Secretary of the Treasury Henry Morgenthau during a discussion of the large number of Jews holding public office in Oregon, "You
can't get a disproportionate amount of any one religion." When he had
been asked by Ed Flynn to appoint three Catholics in Nebraska, Roosevelt refused because they had had their share. When Leo Crowley sought
to debate the point, the president swung into the following lecture: "Leo,
you know this is a Protestant country, and the Catholics and the Jews are
here on sufferance. It is up to both of you to go along with anything that
I want at this time." Although this testimony may well have been garbled
when translated by Crowley for Morgenthau's benefit, it does point up
Roosevelt's keen awareness of the importance of recognizing Catholics,
(for example, by appointing a delegate to the Vatican), but of not going
too far for fear of alienating Protestants (thus, the delegate to the Vatican
was a non-Catholic and was given the special title of "personal representative.")[90]

The president could defend separation of church and state and still
make appointments for religious reasons. Catholics were sensitive to
recognition; such appointments would pay dividends at the polls. When
Roosevelt named Frank Walker as Postmaster General and Frank Murphy

as Justice of the Supreme Court, the Catholic press applauded. Roosevelt, editors noted, had named almost one-half of all Catholics who had ever been named to presidential cabinets. He was the first president to have two Catholics serving in the cabinet at the same time.[91]

Many politicians who applauded the theory of keeping the church out of politics did not hesitate to request support from religious figures whenever such aid was needed. The Committee to Defend America and the America First Committee both sought to recruit Catholic leaders for their cause. Secretary of the Interior Ickes complained about the church in politics but sought to influence the selection of bishops. Even religious figures developed a convenient double standard on the entire question. In July 1940 the Reverend Maurice Sheehy of Catholic University wrote to Roosevelt in support of a third term. Sheehy explained that he was doing his best to promote the idea while he traveled across the country giving speeches. A few weeks later, Sheehy gave the sermon for a special mass for the Catholic Lawyers Guild. He stressed that religion and politics did not mix and that "the effort to coerce any Catholic group, as a Catholic group, to support a particular party or candidate, would, in this country, lead to disaster."[92]

The 1940 election was a classic example of how religion was both in and out of politics and of how Roosevelt understood the distinction. The candidacy of Postmaster General James Farley, an Irish Catholic, raised once again the possibility of a Catholic president, symbol of true assimilation and acceptance to many of that faith. Although public opinion surveys on the chances of a Catholic candidate seemed equivocal and some Catholic leaders had their doubts, Farley, encouraged by his many friends in the party, decided to make the race. His decision was undoubtedly influenced by Roosevelt's hesitancy in announcing he would seek a third term.[93]

In the absence of presidential direction, Farley thought he had a green light. Ed Flynn had reported that Roosevelt wanted to retire, although he might change his mind if events warranted it. As for the problem of Farley's religion, Senator Burton Wheeler of Montana reported a conversation with the president in 1939 in which Roosevelt told him that "if there were an outstanding Catholic Democrat available—someone like my [Wheeler's] colleague, . . . Thomas Walsh,—he could possibly be elected in 1940."[94] Other evidence suggests that the president even entertained the idea of a Catholic for the vice-presidential spot on a ticket headed by himself.[95]

Yet Farley had no sooner thrown his hat into the ring when word came from the White House that his religion would be a disabling factor. Ernest K. Lindley, a prominent Washington reporter, released the story of how Roosevelt had privately predicted another Al Smith debacle if Farley ran. The president suggested that Secretary of State Hull would be called a "stalking horse for the Pope" in the South if he ran with Farley as second man on the ticket. This story gained credibility when the president delayed over a week before telling a press conference of March 19, 1940, that "those of you who know me—that story of Ernest Lindley was made completely out of whole cloth—obviously." He explained his delay in rebutting the story by emphasizing that he never responded to individual stories by columnists and he resented the implication that his silence meant the story was true. Lindley, however, defended his facts and told of receiving several calls from high-placed Democrats confirming the general thesis. In fact, the president had made similar remarks to others, including Secretary of the Interior Ickes. Roosevelt was merely describing political reality as he saw it in March 1940 after having been stung by Protestant reaction to Myron Taylor's appointment. Of course, Roosevelt had other reasons for opposing Farley, who had never been committed to the New Deal. Yet Roosevelt did fear that the religious issue would split the country. The reaction to his Vatican appointment had demonstrated that such sensibilities were still strong.[96]

Farley himself had no reason to be surprised at Roosevelt's attitude. As early as July 1939 George Cardinal Mundelein had approached Farley to discuss the 1940 election. Mundelein spoke of a recent visit with the president and predicted that he would run for a third term. Lest Farley miss the message, the cardinal bluntly explained that the country would not be ready for a Catholic president for many years. He hoped that Farley would do nothing to resurrect the ill-will which had been generated in 1928. Finally, Mundelein urged Farley to support Roosevelt. But Farley remained unconvinced. He cited personal endorsements which indicated he would be a strong candidate. He insisted 1940 was not 1928. Above all, Farley resented the fact that Roosevelt had asked Mundelein to convey this message of despair.[97]

Not only was Farley stubborn, but Roosevelt's expressions of political realism provided another excuse for those Catholics who opposed the president on other grounds, including the issues of a third term and foreign interventionism. This Catholic opposition included such journals as *America*, which editorialized that the issue was not Roosevelt but whether "[we] shall survive as a nation . . . or forsaking democracy, entrust our destiny as a nation into the hands of one man." Reverend John LaFarge of *America* even appeared before a Senate subcommittee to promote a constitutional amendment limiting a president's tenure of office to one term of six years. Reverend James Gillis of the *Catholic World* opposed Roosevelt because of his interventionism and because of the third term. The *Brooklyn Tablet*, another isolationist newspaper, came out strongly against the third term. Individual Catholics who spoke out against Roosevelt's renomination included Archbishop Joseph Schrembs and Archbishop Beckman, and Bishop Thomas J. Toolen of Mobile who warned against the hysteria which might "sweep us into a dictatorship." All of these men were identified with the isolationist cause. The same was true of Father Edward L. Curran of the International Catholic Truth Society, who, along with Dr. Ignatius M. Wilkinson, dean of Fordham University Law School, called for a constitutional bar to a third term. And while this opposition mounted, newspapers reported how Wendell Willkie, the Republican candidate, was dining with various bishops.[98]

To compensate for such defections Roosevelt could count on the support of several important Catholic leaders. Although he did not enter the campaign publicly, Archbishop Spellman of New York made clear to friends that he endorsed Roosevelt for a third term. Joseph Kennedy, now at odds with Roosevelt's foreign policy, remained "on the reservation." John Cort, founder of the American Catholic Trade Union, wrote publicly to explain that Roosevelt had been the champion of American Catholics. Monsignor Ryan of the NCWC wrote letters endorsing the president. More active was Reverend Maurice Sheehy, who even made suggestions to the Democratic National Headquarters on the proper strategy for capturing Catholic votes. The headquarters was manned by two Catholics, Frank Walker and Ed Flynn. In view of this kind of support, one can understand the irritation of Mussolini's ambassador to the Vatican, who asked Cardinal Maglione if it was true that the pope was calling on American Catholics to vote for Roosevelt, the warmonger. Maglione denied the accusation.[99]

Despite such Catholic support, Walker and Flynn were both running scared over possible defections. Flynn became enraged when the president of his alma mater, Fordham, invited Willkie to be his guest at a football game. This nervousness over trivia reflected the reports received from the field which indicated, as columnist Robert S. Allen put it, that Catholics "are off the reservation." A similar conclusion emerged in the columns of Arthur Krock, Joseph Alsop, and Robert Kintner. Rebuttals were issued by such Catholic leaders as Edward J. Heffron of the National Conference of Catholic Men, who denied accusations that Catholics would vote against Roosevelt because of Farley or because of the anti-Axis foreign policy of the United States. Still, Walker, Flynn, and presidential advisor Harry Hopkins worried about the rumors, frequently substantiated by letters from the field containing reports of local priests and diocesan papers pushing Willkie. In addition, Willkie had won by two-to-one over Roosevelt among students polled at St. John's College and by 44 percent to 35 percent at Fordham summer school.[100]

These fears over Catholic defections, however, were exaggerated. The vast majority of Catholic publications remained neutral during the election. The positions taken by the *Catholic World* and *America* were exceptions to the rule. A survey of the foreign language press in the United States revealed that Roosevelt was the clear favorite of Russian, Spanish, and Polish presses. He broke even among German and Italian presses, despite his diplomacy.[101]

An analysis of the presidential vote in 1940 reveals that Catholics remained in the Roosevelt coalition. When such variables as class, age, and ethnic classification were controlled, analysts still found that Catholics voted for Roosevelt more frequently than did Protestants. Catholic manual workers voted for Roosevelt by more than two-to-one over middle-class Protestants. In certain controlled group studies, the Democratic margin among Catholics was never less than 71 percent, regardless of income or social status. Furthermore, Catholic support of Roosevelt was especially high among those Catholics "who regarded their religious group as among the most important to them." The more Catholic, the more Democratic.[102] Roosevelt's coalition held, although Rexford Tugwell probably simplified matters when he wrote, after Taylor's appointment, "even the Catholics had been won over to Franklin."[103]

NOTES

1. White House News Release, December 23, 1939, in *Selected Materials from the Papers of Franklin D. Roosevelt Concerning Roman Catholic Church Matters* (microfilm), Roosevelt Library, Hyde Park, N.Y.); Roosevelt to Pius XII, December 23, 1939, in Myron Taylor, editor, *Wartime Correspondence Between President Roosevelt and Pope Pius XII* (New York, 1947), pp. 17-19.

2. Alex Karmarkovic, "The Myron C. Taylor Appointment: Background; Religious Reaction; Constitutionality" (Ph.D. thesis, University of Minnesota, 1967), pp. 52-53; *Catholic World* 148 (March 1939), pp. 750-751; Anson Phelps Stokes, *Church and State in the United States*, 3 vols. (New York, 1950), vol. 2, pp. 103-110. Formal relations between the United States and the Vatican had been terminated on a mutual sour note in 1868; see Martin F. Hasting, "United States-Vatican Relations; Policies and Problems" (Ph.D. thesis, University of California, 1952); Thomas B. Morgan, *The Listening Post* (New York, 1944), p. 122.

3. Peter Nichols, *The Politics of the Vatican* (London, 1968), p. 103; Morgan, *The Listening Post*, p. 122.

4. *Brooklyn Tablet*, October 28, 1933, p. 2; *New York Times*, June 29, 1933; Joseph Gurn, "Papal-American Relations," *Columbia*, July 1934, p. 11.

5. Karmarkovic, "The Myron C. Taylor Appointment," pp. 44, 47, 49; Steven Early, presidential secretary, to Schramm, May 16, 1934, *Sel. Materials*.

6. Rexford G. Tugwell, *The Democratic Roosevelt* (New York, 1957), p. 513n.; George Q. Flynn, *American Catholics and the Roosevelt Presidency, 1932-1936* (Lexington, 1968), pp. 184-186.

7. Oscar Halecki, *Eugenio Pacelli: Pope of Peace* (New York, 1951), pp. 83-84; Hasting, "United States-Vatican Relations," p. 272.

8. Mundelein to Cicognani, October 6, 1937, in PPF 321, Franklin D. Roosevelt Papers, Hyde Park, New York; Roosevelt to Mundelein, October 22, 1937, in Elliott Roosevelt, editor, *F.D.R.: His Personal Letters*, 3 vols. (New York, 1947-1950), vol. 3, pp. 720-721.

9. *New York Times*: November 5, 1938; November 6, 1939.

10. Morgan, *The Listening Post,* p. 132; Robert I. Gannon, *The Cardinal Spellman Story* (New York, 1962), p. 158; William Phillips, *Ventures in Diplomacy* (Portland, Me., 1952), pp. 222-223, insists Roosevelt arranged the reception to demonstrate American regard for religion to Hitler.

11. Morgan, *The Listening Post,* p. 123.

12. Gannon, *The Cardinal Spellman Story,* pp. 153-154.

13. Karmarkovic, "The Myron C. Taylor Appointment," p. 51; Morgan, *The Listening Post,* p. 157; Halecki, *Pope of Peace,* p. 156; Gannon, *The Cardinal Spellman Story,* pp. 153-154; Carmille Cianfarra, *The Vatican and the War* (New York, 1944), p. 43.

14. Spellman to Maglione, October 25, 1939, in Pierre Blet, et. al., editors, Secrétairerie D'État de sa Sainteté, *Actes et Documents du Saint Siège Relatifs à La Seconde Guerre Mondiale,* 5 vols. (Citta Del Vaticano: Libreria Editrice Vaticana, 1967-), vol. 1, pp. 302-305 (hereafter cited as *Holy See and War*); Gannon, *The Cardinal Spellman Story,* p. 155.

15. Hull to Roosevelt (on board USS *Houston*), [n.d.], *Sel. Materials;* Phillips, *Ventures in Diplomacy,* p. 252; Department of State Memo to Roosevelt, February 24, 1939, in PPF 4129, Roosevelt Papers; *New York Times:* March 9, 1939; March 14, 1939.

16. *New York Times:* April 14, 1939; May 19, 1939; *Boston Pilot,* June 17, 1939, p. 4.

17. Cicognani to Maglione, October 27, 1939, *Holy See and War,* vol. 1, p. 306.

18. Ready to Cicognani, April 15, 1939; Cicognani to Maglione, April 15, 1939, *Holy See and War,* vol. 1, pp. 103-104, 106.

19. Introduction to *Holy See and War,* vol. 1, pp. 1, 10; A. Russell Buchanan, *The United States and World War II,* 2 vols. (New York, 1964), vol. 1, p. 4.

20. Maglione to Cicognani, April 18, 1939, *Holy See and War,* vol. 1, p. 106.

21. Welles to Ready, April 20, 1939, *Holy See and War,* vol. 1, p. 106.

22. Anne (O'Hare) McCormick, *Vatican Journal, 1929-1954* (New York 1957), p. 103, gives this interpretation.

23. *Holy See and War,* vol. 1, pp. 117-118.

24. Notes of Hurley's conversation with Rogers, May 9, 1939, *Holy See and War,* vol. 1, p. 126.

25. Maglione to Cicognani, May 10, 1939, *Holy See and War*, vol. 1, p. 130.

26. Howard Carroll to Cicognani, May 16, 1939, *Holy See and War*, vol. 1, pp. 136-137, 144.

27. Robert A. Divine, *The Reluctant Belligerent: American Entry into World War II* (New York, 1965), pp. 46-47.

28. Cicognani to Maglione, June 11, 1939, and June 27, 1939, *Holy See and War*, vol. 1, pp. 179, 194.

29. *New York Times*: July 16, 1939; July 18, 1939; July 29, 1939; Cianfarra, *The Vatican and the War*, p. 178.

30. The pope was convinced that Phillips had played a key role in obtaining the mission; see Phillips, *Ventures in Diplomacy*, pp. 251-252; Welles to Roosevelt, August 1, 1939, PSF, Vatican, Box 17, Roosevelt Papers; Karmarkovic, "The Myron C. Taylor Appointment," p. 61; Cordell Hull, *The Memoirs of Cordell Hull*, 2 vols. (New York, 1948), vol. 1, p. 713; Hasting, "United States-Vatican Relations," pp. 51, 219; Donald F. Drummond, *The Passing of American Neutrality, 1937-1941* (Ann Arbor, Michigan, 1955), p. 96.

31. Hull, *Memoirs*, vol. 1, pp. 713-714.

32. Spellman to Maglione, October 24, 1939, *Holy See and War*, vol. 1, pp. 302-305; see also Gannon, *The Cardinal Spellman Story*, pp. 162-163.

33. Cicognani to Maglione, October 27, 1939, *Holy See and War*, vol. 1, p. 306.

34. Harold H. Tittmann, Jr., to author, September 10, 1969 (Tittmann became Taylor's assistant in Rome). Hull, *Memoirs*, vol. 1, pp. 713-714; Grace Tully, *F.D.R.: My Boss* (New York, 1949), p. 296.

35. William H. Anderson, "Interview," Columbia University Oral History Project, pp. 57-58; see also Robert Sherwood, *Roosevelt and Hopkins* (New York, 1950), p. 284, who connects the appointment with the desire to have Catholics support aid to Russia, although this suggestion has problems of chronology; Hasting, "United States-Vatican Relations," p. 53. (On voting statistics, see Hasting, Introduction, fn. 16.)

36. Harold L. Ickes, *The Secret Diary of Harold L. Ickes*, 3 vols. (New York, 1953-1954), vol. 3, pp. 55, 65.

37. Taylor, *Wartime Correspondence*, pp. 2, 8; Morgan, *The Listening*

Post, pp. 188, 192. A number of sources accept this moral interpretation of Roosevelt's action: McCormick, *Vatican Journal*, pp. 107-108; *NCWC News Service*, April 22, 1940; *Boston Pilot*, February 24, 1940, p. 1; Cianfarra, *The Vatican and the War*, pp. 7-8.

38. Morgan, *The Listening Post*, pp. 189-190; Hasting, "United States-Vatican Relations," p. 54; Taylor, *Wartime Correspondence*, pp. 3-4.

39. Morgan, *The Listening Post*, pp. 189-190; Hull quoted in Karmarkovic, "The Myron C. Taylor Appointment," pp. 68, 71.

40. Cicognani to Maglione, December 23, 1939, *Holy See and War*, vol. 1, pp. 328-329; Karmarkovic, "The Myron C. Taylor Appointment," p. 78; but see Eleanor Roosevelt, *This I Remember* (New York, 1949), p. 209, who writes that Taylor's mission was only an emergency step due to the world crisis.

41. Press Conference #609, December 26, 1939; Press Conference #614, January 12, 1940, PPF, Roosevelt Papers.

42. News Conference of April 18, 1940, PPF, 1-P, Roosevelt Papers. Tradition in Europe dictated that the ambassador of the Vatican was also dean of the diplomatic corps. This arrangement would have been rather unsatisfactory to members of the Department of State and to domestic opinion. *New York Times*, June 17, 1939.

43. Cicognani to Maglione, December 23, 1939, *Holy See and War*, vol. 1, pp. 327-330; Karmarkovic, "The Myron C. Taylor Appointment," p. 204.

44. Hull had been one of the first to insist that only a personal representative be sent even though Ambassador Phillips suggested that regular diplomatic relations be established; see Hull, *Memoirs*, vol. 1, p. 713; Fred L. Israel, editor, *The War Diary of Breckinridge Long* (Lincoln, Nebraska, 1966), pp. 62-63.

45. Unsigned Department of State Memorandum to Roosevelt, February 9, 1940, PSF, Vatican, Box 17, Roosevelt Papers; Israel, *War Diary*, pp. 82-83.

46. Taylor, *Wartime Correspondence*, p. 6; notes of Maglione conversation with Taylor, March 15, 1940, *Holy See and War*, vol. 1, pp. 368-369.

47. Cicognani to Maglione, December 23, 1939, *Holy See and War*, vol. 1, pp. 328-329; Maglione to Cicognani, December 24, 1939, *Holy*

See and War, vol. 1, p. 336; see also Cianfarra, *The Vatican and the War*, p. 207; Halecki, *Pope of Peace*, p. 161; Morgan, *The Listening Post*, p. 193.

48. Karmarkovic, "The Myron C. Taylor Appointment," p. 141.

49. Robert A. Graham, S.J., *Vatican Diplomacy* (Princeton, N. J., 1959), pp. 327-328.

50. Gannon, *The Cardinal Spellman Story*, p. 165; Karmarkovic, "The Myron C. Taylor Appointment, " pp. 92-93.

51. *NCWC News Service*, January 29, 1940; clipping from the *Erie Daily Times*, January 8, 1940, *Sel. Materials;* Ryan quoted in clipping from the *True Voice*, in letter from Rev. Maurice S. Sheehy to LeHand, January 2, 1940, *Sel. Materials.*

52. Sheen to Roosevelt, telegram, December 24, 1939, *Sel. Materials.*

53. Wilfrid Parsons, "Pope, President, Peace," *Thought* 15 (March 1940), pp. 1-8; *NCWC News Service,* February 2, 1940.

54. *Commonweal*, January 5, 1940, p. 233; *Brooklyn Tablet*, December 30, 1939, p. 10; *Boston Pilot*: January 13, 1940, p. 3; March 2, 1940, p. 4; *Catholic Action*, February 1940, p. 14; *Catholic World* 150 (February 1940), p. 620; *Catholic Transcript*, December 28, 1939, p. 4.

55. Cantrill, *Public Opinion*, January 10, 1940, p. 965.

56. *NCWC News Service*: March 12, 1940; May 17, 1940; May 16, 1940; March 1, 1940; May 6, 1940; Krock, Clapper, and Franklin deplored Protestant criticism. For favorable Jewish reaction, see William Weiss to Roosevelt, December 24, 1939, *Sel. Materials*, and Karmarkovic, "The Myron C. Taylor Appointment," pp. 100, 105.

57. Karmarkovic, "The Myron C. Taylor Appointment," pp. 145-153.

58. Ibid., pp. 124-133. Karmarkovic argues that opinion was divided among Presbyterians, but there seems to have been little positive support for the mission at their various conventions; see *NCWC News Service:* June 28, 1940; May 18, 1940. The Federal Council of Churches was also more negative than positive in its reaction but was embarrassed by Buttrick's role in the original peace suggestion by Roosevelt. The Disciples of Christ were mostly opposed but appeared reluctant to demand immediate recall. As with all surveys of religious groups, the opinions of official journals and resolutions of conventions are the bases for generalization. While this "elite" opinion should not be confused with that of the man in the pew, as an expression of leadership tendencies

it can hardly be ignored. See S. M. Lipset, "Religion and Politics in America," in *Religion and Social Conflict*, edited by R. Lee and M. E. Marty (New York, 1964), pp. 69-126; also Leonard Curry, *Protestant-Catholic Relations in America* (Lexington, 1972), pp. 37-40.

59. Quoted in the *New York Times*, July 24, 1939. Evidence of opposition from Lutherans can be found in Myron Marty, *Lutherans and Roman Catholicism* (Notre Dame, 1968), pp. 11, 112-113; Karmarkovic, "The Myron C. Taylor Appointment," pp. 154-184, 191.

60. Eddie Clayton to Roosevelt, December 23, 1939; clipping from the *Herald of the Epiphany*, Philadelphia, July 15, 1940; Sterling Tracy to Stephen Early, December 24, 1939; all in *Sel. Materials.*

61. Quoted in Karmarkovic, "The Myron C. Taylor Appointment," p. 192. Newton continued his opposition all during World War II. In fact, his opposition was instrumental in the eventual decision to end the Vatican mission.

62. *NCWC News Service*: April 19, 1940; June 12, 1940; May 13, 1940; May 16, 1940; May 21, 1940; Karmarkovic, "The Myron C. Taylor Appointment," pp. 103-106, 109-115; clipping from the *Fort Worth Telegram*, June 16, 1940, *Sel Materials*; Clifford P. Morehouse, editor of the *Living Church*, to Roosevelt, December 24, 1939, *Sel. Materials;* the *Christian Evangelist* (Disciples of Christ) and the *Living Church* (Episcopalian) favored the appointment.

63. *Catholic Herald Citizen,* April 13, 1940, p. 5; *Boston Pilot,* June 1, 1940, p. 4; *NCWC News Service*, April 1, 1940; John Tracy Ellis and John L. McMahon, "Our Envoy to the Vatican," *Catholic World* 151 (August 1940), pp. 573-581.

64. Copy of speech by Most Reverend Francis J. Spellman on occasion of his investiture with the pallium at St. Patrick's Cathedral, New York City . . . March 12, 1940, in *Sel. Materials.* The pallium is a special vestment worn by the pope and conferred on archbishops.

65. *New York Times*, May 12, 1940; also printed in the *Congressional Record*, May 20, 1940.

66. Of course, in some ways the confused thinking in both camps merely reflected a more profound ambiguity between American society and organized religion in the twentieth century, a confusion apparent even in the decisions of the Supreme Court.

67. But see Rexford Tugwell, *The Democratic Roosevelt* (Garden City,

N.Y., 1957), p. 513, who reports that the reaction was "not as adverse as might have been expected."

68. William Langer and S. Everett Gleason, *The Challenge to Isolation*, 2 vols. (New York, 1952), vol. 1, p. 349n; Karmarkovic, "The Myron C. Taylor Appointment," p. 80. Many of the complaints centered on the false impresssion that Taylor was being paid a salary by the government and that his ambassadorial title meant formal diplomatic relations had been established with the Vatican.

69. Karmarkovic, "The Myron C. Taylor Appointment," p. 181.

70. Roosevelt to Josiah W. Bailey, January 12, 1940, in Roosevelt, editor, *F.D.R.*, vol. 4, pp. 988-989.

71. Roosevelt to Buttrick, March 14, 1940, in Samuel Rosenman, *The Public Papers and Addresses of Franklin D. Roosevelt*, 13 vols. (New York, 1938-1950), vol. 9, p. 101.

72. Hull, *Memoirs*, vol. 1, pp. 778-779.

73. Ibid., vol. 1, pp. 715-716; Karmarkovic, "The Myron C. Taylor Appointment," pp. 347-363, goes to elaborate lengths to prove that the appointment was unconstitutional but appears to base his conclusion on a judicial interpretation of the First Amendment made seven years after the Taylor appointment.

74. Roosevelt to Taylor, February 13, 1940, in Roosevelt, editor, *F.D.R.*, vol. 4, p. 999; also see PPF 423, Roosevelt Papers.

75. Notes of Monsignor Hurley of conversation between Taylor and Maglione, March 8, 1940, *Holy See and War*, vol. 1, pp. 352-353.

76. Spellman to Roosevelt, February 5, 1940; Stritch to Spellman, January 20, 1940; Roosevelt to Spellman, February 13, 1940, PSF: Spellman, Roosevelt Papers. Ickes, *Diary*, vol. 3, pp. 36, 45, 403, in which the author indicates that Roosevelt was still seeking the appointment of Sheil as late as January 1941.

77. Roosevelt to Spellman, February 13, 1940, PSF: Spellman, Roosevelt Papers; conversation of Taylor and Maglione, March 8, 1940, *Holy See and War*, vol. 1, p. 353.

78. Phillips, *Ventures in Diplomacy*, p. 207; William L. Langer and S. Everett Gleason, *The Undeclared War, 1940-1941* (New York, 1953), p. 392.

79. Taylor to Roosevelt, February 28, 1940, SDF, 121.866a/31; Hull, *Memoirs*, vol. 1, pp. 777-778.

80. Maglione's notes of conversation with Taylor, March 15, 1940, and conversation with Welles, March 18, 1940, *Holy See and War*, vol. 1, pp. 368-369, 375-376; Taylor to Roosevelt and Hull, March 19, 1940, SDF, 500.421/154; Langer and Gleason, *The Challenge to Isolation*, vol. 1, p. 373.

81. Notes of Hurley, April 24, 1940, *Holy See and War*, vol. 1, pp. 395n, 396; Cianfarra, *The Vatican and the War,* p. 221; Langer and Gleason, *The Challenge to Isolation*, vol. 2, pp. 439, 441.

82. Carlo Falconi, *The Popes in the Twentieth Century*, trans. by Muriel Grindrod (Boston, 1967), pp. 253-254; Valeri to Maglione, May 15, 1940, and Maglione's notes of conversation with Taylor, May 2, 1940, *Holy See and War*, vol. 1, pp. 404, 426; Taylor to Roosevelt, May 17, 1940, SDF, 121.866a/64; Taylor to Roosevelt, May 23, 1940, SDF, 740.0011EW1939/3253½.

83. Cicognani to Maglione, January 16, 1941, *Holy See and War*, vol. 4, p. 344; Cicognani to Maglione, June 4, 1940, *Holy See and War,* vol. 1, p. 449; Taylor, *Wartime Correspondence*, p. 27.

84. Tittmann to Hull, April 26, 1941; Hull to Tittmann, April 29, 1941, in SDF, 740.0011EW1939/10387.

85. Tittmann to Hull, May 5, 1941, SDF, 740.0011EW1939/10672.

86. Tittmann to Hull, May 2, 1941, and May 28, 1941, SDF, 740.0011EW1939/10588 and 11388.

87. Taylor memo to Cicognani, June 7, 1941, SDF, 811.404/221; Hull to Tittmann, June 9, 1941, SDF, 740.0011EW1939/11388.

88. Tittmann to Hull, May 8, 1941, and memo by Sumner Welles, May 8, 1941, SDF, 740.0011EW1939/10735.

89. Tittmann to Hull, June 22, 1941, SDF, 740.0011EW1939/12300; . Saul Friedlander, *Pius XII and the Third Reich: A Documentation,* trans. by Charles Fullman (New York, 1966), pp. 88, 89; notes of Maglione's conversation with Taylor, September 10, 1941, *Holy See and War*, vol. 5, pp. 182-184, 191-194.

90. Morgenthau Presidential Diaries, #4, p. 1020 (November 26, 1941), and #5, p. 1061 (January 27, 1942), Roosevelt Library.

91. *NCWC News Service,* September 3, 1940; William Shannon, *The Am can Irish* (New York, 1964), p. 352; *Boston Pilot*, September 28, 1940, p.

92. Christopher T. Emonett, Jr. to Rev. John Ryan, July 6, 1940, Ryan Papers, Catholic University of America Archives; Sheehy to Roosevelt,

July 24, 1940, *Sel. Materials; NCWC News Service,* September 23, 1940; Ickes, *Diary,* vol. 3, pp. 382-383.

93. For conflicting opinion on the chances of a Catholic candidate in 1940, see George Gallup and Claude Robinson, "American Institute of Public Opinion Surveys, 1935-1938," *Public Opinion Quarterly* 2 (1938), p. 383; Cantrell, *Public Opinion,* p. 95; *NCWC News Service,* March 25, 1940; *Boston Pilot,* April 13, 1940, p. 4. Although in March 1940, 61 percent of those surveyed said they would vote for a Catholic if he was well qualified, in 1937, 67 percent had said yes.

94. James Farley, *Jim Farley's Story* (New York, 1948), p. 227; Wheeler is quoted in Paul A. Carter, "The Other Catholic Candidate," *Pacific Northwest Quarterly* 55 (January 1964), pp. 7-8.

95. David I. Walsh of Massachusetts and Francis T. Maloney of Connecticut were mentioned briefly. See Dorothy Wayman's notes from Diary of Frederick C. Dumaine, May 24, 1939, and Robert Norton to Walsh, June 4, 1939, in David I. Walsh Mss., File 1939, Holy Cross College, Worcester, Mass.; Farley, *Jim Farley's Story,* p. 255.

96. Tugwell, *The Democratic Roosevelt,* p. 490; Tully, *F.D.R.: My Boss,* pp. 181-182; Ickes, *Diary,* vol. 2, pp. 154, 657; Arthur Krock, *Memoirs* (New York, 1968), p. 198; Rosenman, *Public Papers,* vol. 9, p. 110; *New York Times,* March 20, 1940.

97. Ickes, *Diary,* vol. 2, p. 688; Farley, *Jim Farley's Story,* pp. 174-179.

98. *Brooklyn Tablet,* July 15, 1939, p. 10; *New York Times,* September 10, 1940; *Catholic World* 152 (November 1940), pp. 129-138; Miss H. E. MacInnes to Roosevelt, August 4, 1940, OF 76-B, Catholic Church, Box 5, Roosevelt Papers; *NCWC News Service,* October 7, 1940; Toolen quoted in September 30, 1940; October 1, 1940.

99. Gannon, *The Cardinal Spellman Story,* p. 186; *New York Times,* October 29, 1940; Langer and Gleason, *The Undeclared War,* pp. 208-209; *Commonweal:* March 22, 1940, p. 475; August 23, 1940, pp. 360-361; Ryan to Edward J. Dempsey, November 23, 1940, and Ryan to Mrs. Jack Bergin, October 29, 1940, Ryan Papers; Rev. M. Sheehy to Ed Flynn, October 17, 1940, General File, New York Office, 1940, Frank Walker Papers, University of Notre Dame, Archives; Notes of Cardinal Maglione, August 6, 1940, *Holy See and War,* vol. 1, p. 476; Frank J. Comfort to Walker, October 30, 1940, Gen. File, 1940, Walker Papers.

100. Memo, Walker Memoir folder #1; Robert S. Allen to Flynn, September

24, 1940, Gen. File, New York Office; Flynn to Walker, October 28, 1940 James T. Mathews to Walker, October 24, 1940; Mrs. L. A. Daniels to Flyr September 18, 1940; Flynn to Walker, October 26, 1940; all in Walker Pap Heffron to Alsop and Kintner in *NCWC News Service,* September 16, 1940 Joseph D. Lash, *Eleanor and Franklin* (New York, 1971), p. 691; *New York Times:* March 10, 1940; October 25, 1940; August 22, 1940.

101. John J. Carigg, "American Catholic Press Opinion," (M.A. thesis, Georgetown University, 1947), p. 82; Edward Skillin, "The Catholic Press and the Election," *Commonweal,* November 1, 1940, pp. 50-52; Democratic National Committee News Release, November 1, 1940, Gen. File, New York Office, 1940, Walker Papers.

102. Much controversy has surrounded the supposed defection of ethnic groups from the Democratic party in protest against Roosevelt's foreign policy. See S. Lubell, *The Future of American Politics* (New York, 1956), p. 163, who says over one-fifth of the counties which broke with Roosevelt in 1940 were Catholic. See also H. F. Gosnell, *Champion Campaigner* (New York, 1952), p. 187; William Leuchtenburg, *Franklin D. Roosevelt and the New Deal* (New York, 1963), p. 321, who says Willkie cut into Roosevelt's Irish, German, and Italian vote. For evidence that Catholics, regardless of ethnic background, supported Roosevelt with the same consistency as earlier, see Lipset, "Religion and Politics," p. 95; and P. H. Odegard, "Catholicism and Elections in the U.S.," in *Religion and Politics,* edited by Peter Odegard (New Brunswick, N.J., 1960), p. 119 Lipset, however, does find significant Catholic defection from 1940 to 1944 which he explains in terms of opposition to the alliance with Russia.

103. Tugwell, *The Democratic Roosevelt,* p. 530.

5

RUSSIA

One of Roosevelt's biggest diplomatic gambles before Pearl Harbor
was his decision to send aid to Russia. He believed that the Soviet Union
would continue resistance and thereby enhance the prospect for eventual
defeat of the Axis. Yet committing Lend-Lease to communist Russia was
not a trivial step for a Democratic president whose majorities in 1936 and
1940 came in fair part from urban Catholics.[1] To aid a state which
preached an ideological war with Christianity was to court political disaster. The anticommunist attitude of the American Catholic Church was
notorious. Roosevelt was a consensus politician; he would take steps to
reconcile Catholics with the idea of aid to Russia.

1

Catholic attitudes toward the Soviet Union were colored by distaste
for communism. Even before the Vatican condemned communism,
American Catholics had developed a dedicated hatred for Bolshevism.
The antipathy grew directly from the anti-Christian and militant atheism

of revolutionary communism. Under Roosevelt, Catholic suspicions of
Russia had been intensified because of the general improvement in United
States-Soviet relations. In September 1933, when Roosevelt was about to
establish diplomatic relations with Russia, the bishops of the NCWC
presented a memo to the president and to the Department of State arguing against such a move. The bishops reasoned that recognition would
only enhance the prestige of an atheistic state seeking to subvert democracy. Under a "cloak of recognition" communism would spread throughout the United States. The bishops urged reconsideration of the decision
because the country had a "moral responsibility not to recognize a nation
whose principles imperil civilization." Yet they refused to make a public
protest because they were unwilling to become embroiled in "a purely
political affair" and knew that they did not have as much information
as the Roosevelt government. They expressed "trust in the wisdom"
of that government. Well they might. In this earlier crisis, Roosevelt
made sure to mollify Catholic opinion before exchanging ambassadors
with the USSR.[2] But even after the 1933 recognition of Russia, Catholic
suspicions continuously fed on such controversies as the alleged communist-inspired anticlericalism in Mexico during 1935 and Soviet
intrigues during the Spanish Civil War.[3]

Catholics were not alone in their distrust of Russia. Most Americans
shared a dislike of communism. Anticommunism even contributed to the
social integration of American Catholics because it was an issue upon
which they could agree to be faithful both to their church and to their
country at the same time.[4] An interpretation of later Catholic reaction
to the United States-Soviet rapprochement in 1941 must consider this
existing heritage of anticommunism, a heritage which soon received
official encouragement from Rome.

Pope Pius XI reinforced traditional Catholic belief in March 1937 by
issuing the encyclical *Divini Redemptoris,* an authoritative statement
which unequivocally condemned cooperation with communism. In it he
wrote, "Communism is intrinsically wrong and no one who would save
Christian civilization may give it assistance in any undertaking whatsoever."[5] Because of its already cherished tradition of anticommunism,
the American Catholic press endorsed the encyclical with enthusiasm.
The Knights of Columbus held a hugh anticommunist rally in San Francisco later in March to celebrate the launching of a crusade. On the east

coast some 1,000 Knights of Nassau County, New York, heard Reverend John J. Madden call for Catholic leadership in the battle against a cancerous growth which was "eating the vitals of society."[6] Although the pope had specifically avoided condemning any particular nation or people and had written of the "cherished affection" he held for the Russian people, American Catholics easily translated anticommunism into an anti-Russian bias. To Catholics familiar with the writings of such leading publicists as Reverend Edmund A. Walsh of Georgetown University, Reverend Joseph Thorning, Reverend James Gillis of the *Catholic World*, Monsignor Fulton Sheen, and other members of the hierarchy, the papal encyclical simply reiterated an old and familiar message.

The encyclical's appearance led to the renewal of a campaign to frustrate the ambitions of the Soviet Union and its communist agents in the United States. Dr. Charles Fenwick of the CAIP had to revise his writings on Russia because he had taken too optimistic a view of communism. There could be no compromise in the anticommunism crusade, not even with fellow Catholics.[7] The movement swept all before it. The leaders in the crusade included members of the hierarchy, clerical publicists, distinguished laymen, and leaders of Catholic organizations. Frequent admonitions came from the hierarchy about the dangerous growth of communism. The battle provided wonderful opportunities for such prolific polemicists as Father Coughlin, Monsignor Sheen, Father Edward L. Curran of the International Catholic Truth Society of Brooklyn, Reverend Walsh, and Reverend Wilfrid Parsons of *America*. Catholic laymen turned to men such as Curran and Parsons when they wanted information on the communist menace. Congressman John J. O'Connor of New York drew upon the advice of Curran and Coughlin when drafting anticommunist speeches in 1938. An unofficial Catholic anticommunist network developed when O'Connor sent copies of his work to religious groups throughout the nation. Excerpts appeared in diocesan papers and congratulations poured in from all over the country.[8]

Catholic spokesmen, such as Walsh, Sheen, and Thorning, usually embellished their anticommunism with a strong hatred of the Soviet Union.[9] Their negative feelings about Russia seem understandable. The antireligious theory and actions of communism were uncontestable. As practiced in the Soviet Union, communism did not merely dismiss religion as the opium of the people; it methodically set out to destroy the influence and

existence of the church. The campaign was no mere parlor game of words
but a realistic struggle involving disappearing and imprisoned clerics,
closed churches, and confiscated property. The attitude of the papacy and
American Catholics toward such a regime could hardly be dispassionate.
Indeed, Protestant leaders such as Methodist Bishop Raymond J. Wade of
Detroit and President Luther A. Weigle of the Federal Council of Churches
also endorsed anticommunism and anti-Russian sentiment.[10]

For Catholics, however, anticommunism could be a risky enterprise.
The Soviet Union supported collective security against fascism during the
1930s, an approach shared by many American liberals. Under these
circumstances, vigorous opposition by Catholics to cooperation with the
Russians might easily be mistaken for profascism. Indeed, many liberals
categorically accused the Catholic church of being sympathetic to the rise
of fascism, a movement directly antagonistic to democracy and lacking
the redeeming social goals of communism. That Catholic leaders feared
communism more than fascism seemed self-evident to those who thought
the Vatican an arm of the Italian state. As we have seen, liberals had first-
hand evidence of the Catholic enthusiasm for Franco in Spain. Edward J.
Heffron, executive secretary of the National Council of Catholic Men,
kept busy writing letters to the editors of *Time* magazine to deny reports
that the Vatican and German bishops were supporting Italy and Germany
in their fascist policies. No doubt a vast majority of American Catholics
disliked fascism, but too often this sentiment had the character of mere
ritualistic opposition. Catholic dislike of fascism was always diluted by a
consistent tendency to consider it a mere reaction to, or outgrowth of,
the more fundamental threat of atheistic materialism.[11]

Under such circumstances, the church's anticommunism could easily
translate itself into a profascist position. Elizabeth Sweeney of the CAIP
and Reverend Raymond McGowan of the NCWC both agreed that fascism
was more "detrimental" than communism, which at least had a vision of
social justice. But Sweeney reported that "officials at Rome connected
with American religious orders have sent word to their coreligionists here
to soft-pedal any attacks on fascism." The CAIP itself had learned at first-
hand the dangers of equating fascism and communism. Tibor Kerekes of
Georgetown University protested this tendency vigorously in a CAIP-spon-
sored meeting of the Catholic Students Peace Federation. After withdraw-
ing Georgetown from all further participation, Kerekes chastized Sweeney

for failing to understand that "communism is a heresy and cannot be tolerated at any time." But he wrote as early as 1936 that "fascism has never received such a complete . . . repudiation from the Holy Father."[12]

Leading Catholic publicists, such as Bishop Aloysius J. Muench of Fargo, North Dakota, and Reverend James Gillis of the *Catholic World*, considered fascism and communism equally dangerous. But to other Catholic polemicists such as Parsons, Walsh, and Thorning, this was too simple. To their minds, fascism was merely one manifestation of the communist or materialist heresy.[13] Yet it is only fair to emphasize that these men neither admired fascism nor wanted to promote its development in the United States. Despite the Italian character of the Vatican, the sympathy for Franco during the Spanish Civil War, and Father Coughlin's hysteria, most Catholics agreed with the pope. In his encyclical *The Function of the State in the Modern World (Summi Pontificatus)*, Pope Pius XII emphasized the impossibility of reconciling Christianity with any form of totalitarianism. Hitler and Stalin both wanted to eradicate the Catholic church and both received papal condemnation.[14] Still, American spokesmen such as Walsh and Monsignor Sheen insisted that the intellectual shallowness of fascism, as compared to communism, be appreciated. Fascism might have totalitarian characteristics, but it did not have and would never have the rigorous theoretical formulation of communism. To these scholastically trained priests, fascism seemed little more than a jumble of cliches mixed with old-fashioned totalitarianism and some Roman circus. Marxist theory, however, contained a philosophy of human nature, a theory of economics, and a total vision of history that appeared much more portentous. Whatever its intellectual credentials, however, fascism was expanding during 1938.

Among American liberals, Hitler's acts caused more apprehension than did theoretical fears of Russia. Many Catholics reacted the same way and were less anti-Russian than their leaders. In 1938 polling was still in an experimental stage, but it does seem remarkable that only 7 percent of all Americans questioned by the American Institute of Public Opinion thought Russia the nation which "can be least trusted to keep the treaties it makes." Some 65 percent thought Germany fit this description. Public opinion could be fickle, however. In March 1940, 34 percent considered Russia the worst influence in Europe as compared to 55.3 percent who picked Germany for this distinction. The Nazi-Soviet collaboration over

Poland and the occupation of the Baltic countries had influenced American opinion.[15] Secretary of the Interior Harold Ickes had this confusion of public opinion in mind when he discussed the relative danger from Russian and German expansion in early April 1941. He dismissed the communist threat as exaggerated. After certain Catholic leaders had attacked his reasoning, Ickes predicted that a United States-Soviet detente would cause the Catholic church in the United States to support Hitler.[16]

Russian actions were helping American Catholic leaders prove their case. By early 1941 American public opinion had moved toward a more hard-line view of the Soviet Union, one already entertained by leading Catholics. As events in Europe made the Roosevelt administration more and more conscious of keeping Russia friendly as a counterpoise to Germany, American public opinion was simultaneously becoming increasingly negative toward this policy.

Here was the rub. The reasons for Catholic distrust of communism could be dismissed by liberals as clerical eccentricity. More important from a secular point of view was how these attitudes might affect Roosevelt's foreign policy during a period when good United States-Soviet relations seemed wise. Anticommunism made Catholics isolationists and frustrated Roosevelt's attempts at consensus foreign policy. Unquestionably, Catholic isolationism sprang from many diverse sources, some of which had little to do with religion, but anticommunism played a decisive role.[17] If European intervention by the United States meant supporting collective security and if collective security meant closer ties with the Soviet Union, American Catholics could be expected to oppose intervention. The obvious implications of Catholic anticommunism were not lost on such isolationist groups as the America First Committee which, in attempting to win support for a noninterventionist policy, carefully hinted at the possibilities of a United States-Soviet alliance.[18]

The possibility of such an unholy union kept Catholic leaders awake at night long before it was within the realm of possibility. Bishop John A. Duffy of Buffalo articulated this fear in a widely publicized statement as early as 1939. He warned that, in the event of a United States-Soviet alliance, he would "appeal to those within reach of my voice . . . that rather than serve as an ally of a communistic government of atheistic cabal, they refuse to join the armed forces of this country."[19] This was a rather extreme position no doubt, but one repeated by the Jesuit

Thomas E. Davitt, writing in *America* the same year, who argued in Thomistic fashion that Catholics could not in conscience support a United States-Soviet alliance because it would help an atheistic government. No good end could justify such an evil means. Davitt insisted that one could not help the Russian state without helping communism.[20] Reverend Joseph Thorning warned the government that "transporting . . . our young men to Europe in order to pull the chestnuts out of the fire for the Soviet Union" would be a sin against morality and high treason.[21] Reverend Gillis, Reverend Walsh, Monsignor Sheen, and Father Coughlin supported these ideas, as did the major Catholic journals and the diocesan newspapers.[22]

Catholic apprehension rested upon more than mere association with atheistic Russia. There was the very real fear, expressed time and time again, that American intervention in European wars would play into the hands of the Kremlin. To many American Catholics, the Soviet master plan called for the major Western nations to commit suicide. After years of indecisive warfare, the West would be ripe for a communist revolution. Here was the really decisive threat to Western civilization, in contrast to the traditional struggles over national boundaries which seemed involved in German expansion. For the United States to weaken itself by intervening in the preliminary struggle would have been the height of folly in the eyes of many American Catholics.[23] Of course, there was another side to the entire question which became obvious to some American Catholics only after the Soviet-German pact and the conquest of Poland: if Soviet expansion did mean the spread of communism, American Catholics would be wise to advocate an aggressive foreign policy to prevent Marxist penetration into the Catholic nations of Central Europe. Furthermore, if, as Father Parsons and Reverend Thorning suggested, fascism was in league with communism, this called for a counterleague of Christian nations, presumably involving the United States. Such problems were ignored by most American Catholics as events in Europe raced ahead toward the climax of war.

2

As was the case with most Americans, Catholics merely reacted to the crisis in Europe rather than anticipating it. Yet their reaction was different from that of other Americans. It was true that from 1939 to 1941 the American public slowly moved to support a more internationalist foreign policy by Roosevelt. American Catholics participated in this movement, but their pace was inhibited by the issue of anticommunism. Whenever collective security became associated with the Soviet Union, leading Catholics drew back. When Earl Browder of the Communist party recommended a popular front including England, France, the United States, and the Soviet Union, Catholics reacted negatively. Duffy and Davitt's rejection of such an alliance won support from Bishop Gerald Shaughnessy of Seattle and Archbishop Michael J. Curley of Baltimore, among others. When Poland was invaded, American Catholic newspapers even condemned England for trying to reach an understanding with the Soviet Union. The Protestant press in America, which also opposed communism, supported a temporary popular front because it considered Hitler the more immediate threat. But Catholic journalists feared the advantages that an Anglo-Soviet accord would give to communists more than they feared the alternative of a German conquest of Poland.[24]

Much more congenial to Catholic international views was the Soviet-German Nonaggression Pact of August 23, 1939. This collaboration of two apparent enemies appeared to be a victory for Catholic publicists who had long insisted on the identity of the two pagan movements. "I told you so," shouted men such as John LaFarge of *America*, Father Coughlin, and many others. The alliance made matters so clear. To some it was the inevitable drawing together of the pagan forces of the world. Reverend Thorning referred to the "Communist-Nazi plot for conquest of Europe."[25] Yet if American Catholics really believed in a pagan plot to be executed by Russia and Germany it should have been adequate reason for promoting United States intervention on the side of England. As German and Russian troops marched over Catholic Poland, Catholics, instead of merely gloating over proof of their thesis, should have called for a holy war.

A few prelates leaned in that direction. The Reverend Dr. Joseph B. Code of Catholic University denounced neutrality after the rape of Poland and insisted that Americans work for restoration of that nation. "From the standpoint of universal Catholic interest," said Code, justice was on Poland's side. Archbishop Michael J. Curley was equally aggres-

sive. Here was a case in which international indignation became convenient because all of the evil forces were on one side. Poland may not have
been democratic but it was a Catholic state, and Curley condemned
Stalin and Hitler while calling for American Catholics to send succor to
the victims of this aggression.[26] The bishops stopped short of advocating
participation by American troops in the general European war now unfolding.

Russia continued to live up to Catholic expectations as it followed
up the dismemberment of Poland with threats against Finland in October
1939. As Finland enjoyed an estimable reputation in the United States
for having paid its World War I debt and Soviet demands were nakedly
imperialistic, American Catholics expected their distrust of Russia to
soon become official policy. The Roosevelt administration made no
attempt to hide its repugnance at the Soviet invasion of Finland and
instituted a "moral embargo" on the shipment of goods to Russia. The
president was stung into a public condemnation of the Soviet Union.
Sounding much like Pope Pius XI, Roosevelt, on February 9, 1940,
declared his sympathy for the Russian people, but deprecated the "ban-
ishment of religion" and added that the Soviet Union "is a dictatorship
as absolute as any dictatorship in the world."[27]

Naturally, such sentiments met with enthusiastic approval from
Catholic sources. At last it appeared that Roosevelt was becoming disillusioned with Russia. But Catholics wanted more than a moral emgargo.
Reverend Edmund A. Walsh led a faction which saw the Winter War as
the beginning of a new phase of the Russian revolution. Dropping all
pretence to noninvolvement, these men urged United States support for
Finland. Thorning thought the best means of aiding Finland would be
to sever United States-Soviet relations, as had been done earlier with
Germany. Isolationism appeared forgotten when confronted by the
image of an aggressive Russia. The Catholic press reverberated with
suggestions that it would be better to fight the Bolsheviks in Finland
than in New York City.[28] Such an extreme reaction lends support to
the hypothesis that Catholic isolationism was in many cases a function
of anticommunism. If intervention could better serve the cause of anticommunism, it might well be adopted. If communism was really on the
march, such men as Walsh and Thorning would not hesitate to call for

American action since, in their eyes, this would be a crusade to save Christian civilization. In contrast, the antifascist front merely concerned the rearranging of European borders.

3

During 1940, few Catholics complained as the United States maintained formal but cool relations with the Soviet Union. Roosevelt and Hull knew that Russia was providing Hitler with critical supplies in accordance with their treaty, but since the Department of State had already cut Russian trade to the bone, there seemed little more the American government could do. The administration continued to avoid a complete break in relations despite American Catholic protest. Secretary of State Hull expected an eventual collapse of the Russian-German front and hoped to be able to exploit it when it occurred. This interlude came to an abrupt end in early 1941 as Roosevelt moved toward a more active role in the European war with the initiation of Lend-Lease.[29] As we have seen, American Catholics reacted strongly to this major foreign policy commitment by Roosevelt. In November 1940, sixty Catholic interventionists had signed a public statement urging "all possible aid to Great Britain." But these same men also insisted that the dangers of Russian communism could not be ignored. Their advocacy of support for England was on practical grounds and they were careful to emphasize their common identity with traditional Catholic anticommunism.[30]

Roosevelt discovered that attempts to aid England might be jeopardized by Catholic anticommunism. What could be expected if he offered aid to Russia? Such a question had been raised in hypothetical fashion as early as January 1941, long before the German invasion of Russia. In testimony on the Lend-Lease bill before the Senate Foreign Relations Committee, Professor Herbert Wright of Catholic University warned that passage of the act would lead to American aid for Russia. Sam Rayburn warned Roosevelt that an amendment excluding Russia from any future Lend-Lease would greatly speed passage of the bill.[31] Roosevelt and Hull both resisted such a qualification, not because they already foresaw an alliance with Russia, but because they refused to narrow their options. Hull, in particular, was convinced that Germany planned to attack Russia

soon.[32] Rayburn and McCormack received instructions to push for a
general clause which would not specify who would receive aid. But despite
administration desires, the exclusion of aid to Russia became a topic for
debate in Congress. Isolationists began using the issue as a means of gain-
ing Roman Catholic support against the entire idea of foreign aid. Eventually, the administration prevailed as the exclusion idea failed to move
beyond the House Foreign Relations Committee. The bill that Roosevelt
finally signed on March 11, 1941, did not specifically exclude any nation
from aid.[33]

Yet the Lend-Lease debate did have the effect of refocusing American
Catholic attention on the whole concept of United States-Soviet relations.
Suspicions aroused over Lend-Lease seemed confirmed on January 21,
1941, when the year-old "moral embargo" on trade with Russia was officially, if discreetly, abrogated. Hull later explained that this decision really
meant very little in terms of increased trade because most of the items
desired by the Soviet Union were under a strict licensing system as part
of America's strategic preparedness program. The Department of State
lifted the embargo because Russia deserved a "friendly gesture" as Germany became more threatening in Eastern Europe. It was hoped that such
a gesture would help Russia find the nerve to stand up to Hitler.[34] Roosevelt had urged discretion in lifting the embargo because he knew that even
such a modest improvement in United States-Soviet relations would provoke consternation among elements of American Catholicism.

Earlier, when Sumner Welles, assistant secretary of state, tried to launch
a series of intimate talks with Soviet Ambassador Constantine A. Oumansky, there were protests from the Catholic press. John C. LeClair dismissed
the argument that the United States could use Russia to counterbalance
Japanese or German imperialism. A reconciliation with the nation that had
conquered the Baltic states, warned LeClair, could only destroy the moral
position of the United States.[35] Monsignor Fulton Sheen told his friends
of the International Federation of Catholic Alumnae that the United
States could not simultaneously maintain its position as defender of freedom and still be friendly with the pagan power responsible for the war in
Europe. He deplored the tendency of western statesmen to paint the war
against Hitler as a defense of Christianity. How could we claim "to be
fighting God's cause when we call that nation which has driven religion

from its borders, murdered millions, and officially proclaimed atheism, a friendly nation?"[36] Now the United States had lifted its embargo and was trading with the Russians. Arguments advanced by the administration about using the Soviet Union failed to impress these men. LeClair warned that Russia would never be truly neutral because it had a mission to communize mankind. Others warned the Department of State against trying to play sophisticated diplomatic games with Europeans, especially the Russians. In 1917 such attempts had involved the United States in a war. Dealing with the Russians was the equivalent of "supping with a short spoon with the Devil."[37]

To make matters even worse, Russia continued to play the role of a devil by manifesting a dedicated anticlericalism. How could American Catholics be reasonable about Russia when the only Catholic church in Moscow had been sacked for the fifth time in March 1941. Despite repeated protest by Ambassador Laurence A. Steinhardt, the Soviet government appeared indifferent if not actually involved in the incidents.[38] Such obstreperous behavior made it hardly surprising that leading Catholics such as Cardinal O'Connell of Boston and Reverend Dr. John Tracy Ellis of Catholic University should speak out publicly against the danger of the United States becoming involved with Russia. Reverend James Gillis called upon Roosevelt to reject any alliance with Stalin. Monsignor Sheen warned that "the enemy of the world in the near future is going to be Russia."[39]

Hearing such statements, the president knew he would have his hands full if he attempted to achieve a diplomatic rapprochment with Russia. He made his own case even more difficult by failing to prepare Americans in general for such an enterprise. Under his instructions, the Department of State adopted a low key in its negotiations with Soviet Ambassador Oumansky. Publicly, Roosevelt seemed to be increasingly concerned with the dangers of communism. On March 29, 1941, the president provided additional fuel to the anticommunist crusade by using a Jackson Day radio address to warn organized labor against the penetration of Marxists who sought the workers' enslavement. In late May 1941 he condemned the Germans for being "as ruthless as the communists in the denial of God."[40] Men such as Paul Wever, president of the Detroit Association of Catholic Trade Unionists, felt that after months of warning about com-

munist penetration of the American labor movement, the administration
was finally listening. The Catholic press even predicted the launching of
a government investigation into communist work stoppages in defense
industries.[41] In fact, the Department of State now moved against Russian
espionage.

Secretary of State Hull hated to take action, especially in light of his
long-term expectations for the Soviet Union. But the information supplied by the War Department made it quite clear that two Russian
assistant military attachés for air had been caught, and not for the first
time, seeking American military information. On June 10, 1941, Hull
reminded Soviet Ambassador Oumansky of previous warnings and demanded the recall of the two men.[42] In the same month Hull gave
Ambassador Steinhardt in Moscow new, tough guidelines on United
States-Soviet relations. The United States was through trying to meet
Russia halfway. From now on the Department of State would wait for
the Russians to make the first move. American policy would be strict
reciprocity. The Russians must understand that they needed us more
than we needed them.[43] Steinhardt approved of these moves; in fact,
he had personally recommended them earlier. After struggling with the
Russians for months, he concluded that "they do not and cannot respond
to the customary amenities." This was true because "they are not affected
by ethical or moral considerations, nor guided by the relationships which
are customary between individuals of culture and breeding." The ambassador's point in reporting his judgment was not simply to condemn the
Russians as uncouth but to make it clear that they responded only to
firmness.[44]

The new tough policy did not mean that Hull had revised his conviction that Russia could be used against Hitler. He now possessed intelligence estimates predicting an imminent German invasion of Russia. The
Division of European Affairs drafted a memorandum to guide American
conduct in such a contingency. Officially, the United States should be
passive about the invasion. If Russia desired American aid, it should make
the first move. It was agreed that, subject to our primary commitment
to Great Britain, the United States should respond positively to a Russian
request for assistance. Such aid, however, did not mean that the United
States had any illusions about Russia or favored communism.[45]

4

In less than three weeks the State Department memorandum was forgotten. American communists now supported the defense program. Germany had launched "Operation Barbarossa," the invasion of Russia, on June 22, 1941. England immediately pledged support to Russia. A major realignment was under way, one which could conceivably put the United States and Russia in the same camp. On June 23, 1941, Acting Secretary of State Sumner Welles publicly promised aid for Russia before the Soviet ambassador had requested it. However, Welles's promise, fully endorsed by the ailing Hull, made a distinction between the Russian nation and the communist system. Aid to Russia would be a purely selfish act on America's part. Any contribution to Hitler's downfall "will . . . redound to the benefit of our own defense and security." But this did not mean that the United States accepted the antireligious bias which characterized both the Nazi and Soviet systems. As President Roosevelt often declared, this religious right was fundamental to all people.[46] This was a noble sentiment, but would Americans buy the idea of support for Russia?

American Catholics reacted to the German invasion of Russia and the announcement by Welles in predictable fashion. A Gallup Poll revealed that 74 percent of American Protestants desired a Russian victory and 65 percent of American Catholics shared this opinion. In another poll, taken two days after the invasion, 35 percent of all Americans agreed that the United States should supply Russia with war material on the same terms as England. But a rather decisive 54 percent of the respondents objected to such a policy, and 11 percent had no opinion. On August 5, 1941, after time for reflection and after the administration had had time to educate the public, a solid 39 percent still rejected it.[47]

As "Operation Barbarossa" proceeded, American bishops gathered in St. Paul, Minnesota, to open a National Eucharistic Congress. A few bishops in attendance immediately urged that a statement be issued. Monsignor Ready of the NCWC feared that such a statement would condemn the idea of American aid to Russia. He and a group of liberal bishops succeeded in postponing action. Soon Protestant leaders, such as Dr. Rufus Weaver of the Baptists and Dr. Charles Morrison of the *Christian Century*, requested that the Catholic bishops join in a statement denouncing aid to Russia. Ready began to lose control. He feared a split between the Roosevelt administration and the leaders of American Catholicism and turned to Sumner Welles for advice. Ready warned that an embarrassing statement would be forthcoming unless the president could defuse the issue. He recommended that Roosevelt demand Soviet acceptance of the principles of the Four Freedoms as a precondition of aid and also urged continued publicity for Welles's press release because of its realistic approach.[48]

Before Welles or the president could act, a large group of Catholic leaders went on record against any United States-Soviet collaboration. Ready had prevented a joint statement by the bishops, but Monsignor Fulton Sheen and Reverend James Gillis warned that collaboration with the Russians would only lead to future capitulation to communists' demands. Gillis, after taking credit for anticipating the German-Russian struggle, warned that aid to Russia would put the United States in a Faustian position. After the war Stalin would demand his due, including control of Constantinople and the Bosphorus. In addition, such an alliance would destroy what was left of America's moral supremacy. How could our ideals of democracy and Christianity survive such a "covenant with hell"? Reverend LaFarge recommended that Roosevelt blackmail the Russians into granting religious freedom before sending aid. Reverend John Ellis felt that the church should denounce aid to Russia. How could one square the idealism of the Four Freedoms with aid to Stalin? Ellis wondered.[49]

No one, however, went quite so far as the archbishop of Dubuque, Iowa. Archbishop Francis J. L. Beckman was rapidly developing into the leading Catholic isolationist. True, Archbishop Curley of Baltimore, Cardinal O'Connell of Boston, and Archbishop Shaughnessy of Seattle all did their part. But no one overshadowed Beckman. One day before "Operation Barbarossa," he delighted a crowd of America First members by charging that Roosevelt was cheating on his nonintervention pledge made in the 1940 election campaign. By July, Beckman, speaking to a nationwide radio audience, was calling on Congress to keep America out of war, accusing Roosevelt of "coddling" communists, and denouncing the idea of aid to communist Russia. To Beckman and many other Catholic isolationists, the imperialism of Germany and the imperialism of England were identical. Both aimed at the reestablishment of "the shattered boundaries of international finance."[50]

Such rhetoric gave the impression that all American Catholics now opposed aid to Russia. Under such circumstances, Roosevelt would have had real problems if he had decided to declare Russia eligible for Lend-Lease. But gradually a more sympathetic group of American Catholics made itself heard. These men found inspiration in their coreligionists in England. When Arthur Cardinal Hinsley, archbishop of Westminister, was asked the official attitude of British Catholics toward the newly announced government policy of aid to Russia, he made clear his opposition to both Nazism and communism. More to the point, he emphasized that "our country . . . is fighting against the attempt to subjugate Europe." Hitler remained the number one threat despite his recent attempts to paint himself as the defender of European civilization against the communists.[51] Reverend Dr. John C. Heenan and Archbishop Richard Downey of Liverpool echoed this pragmatic argument in radio addresses to their American coreligionists. Of course, these men refused to support an alliance that went beyond the merely negative goal of defeating the Germans.[52]

In the United States, Catholics who had been strong supporters of the New Deal adopted a similar pragmatic argument. Many of these liberals had already endorsed aid for England. Father John Ryan supported aid to Russia because, while the Soviet cause was not just, its enemy in this case was the same as America's.[53] On June 28, 1941, Ryan's name appeared with those of fourteen other prominent American Catholics endorsing aid to Russia. The group admitted that communism remained the foe of Christianity and that in the future Russia might prove to be a grave threat to the United States. But at the moment Hitler was clearly the more dangerous menace.[54] This distinction seemed identical to that made by the Roosevelt administration. Both Nazism and communism were evil. But one had to be realistic. Russia was now fighting the common and most dangerous enemy. A distinction must be made between the Russian government and the Russian people.

The next month Bishop Joseph P. Hurley of St. Augustine, Florida, became the first member of the hierarchy to advocate a similar line in public. Hurley, a junior member of the American hierarchy, had extra prestige because he had spent twelve years in the Vatican diplomatic service. Using material supplied by Assistant Secretary of State Welles, the bishop spoke in favor of aid on CBS radio on July 6, 1941. American

Catholics who insisted that communism was the main danger to the country were distorting reality. Furthermore, papal teaching did not prohibit American Catholics from supporting aid to Russia. Hurley called his address "Papal Pronouncements and American Foreign Policy" and stressed the "striking parallelism" between the moral ideas of the Vatican and the Roosevelt administration. Germany had started the war. American Catholics should support the president's policy.[55] An administration speech-writer could hardly have written a more blanket endorsement.

Anti-aid Catholics immediately challenged Hurley's imprimatur. William T. Leonard of Brooklyn, who served simultaneously as secretary of the Catholic Laymen's Committee for Peace and the local chapter of the America First Committee, dashed off a letter to the hierarchy calling for a clarifying statement lest Hurley's views be considered those of the American episcopacy. Leonard's letter was hardly in the mail before Reverend James Gillis and Archbishop Beckman also complained publicly. Gillis agreed that papal statements must be used in context but still felt that there was nothing equivocal about the condemnation of communism. He urged Catholics who favored aid to Russia to check their views with the Vatican. Beckman called on all bishops to follow the encyclical *Divini Redemptoris* which, to his mind, prohibited all aid to Russia.[56] The apostolic delegate and the NCWC disassociated themselves from Hurley's statement.

Both pro- and anti-aid factions recognized that the key to their positions was how the Vatican viewed Russia and communism. Isolationists felt confident that *Divini Redemptoris* gave them support. Interventionists, on the other hand, substantiated their position by a liberal reading of the Vatican's current international position. The two groups always shared certain ideas. Isolationists emphasized the immediate domestic threat of communism while not denying the repugnance of Nazism. Interventionists acknowledged the atheistic character of Russia but called for a realistic policy of fighting Germany first. The question facing the Roosevelt administration in 1941 was how to encourage the growth of an interventionist interpretation of events without appearing to meddle in church affairs. Obviously, it would not do to have a considerable segment of the Democratic coalition disenchanted over such a basic policy decision as aid to Russia, not to speak of the problems it might cause in obtaining congressional support.

5

The president always viewed the problem of aid to Russia realistically.
German conquest of Russia would make Hitler more of a threat to the
Western Hemisphere. A Russian victory in conjunction with England and
the United States would serve as the basis for international stability.
Roosevelt hoped that Soviet armies, using American military equipment,
might obviate the need for American troops to fight in Europe. With
memories of the slaughter of World War I in mind, the president would
have been happy to use only naval and air forces while leaving the ground
struggle to Europeans.[57] He had to convey this view of international
reality to the American public, including American Catholics, but he held
no illusions about their reaction. He expected Catholics to be bitterly
opposed to aid to Russia.[58] At the same time, he would not permit such
opposition to prevent American aid to Russia even if it had to be on an
ad hoc basis at first.

On June 26, 1941, Welles met quietly with Soviet Ambassador
Oumansky to work out the details of American assistance. All during
July these talks went forward while Catholic criticism mounted. The
United States agreed to receive a Soviet military mission to oversee
military purchases. A number of American bombers and fighter planes
were flown directly to Russia. Harry Hopkins, the confidante of the president, traveled to Moscow to establish liaison with Stalin. On August 2,
1941, Welles informed Oumansky that the United States was willing to
give full assistance to Russia in its stand against aggression. Still, the
Department of State remained suspicious of Russia. Assistant Secretary
of State Adolf Berle advised J. Edgar Hoover of the Federal Bureau of
Investigation to continue surveillance of Soviet agents. United States-Soviet friendship was one of expediency and subject to momentary revision.[59]

Roosevelt continued to be cautious about the method of financing
this aid. He seemed very pleased when Oumansky agreed to accept a
five-year credit to pay for military goods rather than use Lend-Lease.
A credit could be arranged through the Reconstruction Finance Corporation. By early September, however, the ambassador became completely
disenchanted with this method of financing. He complained about making
a mistake in not insisting on Lend-Lease benefits. Paying cash or exchang-

ing Russian goods for military equipment was not possible. When he complained, Roosevelt assured him aid would continue despite financing problems but made no offer of Lend-Lease as the ambassador expected. Such an offer would have brought Congress into the act. Frankly, the president explained, he was not confidant of public support for aid to Russia. Opposition from American Catholics was already bitter and they could be expected to exert great pressure on Congress.[60]

Roosevelt told only half the story. His assessment of Catholic opposition was correct, but the original Lend-Lease bill authorized the president to aid any nation resisting aggression. Under these liberal terms Roosevelt could have given aid to Russia without going to Congress. Yet to have acted without congressional backing would have seemed an assumption of arbitrary executive power, fear of which had upset so many when Lend-Lease was first considered. Second, Congress still had to make periodic supplemental appropriations for Lend-Lease and one was due in October. Finally, Roosevelt was too good a politician to take such a sensitive step as aid to Russia without building up some public sentiment. This support, it was hoped, would crystallize in a vote for the supplemental appropriation. In the meantime, aid to Russia was approached obliquely. Roosevelt eventually arranged a $50 million loan from the Reconstruction Finance Corporation and a $30 million purchase of Russian gold by the Treasury Department. But as late as October 15, 1941, Harry Hopkins warned that "no mention should be made . . . that our government is going to use the Lend-Lease bill to finance Russian purchases." The congressional consideration of supplemental appropriation for Lend-Lease was in progress and the president was still campaigning for public approval of aid to Russia.[61]

Roosevelt's campaign was directed primarily at Catholic opinion and he tried to educate Catholics to the advantages of a Soviet detente. He worked through pro-administration Catholics such as Postmaster General Frank Walker, Associate Justice of the Supreme Court Frank Murphy, and Senator Joseph O'Mahoney of Wyoming.[62] Walker's attitude toward Russia evolved dramatically during 1941. In the period before the German invasion, he was considered a typical hard-liner on communism. A Democratic party worker wrote earlier that America would have "nothing to fear from the communistic party" as long as Roosevelt picked men such as Farley, Frank Murphy, and Frank Walker.[63] Two months before "Operation Barbarossa," Walker addressed fellow alumni of Notre Dame in a speech carried over NBC radio and closed by condemning communism for rejecting God and equating man with a machine.[64] After the German invasion of Russia, Walker spoke again about communism to an audience in Butte, Montana, on July 12, 1941. This time he rejected Hitler's claim to be the defender of civilization, saying that the security of the Western Hemisphere rested upon the strength of British and Russian arms, and called the Soviet struggle "heroic." Later, Walker told Walter Duranty of the North American Newspaper Alliance that American aid to Russia was essential for its self-defense and had nothing to do with the spread of Bolshevism. "Do you realize," Walker continued, "that German bombers could fly from Siberian airports to Alaska and return in less than an hour?" Senator Joseph O'Mahoney, another New Deal Democrat and prominent Catholic layman, made the same strategic point. Responding to hundreds of letters objecting to American aid to Russia, O'Mahoney admitted the antireligious character of the Soviet Union but insisted that Hitler was the main threat to the world.[66]

Associate Justice Frank Murphy also worked to educate American Catholics to the administration program. He expressed deep concern over what he referred to as "the Nazi Revolution in the Catholic Church." He had always lamented the exaggerated Catholic fears of communists. Such attitudes now threatened an important Roosevelt policy and had to be changed. Murphy contrived an invitation to address the 1941 International Convention of the Supreme Council of the Knights of Columbus with the view, as he told the White House, to having them "oriented right" on aid to Russia. He rose to address the Knights gathered at Atlantic City on August 19 as a recognized spokesman for Roosevelt. He spoke to acquaint Catholics with the immediate threat of the Nazis. Religion had no future in a Nazi-dominated world. Alfred Rosenberg, Nazi philosopher, had specifically called for the eradication of Catholicism. Murphy harped upon the thesis that, despite its atheism, Russia was not as much a threat as Germany, with its "superior competence and perverted intelligence, its extraordinary energy and missionary zeal . . . and above all its tremendous military power and skill." The Knights applauded in moderation but Roosevelt and Hull cheered in the distance. A Chicago Irish Democrat appealed to the White House to have the address reproduced and distributed throughout the nation in hopes of offsetting the "un-American opposition to our country and president."[67]

Roosevelt's strategy stood revealed: stress self-defense and insist that Nazism aimed at world conquest, that its ideology, like that of communism, was capable of universal extension. Walker, O'Mahoney, and Murphy all placed emphasis on Nazism as a threat to religion. If Catholic opposition to Russia rested on its antireligious outlook, evidence of a similar attitude by a more aggressive Germany should be equally frightening. The administration made a deliberate effort to dramatize the German threat to organized religion. As early as July 3, 1941, a memorandum reached Roosevelt covering the general attitude of Nazism toward Christianity as gleaned from the writings of its leaders. Needless to say, the report held out little encouragement for the role of the church in the New Order. This information was relayed to both Walker and Murphy. Roosevelt himself supplied the data to friendly senators with the suggestion that it be publicized. He particularly wanted to confirm the authenticity of a campaign for the eradication of the Catholic church in Germany.[68]

When Catholics seemed to ignore these indirect releases, the administration decided to become more blunt. In October 1941 Roosevelt personally briefed Archbishop Spellman and wrote to Myron Taylor in New York City "in great confidence" that information revealing a plan for the establishment of a Nazi church should be passed on to the pope. The same day Assistant Secretary of State Adolf Berle revealed the Nazi plot to found its own church to an audience of the National Council of the Young Men's Christian Association meeting at Columbus, Ohio. Foreign correspondent William Shirer released what he called "the thirty point Nazi religious program" over CBS. Two days later Roosevelt stunned guests of the Navy League dinner at the Mayflower Hotel in Washington by denouncing German plans for the establishment of an "International Nazi church" with *Mein Kampf* as its bible. "The God of Blood and Iron," said the president, "will take the place of the God of Love and Mercy." The administration also leaked to the NCWC a document dated September 13, 1941, "of assured authenticity," concerning the destruction of the Catholic clergy in Slovenia after the German invasion.[69] Secretary of State Hull sent the same information about the formation of a new Nazi church to Harold Tittmann for presentation to the Vatican. If Roosevelt and Hull expected to shock the Vatican, however, they must have been disappointed. As Tittmann admitted, these same documents on a Nazi church had been floating around the Vatican for some time. Their credibility was uncertain; he thought it would be pointless to publicize that the United States had furnished the Vatican with yet another copy.[70] How much effect the campaign had on American Catholics is also open to question. Murphy's speech was given a cool reception. Why should Catholics get excited about Roosevelt's exposure of Hitler's plan for abolishing Christianity? They recalled that similar plans for the church had been put into practice in Mexico and Russia without any remonstrance from the White House.[71]

Roosevelt himself remained dissatisfied with such a negative approach to the question of aid. To prove that Germany was a threat to religion might merely encourage those who hoped that Hitler and Stalin would destroy each other without American interference. The president had to convert American Catholics by rehabilitating the Soviet image. When meeting with Ambassador Oumansky in September, Roosevelt stressed the importance of the Soviet religious policy for American public opinion. The Russian must have been somewhat surprised at the tangential factors which influenced United States foreign policy, but after the president explained the strength of Catholic political power in Congress, Oumansky agreed to ask his government to issue a public statement clarifying its concept of religious freedom.[72]

Superficially, Roosevelt's action appears cynical. Regardless of actual conditions in Russia, a Soviet platitude on religious freedom would "have a very fine educational effect before the next lend-lease bill comes up in Congress."[73] But it seems that the president seriously hoped to promote religious freedom in Russia. He may have adopted a practical tone to impress Oumansky, but other actions reveal his idealism. He was personally conscious of the importance of religion in society. He promoted the principle of religious freedom in November 1933 when he first recognized the Soviet Union. Some presidential advisors even felt he was too sensitive about the religious issue.[74] But they also knew that he really hoped, in the area of religion as in other areas, to bring the Soviet Union closer to the traditions of Western civilization. The religious issue was one of the many barriers to true East-West comity and Roosevelt wanted to remove it. As German troops poured over the Russian landscape, the president thought he detected a general softening of antireligious feeling on the part of the Kremlin. Surely this seemed an excellent time to suggest a softening of official Soviet atheism.[75]

Unfortunately, the president's expectations led him to overreact at the first sign of revision in Russian religious policy. When Polish Ambassador Jan Ciechanowski wrote to Secretary of State Hull on September 29, 1941, that Russia was permitting full religious freedom in the Polish army which was being organized on Russian soil, the information was passed speedily to the chief executive. Earlier, Myron Taylor had reminded Roosevelt that the Soviet constitution of 1936 provided for a form of religious freedom in Article 124.[76] Combining these two facts, Roosevelt felt confident enough to announce the increased liberalization of Russia's religious outlook. On September 30, 1941, he released Ciechanowski's letter to the press. At a press conference the next day, the president began by suggesting that people should read Article 124 of the Soviet constitution if they were skeptical about the assertion of religious freedom for the Polish army. Pressed for a description of this article, Roosevelt at first hedged but finally volunteered that it added up to freedom of conscience and "freedom equally to use propaganda against religion, which is essentially what is the rule in this country; only we don't put it quite the same way." When public reaction to this announcement proved disappointing, Roosevelt asked Secretary of State Hull to cable Ambassador Steinhardt in Russia requesting a Soviet statement confirming the news about the Polish army. The president wanted Russian support for his liberal interpretation, said Hull, "in view of the outstanding importance of this question from the standpoint of public opinion in the U.S."[77] Steinhardt had little luck in his task; Roosevelt had less with Catholics.

Instead, Roosevelt's attempt to draw a picture of religious liberalism in Russia merely irritated leading Catholics. They responded skeptically to the press conference. Bishop Duffy of Buffalo called Roosevelt's statements a provocation which would only serve to "establish a new basis for disunity among the American people who knew that no such freedom existed in the USSR." Bishop Shaughnessy of Seattle deplored the president's analogy of the American and Soviet concepts of religious freedom as an "atrociously false" comparison. Press reaction was equally negative. Editorials in the *Evening Star,* the *Daily News* of Washington, D.C., and the *New York Times* criticized the president for trying to promote aid to Russia by deception. Going to bed with the Soviets was bad enough on a purely pragmatic level. Attempts at painting Russia as a democracy only added hypocrisy to an already morally sordid position. As one editor

wrote, next Americans would hear that the "Internationale" had been re-
placed by the "Te Deum."[78] N. S. Timasheff, a professor at Fordham
University, wrote that the only freedom in the Soviet constitution was
freedom from capitalism. Reverend Edmund A. Walsh of Georgetown
University called a press conference of his own at which he distinguished
between the letter of Soviet law and the brutal atheistic communist
reality behind it. Writing in the *Catholic World*, Paul H. Furfey felt that
the entire episode was only another example of the administration's
left-wing bias. Roosevelt and others were so determined to destroy Hitler
that they refused to see the danger from the Left.[79]

Stung by this criticism, the president sought out Averell Harriman,
who was about to embark on a mission to Moscow to clear up the details
of American aid. Roosevelt told Harriman to explain to Stalin the importance of some sign of amelioration of Soviet antireligious policy to help
the political climate in the United States. Specifically, the president
mentioned the opposition of American Catholics and how this opposition
might be reflected in Congressional appropriations. Surely, Roosevelt
reasoned, Stalin would be willing to endorse religious freedom to win
consensus support for the American aid program.[80] At the same time,
the president called in Monsignor Ready of the NCWC to reassure him.
Ready grew enthusiastic when Roosevelt revealed the details of Harriman's
mission. He later told reporters he had been confused after Roosevelt's
earlier reference to Article 124 in the Soviet constitution. The president,
it seems, had explained his statement about religious freedom as having
been made in the hope that the wish might be father to the act.[81]

On the same day, October 2, 1941, the president released the news
that Harriman had been instructed to raise the religious question with
Stalin. No one envied Harriman his task. German newspapers claimed
that it amounted to convincing Stalin "to join in the singing of 'Onward
Christian Soldiers.' " One of Roosevelt's domestic opponents called it
"asking the dictator to be baptized in the White House swimming pool."
Exaggerations aside, the mission did involve the United States in an
internal Soviet matter. Considering Stalin's view of religion, it could
hardly enhance United States-Soviet relations to push such an issue at
the first meeting. Imagine Harriman's surprise when Stalin proved
receptive to Roosevelt's idea and promised to "give the subject his
attention." Ambassador Oumansky went even further and assured his

American friends that a statement serving Roosevelt's purposes would soon be issued. But Harriman remained pessimistic. While Stalin might give verbal endorsement to religious freedom, Harriman had doubts about any real progress for religion in communist-dominated Russia. Furthermore, the United States had little leverage to exert because a bitter controversy at this stage of United States-Soviet Union negotiations would only help Hitler.[82]

Yet Stalin and Oumansky did fulfill their promises. An official Soviet statement was issued concerning religious freedom shortly after Harriman's departure from Moscow. Solomon Abranmquick Lozovsky, assistant commissar for foreign affairs, made a statement which may have fulfilled Oumansky's promise but which must have disappointed Roosevelt. Lozovsky noted Roosevelt's interest in the religious situation in Russia, congratulated him on his correct perception of the Russian constitution, and insisted that "freedom of worship exists in the USSR." The assistant commissar emphasized that religion was a private affair which the citizen was free to pursue or ignore. The state, however, would not tolerate any religion or church used "for the overthrow of the existing authority . . . in the country."[83] Since Roosevelt had implicitly asked the Russians to adopt an American view of religious freedom, an inadequate Soviet reply was virtually inevitable. Roosevelt decided against pursuing the topic further. He agreed with Harriman that it would be poor timing to press Stalin about religion at a moment when the Soviet regime was tottering. When Representative John McCormack, majority leader in the House, suggested that the Department of State induce the Russians to free some 135 priests allegedly held prisoners, the administration became embarrassed. Adolf Berle agreed with McCormack that such a step would help "in allaying some of the Catholic opposition to Russia," but such a topic had to be approached gingerly. It was at heart an internal Soviet matter.[84] After a preliminary inquiry met a glacial Soviet response, no more was heard of this matter.

Harriman's failure to get more from the Russians than the usual banalities dismayed expectant Catholics. Reverend Edmund A. Walsh dismissed Lozovsky's entire statement as shadow boxing. The priest asked whether America should send aid to a nation which had rejected the Four Freedoms. Stalin would not cease persecuting religion even though it helped legitimize Hitler's claim of fighting a war against the

enemies of Christianity. Walsh emphasized that "there is only one voice
to be heard from now." The last word would come from Roosevelt, who,
Catholics hoped, would demand Soviet cooperation.[85]

6

The president refused to play the game of baiting Stalin. His dealing
with Russia had been a disappointment, but perhaps he would have better
luck with the Vatican. He had always believed that Vatican disapproval
of Russia was the linchpin of American Catholic opposition to aid to
Russia. If the Vatican would moderate its anticommunist position, there
might be a corresponding moderation of domestic criticism. Roosevelt
actually thought of this long before the German invasion of Russia. In a
private conversation with Apostolic Delegate Cicognani in January 1941,
he had emphasized that communism was losing momentum in America.[86]
Later, when he realized that Germany planned to invade Russia, Roosevelt told the Vatican of his displeasure with the exaggerated anticommunism of American Catholics. In early June, Myron Taylor, Archbishop
Spellman, and Frans Van Canwelaert, a Belgian statesman, all explained
Roosevelt's dissatisfaction with the American hierarchy to Cicognani.[87]
Cicognani, in turn, reminded his visitors of the pope's 1937 encyclical
against the Nazis and assured them of the pontiff's abiding concern for
peace.[88]

References to a four-year-old encyclical failed to satisfy Roosevelt.
With German tanks rolling across the Ukraine, he feared that the Vatican
would publicly endorse an anti-Bolshevik campaign. Pope Pius XII's hatred
of communism was well known. Diplomatic sources predicted that Musso-
lini would exert pressure on the Vatican to join the crusade against the
Bolsheviks. Hitler had already justified his invasion as an attempt to defend
European civilization against communism.[89] Harold Tittmann at the
Vatican reported a reserved reaction to the German invasion of Russia.
Officially, the Vatican remained "equidistant" from both powers, but
Tittmann was convinced that militant atheism "is still regarded as more
obnoxious than the modern paganism of [Germany]." Although Vatican
officials had every reason to applaud the mutual destruction of its enemies,
they knew that a decisive victory by either power would upset the European balance of power. Tittmann became worried because Vatican

sources assumed that the German invasion had confused the American people "and slowed the U.S. war effort." He requested immediate policy guidance.[90] Washington replied bluntly that the Vatican should avoid encouraging Germany. Considering the present state of Vatican-German relations, the recommendation had a gratuitous ring to it. In talks with papal officials, Tittmann reiterated Welles's point that the United States rejected both communism and Nazism. But it remained the official policy of the United States to aid victims of aggression. No direct mention was made of aid to Russia because Russia had not yet approached the United States.[91]

Tittmann continued to worry because militant anticommunists manned the Vatican bureaucracy. He suggested that the Department of State could help him soften their attitude by sending him evidence of a liberalization of Soviet religious policy. The request arrived in late July 1941; Welles replied that no such evidence existed. But Tittmann's request undoubtedly contributed to Roosevelt's later decision to seek a liberal interpretation from Russia.[92]

The Russian campaign failed but Roosevelt had higher hopes for his plan to convince the pope to revise his anticommunist encyclical. Such a revision would ameliorate American Catholic opposition to Lend-Lease. Roosevelt reasoned that it would be easier to convert the pope to a new view of Russia than to badger with innumerable American bishops. He had been urged to take just such a step by two leading American clerics.[93] On August 21, 1941, Acting Secretary of State Welles spoke at length with Archbishop Mooney and Monsignor Ready. Both prelates wanted to help the administration; both accepted the need to aid Russia. They feared that American Catholics might appear disloyal to the nation if they persisted in their criticism of Roosevelt's policy. Most important, they warned that an anti-Roosevelt faction within the American church was using fear of communism to promote noninvolvement and anti-administration sentiment. Mooney personally believed that such isolationist clerics were misusing the papal enclyclical on communism. He intimated that he would personally seek Vatican clarification of the document. In the meantime, both priests urged Welles to undercut the anticommunist campaign by constantly stressing the distinction of the Russian state from communism, by prosecuting communists in the United States to prove the sincerity of the administration, and by urging Russia to liberalize its religious policy. Should Russia accept this last idea, American aid would appear almost "providential." Welles immediately passed this information on to the president who prepared to dispatch Myron Taylor to revisit the pope.[94]

On September 4, 1941, the *Yankee Clipper* left for Lisbon. On board, Myron Taylor went over his plan to convert the pope to Lend-Lease for Russia. The mission was supposed to be secret but even the Germans reported Taylor's trip as part of the campaign to win Catholic support for the Bolsheviks.[95] Within the next few weeks so many American officials appeared at the Vatican that their presence began to embarrass papal officials concerned about the pope's reputation as a neutral. Taylor arrived in Rome on September 9 after a brief stop in Barcelona. He carried with him a memorandum spelling out the similarities of the Atlantic Charter to the teachings of the New Testament and of the pope. The next day he delivered a personal letter from Roosevelt. "In so far as I am informed," the president wrote optimistically, "churches in Russia are open." Roosevelt claimed that the present war might be the occasion for a religious revolution in Russia which would place freedom of worship on a better plane than it was in Germany. We all know, he continued, that Russia is ruled by a dictatorship similar to Germany. The big difference, however, is that Germany seeks to export its diabolical system through forces of arms while Russia uses only primitive propaganda. Russia is less a threat to organized religion than Germany. Concluding, the president explained why he brought these opinions to the attention of the Holy Father and said that he felt that "the leaders of all Churches in the United States" should agree with him. Furthermore, these leaders should not "by their present attitude on this question directly assist Germany in her present objectives."[96] Myron Taylor then offered to campaign personally for an improvement in Vatican-Russian relations.

The Vatican had expected such a proposal. Before Taylor arrived, Cicognani had warned Cardinal Maglione that Archbishop Mooney, chairman of the NCWC, sought aid from the pope in a delicate situation. According to Mooney, certain American Catholics were leading the opposition to Roosevelt's foreign policy by using quotations from *Divini Redemptoris*. Mooney was concerned, not merely because he felt that the encyclical was being quoted out of context, but because such opposition to the administration "will cause serious embarrassment to the church and will create grave dissensions within the hierarchy." Furthermore, the loyalty of Catholics might well be called into question if criticism of the president continued. Catholic leaders worried about a Protestant backlash. Monsignor Ready of the NCWC joined Mooney in requesting that the Vatican make a public statement which would undermine Catholic criticism of Roosevelt's foreign policy.[97]

Despite this coordinated lobbying by the president and the NCWC, the Vatican reacted coolly. Men such as Maglione and Dominico Tardini, secretary for the Congregation for Extraordinary Ecclesiastical Affairs, dismissed Taylor's mission and Mooney's request as an obvious attempt to make the pope a pawn in Allied diplomacy. The United States, wrote Tardini, seeks to compromise the neutrality of the Holy See "in order to conquer the difficulty that they encounter domestically . . . because of this practical union with bolshevism." Maglione could not believe that anyone would interpret the papal encyclical as a condemnation of the Russian people. He reminded the American bishops that they were quite free to make such a distinction on their own. In fact, he recommended that the "clergy . . . would do very well to inculcate in everybody the duty of good citizenship, and to leave to the competent government authorities the responsibility of decisions as regards the preparation of war."[98]

Yet both men refused to have the Vatican make the type of clarifying statement that Taylor and Mooney wanted. Above all, the nonpartisanship of the pontiff must be preserved. For the Vatican to issue a statement on the encyclical immediately after Taylor's arrival would make it appear that Pope Pius was in the pay of Roosevelt. Furthermore, could the encyclical be twisted to fit the needs of the president? No one at the Vatican agreed with Roosevelt's analysis of either the European situation or Russia's attitude toward religion. Only a few days before Taylor's arrival, the Vatican announced that of the thirteen apostolic administrators in Russia, eleven were either in prison or in exile, and the other two had simply disappeared.[99]

Tardini personally tore the Roosevelt assessment apart, refuting it line by line. Churches remained closed. The killing and deportation of priests continued. Most serious, Tardini thought the president completely misunderstood the dynamics of communism and its relationship to the Soviet state. Reflecting an easy American pragmatism, Roosevelt ignored the theoretical question of communism, passed off Stalin as just another dictator, and predicted a rosy future. Upon reflection, Tardini thought he understood why the president was so cavalier in his treatment of communism. Roosevelt had written the letter as a politician seeking aid in overcoming a practical problem in the United States, namely, domestic opposition to his program; he wanted the Vatican to help him to bring American bishops into line. Vatican officials might agree that bishops should be silent in areas of politics where their information was limited, but how could the pope ask these men to support a program which looked with equanimity upon the survival of communism? Such was Roosevelt's proposal.[100]

This rejection of Roosevelt's suggestion did not imply Vatican support for the Nazi war effort. Repeatedly the Vatican denied German press releases on how the advancing troops of the Third Reich were spreading religious freedom.[101] The Vatican prided itself on its realism and breadth of vision in diplomacy. While nations shifted their interests and diplomatic goals, in Vatican City a sense of continuity and endurance permeated all decisions. Hitler and Stalin were transitory figures. The world had seen their types before. They would pass from the scene but the church would go on. The Vatican was also keenly conscious of its geographical vulnerability to the Axis. Finally, if the pope had any hopes of acting as a peacemaker, he must maintain his neutrality. Only then could he play the role of honest broker at the conference table. Vatican officials speculated on postwar developments and perceived dangers in a victory by either Russia or Germany. Should both nations be destroyed by the war, Europe might enjoy a period of tranquility. But if, for example, only communism survived, it would meet little resistance as it spread throughout the Germanic and Latin peoples. A few years after the defeat of Germany, a giant Soviet bloc would face England and America. World War III would swiftly follow.[102]

Myron Taylor sought desperately to revise this world view and to bring it into line with Allied thinking about the war. The ambassador painted his own picture of a religious revival in Russia. After the war, Catholicism would play a leading role in the Soviet Union, he explained. Even Eugene Cardinal Tisserant of France agreed with Taylor that Russia was on the verge of a religious revival. But Taylor had less success in his discussions with Tardini, who kept bringing up specific charges of persecution which proved impossible to refute. Next to these names and places Roosevelt's glittering generalities about Soviet reform were embarrassing.[103]

Still, it would not do for the Vatican to dismiss the President of the United States as ill-informed. Roosevelt's request for Vatican cooperation to defuse Catholic anticommunism must be answered. Maglione attempted to satisfy Taylor by promising to "write to the apostolic delegate [Cicognani] that privately and discreetly" he should explain to the bishops that "there is nothing in the encyclical of Pius XI against the Russian people."[104] But Taylor preferred a written statement by the pope in reply to Roosevelt's letter. Both Tardini and Maglione advised the pontiff against such a course. To them, Roosevelt's letter was a political ploy. The pope should reply in generalities so as not to hand the president a papal crutch for Allied diplomacy. More to the point, Tardini really believed that Catholic theology did prohibit aid to Russia. One could distinguish between the Russian people and the Soviet state, but was this not just excessive sophistry? A Russian victory would be a communist victory.[105]

The pope decided on a compromise. Privately, he wrote Taylor on September 16, 1941, that he was quite willing "to accede to the wish of your esteemed President" by repeating what he had said in October 1939 in *la Summi Pontificatus* and in the papal Christmas messages of 1939 and 1940. He would again express his eternal affection for the Russian people. As for the Lend-Lease issue, this was a military problem to be solved by the United States and Russia without Vatican interference. The pope also insisted that his statement about Russia must be delayed lest it appear "as concession to pressure of the United States and not a free statement, making it useless."[106] Since Roosevelt required a courtesy reply, however, Pope Pius wrote to him on September 20, 1941, expressing gratitude for the information on what Americans were thinking. The note failed to mention Russia, communism, or Lend-Lease. Finally, in his Christmas message of 1941, the pope reiterated his long-standing affection for the Russian people but did not mention the anticommunist encyclical *Divini Redemptoris.*[107]

Maglione did more for the Americans. Discreetly, he informed Cicognani that the encyclical *Divini Redemptoris* merely condemned Catholic collaboration with communists in humanitarian enterprises.

The pope had no wish to denounce the Russian people. Yet, lest Americans think the Vatican had changed its mind about communism, Tardini also wrote to Cicognani and told him that, when Mooney and the other bishops used the Maglione revision or elaboration of the encyclical, they were not to attribute it to Rome. Concern over appearing a mere pawn of the United States and guilt over such a literal approach to the encyclical probably explain Vatican reluctance to admit involvement in this revision.[108]

Knowing of these messages, Myron Taylor returned to the United States expecting Cicognani to make a public pronouncement correcting those Catholic isolationists who had adopted a hard-line interpretation of the encyclical. But days and then weeks passed without a word. When Taylor finally approached Cicognani and the latter admitted having received new instructions from Rome, Taylor sensed Cicognani's reluctance to engage in a public fight with fellow clerics and made arrangements for him, Archbishop Mooney, and Monsignor Ready to meet quietly with Roosevelt. It was Taylor's hope that a coordinated plan could then be formulated. Roosevelt looked forward to such a meeting, but Ready demurred. He feared that news of such a visit might be connected with revision of the encyclical. If American Catholics thought the president had a hand in rewriting a church policy, there would be the devil to pay.[109]

Roosevelt could well appreciate such a warning. During Taylor's visit to the Vatican, Catholics in the United States had increased their criticism. An alliance between secular isolationists and American Catholics over anticommunism was becoming more of a possibility each day. William P. Leonard's poll of the Catholic clergy in America on the question of aid to Russia gratified isolationists. Of those polled, 35 percent, a total of 12,827, replied to the question, "Do you favor aid to Russia?" Ninety percent opposed aid. In addition, 91.5 percent opposed the United States entering any war outside the Western Hemisphere. As Philip Burham wrote in the *Commonweal*, since American priests were now on record against the war, if the United States did get involved, the Catholic church would be suspected of disloyalty.[110] Roosevelt could take little satisfaction because the polltakers were biased and partisan. The trend was clear. During the same month of September three important members of the American hierarchy made public statements denouncing aid to Russia. Archbishop Beckman of Dubuque called upon his congregation to understand that the common enemy of the day was communism. Bishop Shaughnessy offered prayers in Seattle for those in Russia persecuted for their faith. Archbishop Curley offered condolences in Baltimore for Poland, now under the tyrannical heels of the "murderer of Moscow and the Mad Man of Berlin." In Springfield, Illinois, Bishop James A. Griffin feared there was a German plot to divide American Catholics. He thought it was succeeding.[111]

7

Increasingly, Catholic criticism of aid to Russia became a campaign of suspicion against the Roosevelt administration. One popular reason for Catholic opposition to aid was a fear that such an understanding would pave the way for the internal subversion of the country by communists. In light of the "Red Scare" which occurred after World War II, it is enlightening to note that many Catholics thought they saw the beginnings of a domestic sell-out in 1941. Paul Furfey of the *Catholic World* emphasized that American aid would only help the communists to defeat Germany and occupy most of Eastern Europe. Such a victory would aid the Communist party in the United States in its attempts to take over. Marxism appeared to be the wave of the future.[112] Noted journalist Eugene Lyons wrote in the *Sign* that the current "beatification of Stalin" was a "moral obscenity." Instead of merely aiding Russia on realistic and pragmatic grounds, as Welles had suggested in June, the United States was trying to identify it as an ideological ally. The failure to distinguish between aid to the Russian people and their bloodthirsty leaders was merely preparing the way for a considerable Soviet penetration of American schools, unions, and government. The Soviet influence in the Roosevelt administration, noted Lyons, was already obvious. He concluded that we were building a "Red Frankenstein."[113] *America* repeatedly editorialized that the decision to aid Russia was part of a larger plan of sympathy for the leftists on the part of the Roosevelt administration. At such a time, wrote the editors, it is imperative to launch a campaign to root communists out of American life.[114]

Many non-Catholics agreed. The American Federation of Labor, meeting in Seattle, passed a resolution which admitted the practical necessity of such aid but warned against forming any true alliance with the Soviets.

Patriotic groups such as the American Legion joined the Ancient Order of Hibernians to condemn aid to Russia. Protestant journals, in contrast, took a more liberal attitude toward aid, feeling that Germany was the primary threat. General public opinion was difficult to gauge. The only poll to test the question was worded in a rather curious fashion. Asked the question, "Regardless of how you feel toward Russia, which of these policies do you think we should pursue toward her now?" in October 1941, the American public responded as follows: 13.5 percent thought we should "leave Russia strictly alone and give her no help or encouragement of any kind"; 51.4 percent wanted to "work along with Russia and give her some aid if we think it will help beat Hitler"; 13.2 percent failed to register an opinion.[115] Many Americans were willing to aid Russia on pragmatic grounds, to buy time for the United States, but they had not grown to like the Soviet Union. An idealistic approach to Moscow had within it the seeds of disillusionment.

Both Roosevelt and Bishop Mooney hoped to frustrate this rabid anticommunist campaign but they had to proceed with caution. Now, after working through the Vatican, the president expected a clarification of *Divini Redemptoris*. Cicognani, Ready, and Mooney refused to visit the White House but did agree that the best man to announce the revision would be Archbishop McNicholas of Cincinnati. His loyalty to the Holy See, venerable episcopal status, and reputation as a moderate on foreign policy questions made it unlikely that he would appear a mere mouthpiece for the administration. On October 14, 1941, McNicholas met with Cicognani and agreed to the assignment with the stipulation that the address take the form of a diocesan letter so that he would not appear to be instructing the other bishops. Unfortunately, before McNicholas could speak and despite the discretion of Cicognani and Ready, word of the plan leaked out. On October 19, 1941, Archbishop Beckman went on the radio predicting such a statement and denying any distinction between the communist army and the Soviet state. Cicognani quickly intervened and prevented Archbishop Shaughnessy from joining Beckman in this attack, but the damage had been done.[116]

Cicognani was upset. He even accused the Roosevelt administration of leaking the story to Beckman in order to force the issue. Now, in late October, there was nothing to do but issue the McNicholas letter. First, Ready sent a copy to Welles, who considered it an important item in light of the fact that McNicholas was "generally regarded as one of the extreme isolationists among the members of the Catholic hierarchy." Apparently Welles did not share Ready's assessment of the bishop as a moderate, but he did predict that the letter would "have a most beneficial effect." McNicholas' document of October 27, 1941, sought to explain what Pope Pius XI really had in mind in his encyclical on communism of March 19, 1937. The pope was not, he emphasized, shaping United States policy toward Russia. In addition, the papacy clearly distinguished between the Russian government and the Russian people, expressing great affection for the latter. As was the wont of certain American bishops speaking on politically sensitive issues, McNicholas stressed that he was not entering politics but was disturbed over the dissension arising among his coreligionists on the issue of aid to Russia.[117]

Altogether, McNicholas said nothing new. After all of Roosevelt's and Taylor's efforts, the statement appeared intellectually shallow. McNicholas's reasoning was uninspiring even in American Catholic circles. Ironically, there was already a sophisticated theology at hand which could justify aid to Russia while remaining on morally sound ground. In 1939, Reverend Edgar R. Smothers, S.J., writing for the *Ecclesiastical Review*, had applied modern moral theology to the problem of dealing with Russia. He stressed that the Soviet regime was clearly illegitimate by virtue of its official and militant atheism. Yet above all, his argument called for "great practical prudence" and a consideration of particular circumstances. After warning against any dealings with such a regime, Smothers refused to declare it "antecedently certain" that such dealings were illicit. The Soviet state had to perform many morally acceptable acts to keep the nation functioning. It had to do certain licit things to exist internationally. Furthermore, the Soviet citizen could still lead an honest life although forced to live under a godless tyranny. While unquestionably a Soviet citizen would not be justified in fighting to advance the communist cause, the defense of Russia against any unprovoked invasion was another matter. Smothers declined to pass a "peremptory prohibition" on such defensive action. Likewise, he refused to rule out international relations with Russia; indeed, he pointed out that the Vatican itself had mounted a relief expedition in the early 1920s. Cooperation with Russia could not be declared intrinsically evil, nor was it inherently forbidden.[118]

No doubt Lend-Lease aid would help Stalin. Yet according to Smothers' ethical distinctions, the promotion of an evil result in such a case would be attributed to the character of Stalin rather than to the act of aid. Obviously, a military alliance with Russia would be "most deeply fraught with moral menace" and "the moral liabilities . . . very grave." But, even so, a nation was not bound to suffer any alternative rather than enter into such an alliance with Russia (Smothers here had in mind Poland in 1939). The entire argument seemed to support the type of moral distinctions embodied in the practical approach Welles had adopted in his statement of June 1941.[119]

Here was a perfectly legitimate theology to answer the question of whether or not Catholics could support aid to Russia. In contrast, McNicholas' reasoning lacked substance and cogency. To emphasize that the papacy had not condemned the Russian people was pointless; none of the critics had condemned the Russian people. The distinction between the Russian people and the Soviet government was important only if it could be proved that aiding Stalin's defense of Russia would ultimately help him to maintain control over his people since, in that case, the people would benefit more from the disintegration of the regime. To say that the encyclical *Divini Redemptoris* was not a moral directive to the United States government was to beg the question. Presumably, the pope was guiding Catholics who were bound up in the decisions made by their government. McNicholas also failed to explain away paragraph 57 of the encyclical which prohibited cooperation with communists even in affairs to promote humanitarian interests "which are in perfect harmony with the Christian spirit." Altogether, Mc-Nicholas' arguments seemed much weaker than the pragmatic ones used by English Catholics and advanced by Smothers. It was further weakened when critics remembered that McNicholas himself, in an address two weeks earlier, had denounced "the murderous brutality of Nazism and Atheistic Soviet Communism." He had prayed that the United States would stay out of war, called upon citizens to make their judgment known to Congress, and warned against trusting the Soviets. He then concluded that one must sympathize with the Russian people but that "it is impossible to distinguish between the Soviet government and the theory of communism."[120]

McNicholas' most recent change of heart did not convince Catholic isolationists. True, Shaughnessy had been silenced, but Beckman continued to hurl brickbats, as did Archbishop Curley. If the pope had called for a moratorium on criticism of Roosevelt, as Cicognani insisted, word had not reached Curley. In a tone that was surprisingly vitriolic, he lashed out at Stalin in a public interview with the *Baltimore News-Post*. The idea of the United States fighting side by side with the Soviet murderer gave him nightmares. He even took time to heap ridicule on the entire New Deal establishment: "These American flops—these moronic Hollywood 'geniuses,' these scions of millionaire families, these jewel-bedecked 'thinkers' in Washington, these university professors, these writers—they flopped from one side to another according to the changes as dictated by the Browder boys." Five days before Pearl Harbor, Curley predicted that the communists would take advantage of collaboration to achieve their long-stated objective of destroying the United States government.[121]

8

Roosevelt was no longer listening. He moved ahead in his aid program, encouraged by an unobtrusive vote in Congress. On October 10, 1941, the House considered the supplement to the initial Lend-Lease appropriation. Representatives rejected an amendment to prohibit aid to Russia by a vote of 162 to 21. On October 23 the Senate concurred in this decision. This congressional action and growing support for aid by such groups as the American Federation of Labor influenced Roosevelt's final decision. Clearly, he had made a basic commitment to aid Russia as early as June 23. The problem of finding the proper method of financing such aid had created the major delay. After having exhausted a number of approaches to soothe Catholic feelings, the president went ahead with his original intention.[122] On October 30, 1941, he assured Stalin in a private letter that "immediate arrangements are to be made so that supplies up to one billion dollars in value may be effected under the Lend-Lease Act." On November 7, 1941, Roosevelt wrote Lend-Lease Administrator Edward R. Stettinius authorizing immediate steps to transfer supplies to Russia.[123]

The president sent aid to Stalin despite the absence of a consensus on the matter. In mid-November the annual joint meeting of the administrative board of the NCWC brought together the leaders of the American hierarchy. Seven days after Roosevelt began sending aid to Russia, the largest and most representative organization of the American Catholic church issued a statement of guidance for the times. Called *The Crisis of Christianity*, it was an ambiguous document. Still, several basic themes emerged. First, Nazism and communism were condemned equally. Second, people suffering under both systems were extended Christian affection. Third, the bishops reminded the faithful of their duty to obey properly constituted civil authority, deplored dissension in the republic, and endorsed all steps for national defense. The bishops also discussed other issues and expressed sympathy for the persecuted Jews. Above all, the statement revealed the attempts of the bishops to be flexible, to satisfy both isolationists and interventionists in the church, and to remove any question of Catholic loyalty to the government.[124]

The president had no comment on the episcopal statement. He had already committed himself to aid to and friendship with Russia. He did so on the basis of military reality and with high hopes for the future of Soviet-Western relations. Yet he did so while a large segment of the American population, especially Roman Catholics, were still hostile to this new ally. Within a few weeks the United States would enter the war. Catholics would rally to the flag, but distrust of the Soviet Union would remain. Like a low-grade infection, it could flare up at the first weakening of the wartime coalition.

NOTES

1. Seymour M. Lipset, "Religion and Politics in the American Past and Present," in *Religion and Social Conflict*, edited by Robert Lee and Martin E. Marty (New York, 1964), pp. 92-93, shows how Catholic laborers and non-manual workers supported Democrats in 1936 and 1940. Also see Raymond H. Dawson, *The Decision to Aid Russia, 1941* (Chapel Hill, N.C., 1959), pp. 85-96.

2. Rev. John J. Burke to Hon. William Phillips, September 30, 1933, State Department File 861.01/2046, National Archives, Washington (hereafter cited as SDF).

3. George Q. Flynn, *American Catholics and the Roosevelt Presidency, 1932-1936* (Lexington, 1968), pp. 150-194 passim; also see Chapter 2 of this book.

4. David O'Brien, *American Catholics and Social Reform* (New York, 1968), pp. 81-96.

5. The binding power of an encyclical on the faithful is a source of debate among modern theologians. The consensus, however, agrees that,

while not possessing the "charism of infallibility," such teaching should
be accepted "with all reverence." It seems safe to say that most American
Catholics probably shared Al Smith's reported ignorance over the definition of an encyclical. Yet the American clergy understood it and consistently applied such teaching as binding on the faithful. See George D.
Smith, *The Teaching of the Catholic Church*, 2 vols. (New York, 1956),
vol. 2, p. 719; William E. Langer and S. Everett Gleason, *The Undeclared
War, 1940-1941* (New York, 1953), pp. 542-543.

6. *NCWC News Service:* March 29, 1937; March 19, 1937.

7. McGowan to Thorning, April 17, 1937; Elizabeth Sweeney to Fenwick, April 22, 1937; Thorning to Sweeney, March 25, 1937; all in CAIP
Mss.; *NCWC News Service,* April 16, 1937.

8. *NCWC News Service,* April 4, 1938; O'Connor to Curran, June 6,
1938, and John M. O'Shea to O'Connor, July 1, 1938, Communism
File, 1938, John J. O'Connor Mss., Lilly Library, Bloomington, Ind.

9. Fulton Sheen, "Primacy of Ethics over Politics" (radio address of
October 27, 1940), reprinted in *Catholic Mind* 38 (December 22, 1940),
pp. 538-544; *NCWC News Service,* November 7, 1940.

10. *Time,* October 13, 1941, p. 46.

11. Harold Ickes, *The Secret Diary of Harold Ickes,* 3 vols. (New York,
1954), vol. 3., p. 231; Theodore Maynard, "Catholics and the Nazis,"
American Mercury 53 (October 1941), pp. 391-400, which was written
in response to accusations of Catholic sympathy for Germany; Heffron
letter in *NCWC News Service,* September 23, 1940.

12. Sweeney to Mary J. Workman, February 2, 1937; Workman to
Sweeney, November 27, 1937; Tibor Kerekes to Sweeney, December 17,
1936; all in CAIP Mss.

13. *NCWC News Service*: April 30, 1937; July 5, 1937; August 17,
1937; November 18, 1940.

14. Maynard, "Catholics and Nazis," pp. 391, 393-395.

15. Hadley Cantrill, editor, *Public Opinion, 1935-1946* (Princeton,
N.J., 1951), p. 1055; *Catholic Herald Citizen,* April 9, 1938, p. 9; *NCWC
News Service,* April 8, 1938.

16. Ickes, *Diary,* vol. 2, p. 231.

17. Maynard, "Catholics and Nazis," pp. 396-398, feels Catholic
isolationism was similar to that of Wheeler and Lindbergh. But see James
O'Gara, "The Catholic Isolationist," in *Catholicism in America: A Series*

of Articles from "The Commonweal" (New York, 1954), p. 116, who agrees on the importance of anticommunism in explaining Catholic isolationism.

18. Wayne Cole, *America First* (Madison, Wisconsin, 1953), pp. 86-87.

19. Quoted by Gillis, *Catholic World* 152 (February 1941), p. 522.

20. Thomas E. Davitt, S. J., "Can We Ally with Russia?" *America*, April 1, 1939, p. 605, which provoked a lively exchange of letters, one of which refuted Davitt by pointing out that what was decisive for American moral integrity was the posture of the United States vis-à-vis the war. If our cause was just, it did not matter what Russia was doing. Another wrote that cooperation with atheism did not imply encouragement in its expansion (see *America*: April 22, 1939, p. 44; May 13, 1939, p. 113).

21. Quoted in the *Brooklyn Tablet*, May 6, 1939, p. 12.

22. *Brooklyn Tablet*, January 15, 1938, p. 9; May 6, 1939, p. 12; *Our Sunday Visitor*, May 14, 1939, p. 1; Ronald E. Magden, "Attitudes of the American Religious Press Toward Soviet Russia, 1939-1941" (Ph.D. thesis, University of Washington, 1964), pp. 3, 8, 11; Wilfrid Parsons, "Shall We Choose War?" *Columbia*, January 1937, p. 7; Sheen, "The Primacy of Ethics," pp. 538-544.

23. Magden, "Attitudes," p. 86; *Sign* 20 (November 1940), p. 196; John C. LeClair, "No Friendship Wanted Between the U.S. and USSR," *America*, September 28, 1940, pp. 679-680.

24. S. R. Herbert, "The Vatican and the Nazi-Soviet Pact," *Protestant Digest* 3 (June-July 1941), pp. 54-65; *Boston Pilot*: December 24, 1938, p. 11; January 14, 1939, p. 4; Magden, "Attitudes," pp. 9, 20.

25. Magden, "Attitudes," pp. 52, 60; *NCWC News Service*: March 2, 1940; February 19, 1940.

26. *NCWC News Service*: Code quoted in April 12, 1940; May 14, 1940.

27. Ibid., February 10, 1940; Cordell Hull, *The Memoirs of Cordell Hull*, 2 vols. (New York, 1948), vol. 1, p. 685.

28. *Denver Catholic Register*, December 7, 1939, p. 4; *NCWC News Service*: February 9, 1940; February 24, 1940; February 26, 1940; April 1, 1940; Magden, "Attitudes," pp. 95, 120.

29. Warren Kimball, *The Most Unsordid Act: Lend-Lease, 1939-1941* (Baltimore, 1969), is the most complete treatment; Langer and Gleason, *The Undeclared War*, p. 224; John M. Blum, *From the Morgenthau*

Diaries, 3 vols. (Boston, 1959, 1965, 1967), vol. 2, pp. 211-225 passim.

30. *NCWC News Service*, November 8, 1940.

31. Blum, *Morgenthau Diaries*, vol. 2, pp. 224-225; Langer and Gleason, *The Undeclared War*, pp. 268, 278-279.

32. Kimball, *The Most Unsordid Act*, pp. 198, 200.

33. Langer and Gleason, *The Undeclared War*, pp. 257, 280; Cole, *America First*, p. 46.

34. Roosevelt approved the move so long as it was not widely publicized; see Hull, *Memoirs*, vol. 2, p. 969; Blum, *Morgenthau Diaries*, vol. 2, p. 256; Langer and Gleason, *The Undeclared War*, p. 338.

35. LeClair, "No Friendship Wanted," p. 679.

36. *NCWC News Service:* December 8, 1940; quote in January 20, 1941.

37. J. LeClair, "Tragic Folly," *America*, March 15, 1941, p. 626; editorial, "Supping with Soviets," *America*, March 15, 1941, pp. 630-631.

38. *NCWC News Service*: March 3, March 7, March 8, 1941.

39. Ibid.: April 1, 1941; April 5, 1941; James Gillis, "Russia As An Ally," *Catholic World* 153 (May 1941), pp. 130-136; *NCWC News Service:* June 13, June 20, 1941.

40. *NCWC News Service:* March 31, 1941; quote in May 30, 1941; June 2, 1941.

41. Ibid., June 2, 9, 13, 16, 23, 1941.

42. Department of State, *Foreign Relations of the United States, Diplomatic Papers, 1941*, 7 vols. (Government Printing Office, Washington, D.C., 1958), vol. 1, pp. 621-623 (hereafter cited as *USFR 1941*).

43. Ibid., vol. 1, p. 758.

44. Ibid., vol. 1, pp. 764-765.

45. Ibid., vol. 1, p. 766.

46. Ibid., vol. 1, p. 767; Hull, *Memoirs*, vol. 2, p. 967.

47. Magden, "Attitudes," p. 128; Cantrill, *Public Opinion*, p. 411; Thomas Bailey, *The Man in the Street: The Impact of American Public Opinion on Foreign Policy* (New York, 1949), p. 206.

48. Ready to Welles, July 2, 1941, SDF, 861.24/517¼.

49. Dawson, *The Decision to Aid*, p. 91; *NCWC News Service*, July 14, 1941; James Gillis, "Covenant with Hell," *Catholic World* 153 (August 1941), pp. 513-517; John J. Carrigg, "American Catholic Press Opinion

Opinion with Reference to America's Intervention in the Second World War (M.A. thesis, Georgetown University, 1947), p. 125.

50. Beckman quoted in *NCWC News Service,* July 28, 1941; see also Dawson, *Decision to Aid,* p. 90.

51. *NCWC News Service,* July 3, 1941.

52. "English Catholics and Russia," *Commonweal,* August 15, 1941, pp. 399-401; *NCWC News Service*: July 3, 18, 1941; September 1, 15, 27, 1941; October 20, 1941.

53. F. L. Broderick, *The Right Reverend New Dealer: John A. Ryan 1945* (New York, 1963), pp. 259-260.

54. Dawson, *Decision to Aid,* pp. 87-88. The group included William J. Donovan, Reverend George B. Ford, Michael Williams, Francis E. McMahon, Dr. William A. Agar, and others. Not one bishop was included and the group did not represent much ecclesiastical muscle. Nor was it geographically or ideologically representative of American Catholicism, being primarily eastern and urban in composition; see *NCWC News Service,* June 30, 1941.

55. Hurley quoted in *NCWC News Service,* July 7, 1941; see also *Catholic Action,* June 1941, p. 18.

56. Gillis, "Covenant with Hell," pp. 518-519; Dawson, *Decision to Aid,* pp. 89-90; see also Chapter 3 of this book.

57. Averell Harriman to the author, January 31, 1969; Langer and Gleason, *The Undeclared War,* pp. 543-544.

58. Langer and Gleason, *The Undeclared War,* p. 540; Dawson, *Decision to Aid,* p. 147; James M. Burns, *Roosevelt: The Soldier of Freedom, 1940-1945* (New York, 1970), p. 112.

59. *USFR 1941,* vol. 1, pp. 769, 789-790, 795-798, 815.

60. Ibid., vol. 1, pp. 779-780, 827, 832-833; Blum, *Morgenthau Diaries,* vol. 2, pp. 262-268; Dawson, *Decision to Aid,* p. 217.

61. Langer and Gleason, *The Undeclared War,* p. 815; *USFR 1941,* vol. 1, pp. 815, 835, 836, 847-848, 848n.

62. Robert E. Sherwood, *Roosevelt and Hopkins* (New York, 1950), p. 384, also mentions another Catholic advocate, Philip Murray, president of the Congress of Industrial Organizations.

63. Jane Purcell to James Farley, June 24, 1940, General File, 1940, Frank Walker Papers, University of Notre Dame Archives, South Bend, In

64. *NCWC News Service,* Chicago, April 21, 1941.

65. Dawson, *Decision to Aid,* p. 149; Langer and Gleason, *The Unde-*

clared War, p. 547; quote in memorandum by Walter Duranty, August 4, 1941, General File, 1940, Walker Papers.

66. Senator O'Mahoney to Mrs. Rose Goggin, November 11, 1941, Box 48, O'Mahoney Papers, University of Wyoming Archives, Laramie.

67. Memo from GGT to Roosevelt, August 19, 1941, Official File 41-A, Box 118, Roosevelt Papers, Hyde Park, New York; Dawson, *Decision to Aid*, p. 232; Langer and Gleason, *The Undeclared War*, p. 793; Murphy quoted in *NCWC News Service*, August 22, 1941; William T. O'Donnell to Stephen Early, August 20, 1941, Official File 41-A, Box 118, Roosevelt Papers.

68. Roosevelt to Senator James M. Mead (D.-NY), October 9, 1941, in Elliott Roosevelt, editor, *F.D.R.: His Personal Letters*, 4 vols. (New York, 1947-1950), vol. 4, p. 1220.

69. Roosevelt to Spellman, October 25, 1941, PSF: Spellman, Roosevelt Papers; FDR quoted in *New York Times*, October 28, 1941; *NCWC News Service*: October 28, 1941; November 3, 1941.

70. Hull to Tittmann, October 29, 1941, SDF, 862.404/321; Tittmann to Hull, November 1, 1941, SDF, 862.404/326; Tittmann to Hull, November 6, 1941, SDF, 862.404/329; see also Roosevelt to Taylor, October 25, 1941, PSF, Taylor folder, Roosevelt Papers.

71. *Catholic Herald Citizen* (Milwaukee): August 23, 1941, p. 23; November 1, 1941, p. 23.

72. Langer and Gleason, *The Undeclared War*, pp. 797-798.

73. Quoted in ibid., pp. 797-798.

74. When he returned from his Atlantic Charter meeting with Churchill, Roosevelt was reminded that freedom of religion was not covered in the statement of principles agreed upon. The president then made a special correction of this oversight in his report to Congress, commenting that "it is unnecessary for me to point out that the declaration of principles includes of necessity the world need for freedom of religion." Quoted in Langer and Gleason, *The Undeclared War,* pp. 690-691; Sherwood, *Roosevelt and Hopkins*, p. 384.

75. Averell Harriman to author, January 31, 1969; Myron C. Taylor, *Wartime Correspondence Between President Roosevelt and Pope Pius XII* (New York, 1947), p. 58.

76. *USFR 1941*, vol. 1, p. 999n; Dawson, *Decision to Aid*, pp. 235-237.

77. Hull to Steinhardt, October 2, 1941, *USFR 1941*, vol. 1, p. 1000;

Langer and Gleason, *The Undeclared War*, p. 816. The article in question reads: "In order to insure to citizens freedom of conscience, the Church in the Union of Soviet Socialist Republics is separated from the State and the School from the Church. Freedom of religious worship and freedom of anti-religious propaganda is recognized for all citizens."

78. *NCWC News Service,* October 2, October 6, October 14, 1941; *Extension Magazine,* November 1941, pp. 18-19; Dawson, *Decision to Aid,* pp. 258-259.

79. *NCWC News Service:* March 22, 1937; October 2, 1941; December 5, 1941; Paul H. Furfey, "Glance to the Left," *Catholic World* 154 (November 1941), p. 148.

80. Harriman to the author, January 31, 1969; Langer and Gleason, *The Undeclared War*, p. 817.

81. Cicognani to Maglione, October 7, 1941, Pierre Blet, et al., editors, Secrétairerie D'État de sa Sainteté, *Actes et Documents du Saint Siège Relatifs à La Seconde Guerre Mondiale,* 5 vols. (Citta Del Vaticano: Libreria Editrice Vaticana, 1967-   ), vol. 5, p. 261 (hereafter cited as *Holy See and War*); Dawson, *Decision to Aid,* p. 263; *NCWC News Service,* October 3, 1941.

82. Steinhardt to Hull, October 4, 1941, *USFR 1941,* vol. 1, pp. 1001, 1001n, 1003n; Langer and Gleason, *The Undeclared War,* pp. 816-817.

83. Quotes in Steinhardt to Hull, October 4, 1941, *USFR 1941*, vol. 1, pp. 1002-1003; see also Dawson, *Decision to Aid*, p. 264.

84. *USFR 1941*, vol. 1, pp. 1003-1004, 1004n.

85. *NCWC News Service,* October 3, 6, 20, 1941; Walsh quoted in Dawson, *Decision to Aid*, p. 264.

86. Cicognani to Maglione, January 16, 1941, *Holy See and War*, vol. 4, p. 344.

87. Cicognani to Maglione, June 17, 1941, *Holy See and War*, vol. 4, pp. 555-558.

88. Ibid.

89. Camille M. Cianfarra, *The Vatican and the War* (New York, 1944). pp. 268-269.

90. Tittmann to Hull, June 30, 1941, SDF, 740.0011EW1939/12651; Tittmann to Hull, July 2, 1941, SDF, 740.0011EW1939/12725.

91. Notes of Monsignor Montini, June 28, 1941, *Holy See and War*, vol. 4, p. 575; Martin F. Hasting, "United States-Vatican Relations: Policies and Problems" (Ph.D. thesis, University of California, 1952), p. 221;

Oscar Halecki, *Eugenio Pacelli: Pope of Peace* (New York, 1951), p. 166; Tittmann to Hull, July 11, 1941, SDF, 740.0011EW1939/13727.

92. Welles to Phillips, July 31, 1941, *USFR 1941*, vol. 1, p. 999.

93. Langer and Gleason, *The Undeclared War*, p. 794.

94. Memo of conversation on August 21, 1941, of Mooney, Ready, and Welles in Cicognani to Maglione, September 1, 1941, *Holy See and War*, vol. 5, pp. 173-174.

95. Saul Friedlander, *Pius XII and the Third Reich: A Documentation*, trans. by Charles Fullman (New York, 1966), p. 87.

96. Roosevelt to Pius XII, September 3, 1941, PSF, Vatican Box 17, Roosevelt Papers; Taylor, *Wartime Correspondence*, pp. 61-62; Halecki, *Pope of Peace*, p. 168; Langer and Gleson, *The Undeclared War*, pp. 794-795.

97. Cicognani to Maglione, September 1, 1941, *Holy See and War*, vol. 5, pp. 172-173.

98. Tardini notes, September 5, 1941, and Maglione notes, September 10, 1941, *Holy See and War*, vol. 5, pp. 185, 191-193.

99. *NCWC News Service*, Vatican City, July 21, 1941.

100. Tardini notes, September 12-13, 1941, *Holy See and War*, vol. 5, pp. 202-206.

101. The Secretariat of State for the Vatican rejected the crusade idea; see *New York Times*, August 25, 1941; Dawson, *Decision to Aid*, p. 93; *NCWC News Service:* London, January 27, 1941; August 25, 1941.

102. Langer and Gleason, *The Undeclared War*, p. 796; Halecki, *Pope of Peace*, pp. 145-147, 166; memo of conversation between Tardini and Taylor, September 17, 1941, *Holy See and War*, vol. 5, p. 224.

103. Tardini to Taylor, September 20, 1941, *Holy See and War*, vol. 5, pp. 241-243; Tittmann to Hull, July 21, 1941, SDF, 740.0011EW1939/13352.

104. Maglione notes, September 11, 1941, *Holy See and War*, vol. 5, pp. 199-200.

105. Notes of Tardini, September 14-15, 1941, *Holy See and War*, vol. 5, pp. 215-218.

106. Pius XII to Taylor, September 16, 1941, *Holy See and War*, vol. 5, p. 219; Halecki, *Pope of Peace*, p. 169.

107. Pius XII to Roosevelt, September 20, 1941, in Taylor, *Wartime Correspondence*, pp. 63-64.

108. Tardini to Cicognani, September 20, 1941, *Holy See and War*, vol. 5, pp. 240-241.

109. Presidential memo, October 9-October 10, 1941, in *Selected Materials from the Papers of Franklin D. Roosevelt Concerning Roman Catholic Church Matters* (microfilm), Roosevelt Library, Hyde Park, N.Y.; Cicognani to Maglione, October 28, 1941, *Holy See and War*, vol. 5, pp. 285-288.

110. Philip Burham, "Clergy Poll," *Commonweal*, October 31, 1941, pp. 37, 38; Cole, *America First*, p. 87; Magden, "Attitudes," p. 135. Altogether, some 34,616 questionnaires were sent out and 13,155 or 37.6 percent replied. Two questions were asked: "Do you favor the U.S. engaging in a shooting war outside of the Western Hemisphere? Are you in favor of the U.S. aiding the communistic Russian government?" 12,038 said no to the first question, only 885 yes. While New York, New Jersey, Massachusetts, Pennsylvania, Illinois, California, and Ohio accounted for over 50 percent of the replies, there seemed little geographical difference in the responses from other sections. All areas were over 90 percent negative on both questions; see *Commonweal*, October 31, 1941, p. 38, and *Catholic Herald Citizen*, October 25, 1941, p. 3, for conflicting reactions to the poll.

111. *NCWC News Service:* Beckman quoted in September 16, 1941; September 26, 1941; Curley quoted in September 23, 1941; *Catholic Herald Citizen*, September 27, 1941.

112. Paul H. Furfey, "Glance to the Left," pp. 145-147.

113. Eugene Lyons, "Our Muddled Russian Policy," *Sign*, December 1941, pp. 261-264.

114. *America*: March 1, 1941, pp. 574-575; July 5, 1941, pp. 350-351; July 12, 1941, p. 378.

115. Cantrill, *Public Opinion, 1935-1946*, p. 961; *NCWC News Service:* Washington, October 10, 1941; Seattle, October 6, 1941; San Jose, September 5, 1941; Milwaukee, September 19, 1941; Magden, "Attitudes," p. 153.

116. Ready to Welles, October 28, 1941; Welles to Hull, October 29, 1941; Welles to Ready, October 29, 1941, SDF, 811.404/258; Cicognani to Maglione, October 28, 1941, *Holy See and War*, vol. 5, pp. 285-288.

117. Welles quoted in *Holy See and War*, vol. 5, pp. 285-288; for letter by McNicholas see *NCWC News Service*, Cincinnati, October 27, 1941; see also *Catholic Action*, November 1941, pp. 9-10. The Fight for Freedom Committee attempted to solicit widespread Catholic support for the statement, but see Mark Chadwin, *The Warhawks: American Interven-

tionists Before Pearl Harbor (New York, 1968), pp. 248-249, who concludes that this statement had little effect on Roosevelt.

118. Edgar R. Smothers, S. J., "The Moral Aspects of Certain Relationships with Russia," *Ecclesiastical Review* 101 (July 1939), pp. 50-54. In fairness to Smothers, it should be noted that he closed his piece with a warning against any American-Soviet detente. He even suggested a moral and religious front of all churches to oppose such an alliance. But his theology allowed for circumstantial considerations; it could bend with the world.

119. Ibid.

120. Quoted in *NCWC News Service*, Cincinnati, October 13, 1941.

121. Ibid., Baltimore, December 2, 1941.

122. Langer and Gleason, *The Undeclared War*, p. 818. Burns, *Roosevelt: Soldier*, p. 112, points out that Roosevelt had access to polls by Hadley Cantrill. The amendment to prohibit Lend-Lease to the USSR was offered by Robert F. Rich of Pennsylvania, who based his position squarely on religious factors. He did not think the U.S. should help a nation which persecuted religion; he quoted Pius XII about the hatred of Russia for religion. His colleagues in the House responded by arguing that aid was to help defeat Hitler rather than to assist the USSR. The Rich amendment failed by a voice vote: yeas 21, nays 162. Later the same day, the supplemental appropriation passed with 328 yeas and only 67 nays. The administration received support from men of a variety of ethnic origins: Capozzoli, Casey, Flaherty, O'Brien, O'Toole, Kocialkowski, McCormack, and others. The Senate passed the same bill later by a vote of 59 to 13 with 21 not voting. There was no special amendment in the Senate to bar aid to the USSR. See *Congressional Record*, 77 Cong. 1 Sess. (October 10 and 23, 1941), pp. 7820-7823, 8204.

123. Roosevelt to Stalin, October 30, 1941; Roosevelt to Stettinius, November 7, 1941, *USFR 1941*, vol. 1, pp. 851-852, 857.

124. Raphael M. Huber, *Our Bishops Speak: National Pastorals and Annual Statements of the Hierarchy . . . , 1919-1951* (Milwaukee, 1952), pp. 102-109; Thomas T. McAvoy, "American Catholics and the Second World War," *Review of Politics* 6 (April 1944), p. 135. The reaction to the statement was favorable in the isolationist's camp. The *Brooklyn Eagle* said the bishops' statement would surely take the wind out of Catholics who called communism a lesser evil than Nazism. Other papers said it would straighten out clerics soft on communism. See *NCWC News Service*, December 2, 1941, for general press reaction.

6

THE THEOLOGY OF WAR

The religious skeptic could ask for no more potent ammunition for his cause than the manner in which the Christian church, Protestant and Catholic, has always marched to war. Things were a bit different for the generation of the 1960s, which was confronted with a never-ending conflict in Vietnam. Newspaper headlines related the decision of the United Methodist Church to allow every member of the denomination the right to consult his own conscience about serving in Indo-China. Protestants and Catholics in general seemed almost up in arms over that conflict. Headlines reported such items as a priest being arrested for pouring blood over draft records. Another priest was implicated in a plot to kidnap a high government official in hopes of forcing the government to change its foreign policy. Nuns and priests marched in protest against the war in Southeast Asia. Young members of the Catholic Worker Movement burned their draft cards. One young man immolated himself as a protest against the injustice of American policy in Vietnam.

A generation earlier the Christian conscience had reacted to war in a different manner. The scene is a mountain top where a young soldier, dressed in the uniform of 1917, sits pondering the Bible in his hand. His struggle is the age-old one of reconciling a Christian conscience with the requirements of war. As clouds rush by the mountain, a gust of air flips open the Bible to a passage in Matthew (chapter 22, verse 21): "Render, therefore, to Caesar the things that are Caesar's, and to God the things that are God's." Here is the way out of the dilemma for the young soldier. He mutters to himself: "God and country, God and country." The background music rises to a crescendo; the two concepts become one; Alvin York descends from his mountain and marches off to slaughter Germans with a good conscience. York marched off to fight World War I, but American moviegoers watched "Sergeant York" as they prepared to fight in World War II.

American Catholics in 1941 applauded York's decision and the moral of the scene. As bombs rained down on Pearl Harbor, they stopped debating foreign policy and started pushing patriotism. The leaders of the church enlisted for the duration. Some clerics set a high level of commitment. One would have thought the church was filled with potential chaplains. The Reverend John J. Dillon, president of Providence College, spoke for many of his colleagues when he told alumni that the United States was fighting a just war. "Any friend or ally of Japan is an enemy of ours," Dillon said. Archbishop Michael J. Curley, long a critic of Roosevelt, announced that "today there is no place for discussion between isolationists and interventionists. The die is cast—it is a matter of defense of the nation."[1] American Catholics marched to war secure in the conviction that God was on their side.

1

How can one explain the paradox between the Christian conscience in the 1960s and in 1941? It is easy to emphasize the moral ambiguity of Vietnam and the moral clarity of World War II, but more is involved. Vietnam once appeared morally clear to most Americans. An explanation of the events of that earlier war may help us understand how the Catholic conscience shapes itself during a crisis. Most explanations of why American Catholics gave moral endorsement to the war of 1941-1945 rest upon nonhistorical assumptions. One argument is that Hitler was a demonic force in history, that the United States represented Providence, that the purpose

of the war was to promote a world of liberty and goodness. Catholic periodical literature repeatedly explained Hitler in terms of his alliance with
the devil. Equally pervasive and traditional was the assumption that a
special providential hand guided the United States. In 1884, when the
American bishops gathered at the Third Plenary Council of Baltimore,
they affirmed their belief that the creation of the United States had been
under the special direction of God. The bishops who guided Catholics
during World War II held a similar belief.

Historians have difficulty with these ideas. Painting Hitler as super-
human makes rational analysis of his actions difficult. A political scientist
may have trouble discussing the United States if he insists that it has been
lifted out of history by some special act of Providence. The diplomatic
historian who seeks to understand the issues of World War II must pay less
attention to eschatological concepts and to the speeches of statesmen and
more to the actions of politicians. Students who are unwilling to examine
the process by which the United States and World War II were lifted out
of history and made part of a morality play can never hope to understand
why the Catholic leadership in this nation acted the way it did in the early
1940s. Without such an understanding, we cannot sense why Catholic
leaders supported Roosevelt's diplomacy, nor why they eventually rejected it.

It is true that in some sense many Catholics did not need the disaster
of Pearl Harbor to enlist them against Hitler's Germany. While archbishops
Francis J. L. Beckman, Michael J. Curley, O'Connell of Boston, Father
Coughlin, and a few others had maintained a vigorous isolationist position
up to December 7, 1941, most Catholics had already come to accept
Roosevelt's assessments at face value.[2] Even the Vatican, occasionally
taking part in the affairs of the American church, sought to discourage
criticism of the president. On the question of isolationism and on the
problem of aid to Russia, Roosevelt succeeded in having the Vatican put
pressure on domestic prelates who objected to his foreign policy. There
were many American clerics who, although still suspicious of Russia, had
always been quite willing to work with the president. The American
church remained anticommunist but already had joined the Roosevelt
diplomatic consensus.

With the attack on Pearl Harbor, the flood gates opened. Writing in
the name of his fellow bishops, the religious leaders of 20 million Ameri-

can Catholics, Archbishop Edward A. Mooney informed President
Roosevelt on December 22, 1941, that "we will marshal the spiritual
forces at our command to render secure our God-given blessings of freedom." The bishop cited the Third Plenary Council of Baltimore as evidence
of the historic commitment of American Catholics to the United States.
In a spirit resembling that of the German hierarchy, Mooney stated, "We
place at your disposal in that service our institutions and their consecrated
personnel."[3] The president thanked the bishop for making a commitment
to national unity "so necessary in our all-out effort to win the war." More
important, Roosevelt reinforced the bishops' theological interpretation of
the conflict: "We shall win this war and in victory we shall seek not vengeance but the establishment of an international order in which the spirit
of Christ shall rule the hearts of men and of nations."[4] Never mind the
practical political objectives of the war. Roosevelt stressed the moral ideals
which had led to the Atlantic Charter and the Four Freedoms.

Other church leaders, in their individual reactions to Pearl Harbor, sus-
tained this level of enthusiasm. The America First Committee disbanded.
In the words of the *Denver Catholic Register*, "any half-hearted or inimical
attitude toward national leaders is treason." Bishops such as Thomas J.
Toolen of Mobile, Duane G. Hunt of Salt Lake, and Samuel Stritch of
Chicago emphasized that American patriotism required united support of
the president. Catholic sources which had been suspicious of Roosevelt's
diplomacy capitulated. The *Sign* wrote that "as far as the war is concerned
we are no longer Democrats or Republicans, isolationist or interventionist.
We are Americans." Archbishop Curley, who had predicted that Roosevelt
would get the United States into war, now forbade any dissent, any discussion of isolationists vs. interventionists, and called for all to be Americans.
Those critics who in 1939 and 1940 had predicted war with Japan if the
Department of State continued its policies were now forgotten.[5]

Such emphasis on patriotism seemed normal in the wake of Japan's
treachery. Bands played and flags waved, although not with the exuberance of 1917 because now the nation was responding to a direct attack.
Still, the frustration in avenging the disgrace to American national honor
was conducive to hyperbolic statement. The clergy did its part. The Catholic liturgy was changed by adding the prayer *A Tempore Belli*. Bishop John
A. Duffy of Buffalo, who had earlier called for Catholics to refuse to serve
if drafted, organized a prayer crusade after Pearl Harbor. Each child in the

parochial schools was to adopt a serviceman for whom he would intercede with God. Blank forms were run off by the diocese.[6]

On a more theoretical level, Catholic spokesmen presented a moralistic interpretation of the war which came close to identifying the diplomacy of the United States with the will of God. The *Catholic Standard and Times* of Philadelphia announced that Catholics understood and accepted the idea of total war and that distinctions could hardly be made between civilians and soldiers. Bishop James Ryan of Omaha said that Americans should feel free of guilt because they had done all they could to stay out. Now that America had been attacked, "we are in conscience obliged to do all we can to promote and further the efforts of the National Government looking toward the complete defeat of our enemies." As Bishop A. J. Muench of Fargo wrote, "When a government speaks with the voice of authority, it speaks with the voice of God." Bishop Gannon of Erie, Bishop John Swint of Wheeling, and Francis P. Matthews of the Knights of Columbus were other leading Catholics who helped to reinforce the idea of commitment. The *Southwest Courier* of Oklahoma City found it a good omen that the declaration of war came on the Feast of the Immaculate Conception, since the Blessed Mother was the patroness of America. Bishop Lucey of San Antonio felt that going to war was the working out of divine will, a mission "to redeem the Christian Church from oppression and to salvage what is left of Western Civilization." America would save the Japanese by defeating them. In New York City, the military vicar, Archbishop Spellman, reported to his Commander-in-Chief that 500 Catholic chaplains were on duty. "As an American and one of the 25 million Catholic Americans I follow the identically glorious traditions of my country and my religion."[7]

A certain desire for conformity was at work here, quite apart from any feeling that after December 7, 1941, all Americans had to stand up. There were fears about the integration of Catholics into American society, especially after the controversy over Spain and neutrality. The *Western Catholic* of Quincy, Illinois, stressed that "there are no traitors among Catholics." Bishop Francis Keough of Providence emphasized that patriotism held an honorable place in Catholic teaching. All of this seemed understandable, but Catholics might have put some qualifications on their commitment; to identify God with any nation was a heresy in doctrine. Yet one searches in vain during the days following Pearl Harbor for reservations voiced by the bishops.[8]

The closest thing to dissent came from the Catholic Worker Movement in New York City, hardly representative of the American church. In New York, on January 2, 1942, Dorothy Day wrote an editorial reaffirming pacifism. The members of the Catholic Worker Movement would not enter the military, make munitions, or buy government bonds. In Chicago, the student newspaper at DePaul University editorialized that although we might fight, we must reject hate. The editor would have none of the idea that soldiering for the United States amounted to missionary work. Thomas Maguire, editor of the *Sign*, wrote in January 1942 that Catholics must not lose their moral faculties in this war no matter how just it appeared.[9]

These voices were lost in the storm of enthusiasm for the war effort. A high point came in early 1942 when the Vatican became an instrument for lining up American Catholics behind Roosevelt. Apostolic Delegate Cicognani traveled across the country speaking privately with those bishops most noted for their anti-administration views. He told Archbishop Beckman of Dubuque, Bishop Ryan of Fort Wayne, Archbishop Curley of Baltimore, and Bishop Shaughnessy of Seattle that the Holy See would frown upon public statements which would "create disunity in the United States and . . . lessen in any way popular support of the policies of the administration."[10]

Even without Vatican guidance, American Catholic leaders had concluded that World War II satisfied the criteria for a just war in accordance with the definition of that concept in Catholic theology. The problem was whether a modern war, with its unprecedented destruction, could be evaluated by traditional morality. Before Pearl Harbor, a few American bishops had denounced the blockade employed by the British as an immoral action not justifiable by theology.[11] Other Catholics had disagreed. What was Catholic doctrine toward total war? As early as December 1939, the Catholic philosopher Jacques Maritain, fearing the conquest of France, wrote that the struggle against Hitler was a fight to "prevent the world's being enslaved." While Maritain drew the line at calling the war holy because of its temporal character, he did think that it was just and that the Allies could "count upon the help of God." The Allied cause derived its justice from the fact that these nations had entered the war to defend themselves against Nazi aggression.[12]

The same reasoning could now apply to the United States. Bishop Francis C. Kelley of Oklahoma City said there could be "no question as to the justice of this war of defense." Father Dillon of Providence College announced that the United States "is fighting a just war" and hoped that "there are no conscientious objectors among you who would shirk your duty believing this war to be unjust." Father Robert I. Gannon of Fordham University publicly admitted that he had been wrong and Roosevelt correct in promoting intervention. Archbishop Philip G. Scher of Monterey-Fresno explained to his people that after applying the test of Catholic dogma, he had concluded that the war was just and that one must render to Caesar the things that are Caesar's. Even after the enthusiasm of Pearl Harbor had been tempered by time, Catholic theologians defended the justice of the war. When in July 1944 a Catholic writer wondered how we could consider the war just when the United States was aiding Russia, fighting Catholics in Germany and Italy, and even bombing the Vatican, the editor of the *Sign* answered that the war was just because America had been attacked and was defending itself. Citing *Principles of Ethics*, a textbook by Dom Thomas Moore, the editor quoted: "A citizen owes his state support in time of war. The judgment as to whether or not war is to be declared must rest with those in authority. . . . A citizen should so far acquiesce in the judgment of the government as to place his financial aid and personal services at the disposal of the government." Using such a strategy, the Catholics in Germany could accept the justice of their cause with the same serenity of conscience that American Catholics adopted for their cause.[13] The few American Catholics who renounced all use of force and became conscientious objectors found comfort in an Association of Catholic Conscientious Objectors sponsored by the Catholic Worker Movement.[14]

American Catholics concluded that they were engaged in a just war, but problems emerged when they sought to go beyond this moral prescription to discuss issues of the war, the ethics of combatants, and the objects, tactics, and strategy of the conflict. It did not follow that because the United States had entered the war in a morally legitimate fashion everything about the war was legitimate. "A Nation may win a war and lose its soul," wrote the editor of *America*.[15] The way Catholic leaders adopted the dubious garb of moral cheerleaders for the United States, however, led to an atrophy of their ethical feelings.

President Roosevelt may have given American Catholics more leader-ship in this moral interpretation of the war than he realized. The president expressed an elevated ethic about the war. His idealism came across to an ear attuned to spiritual resonances. He became the moral leader of the nation by stressing the spiritual dimension of the Allied cause as expressed in the Atlantic Charter. Even before Pearl Harbor, the president also had tried to explain the threat of Hitler to the Christian religion. Elmer Murphy of the *NCWC News Service* joined with other Catholics to praise the deep spiritual understanding that Roosevelt brought to foreign policy. The declaration by the United Nations on January 1, 1942, was a case in point, as it reaffirmed the principles of the Atlantic Charter, including the idea of religious freedom. Roosevelt himself took credit for convincing Lit-vinoff, the Soviet delegate, to accept this idea. The president recalled the criticism he had received earlier by omitting such a principle in his con-ference with Churchill at Argentia Bay. When he set aside New Year's Day, 1943, as a National Day of Prayer, Roosevelt called upon all churches to sponsor a week of meditation: "Without spiritual armor we cannot hope to win this war . . . cannot be worthy of victory." Against the "new order" of Hitler, the president proposed a greater concept, the "moral order." The United Nations fought for freedom of speech and freedom of religion for all men. The Atlantic Charter and the Four Freedoms, while disclaim-ing territorial ambitions by the Allies, projected a reeducation of the world along the lines of Western morality and Judaeo-Christian principles. As the president wrote to the National Conference of Christians and Jews, the United States fought for the right of men "to live together as members of one family rather than as masters and slaves. It is our promise to extend such brotherhood earthwide which gives hope to all the world." Vice-presi-dent Wallace also contributed to a spiritual concept of the war by announc-ing to the American Free World Association at their annual banquet in New York on May 8, 1942, "The people's revolution is on the march, and the devil and all his angels cannot prevail against it. They cannot prevail for on the side of the people is the Lord." As Roosevelt had promised Catho-lics a peace based on the spirit of Christ in 1941, in 1943 he promised that the Sermon on the Mount would guide the Allied cause.[16]

When Allied troops massed to invade Europe, the Association of Army and Navy Wives requested that all places of public worship remain open. As the invasion unfolded, President Roosevelt went on radio and led the nation in the following prayer: "Almighty God—Our Sons . . . have this day set forth upon a mighty endeavor, a struggle to preserve our Republic, *our religion*, [my emphasis], and our civilization and to set free a suffering humanity. Lead them straight and true, give strength to their arms."[17]

Catholic leaders eagerly sought to help their political leaders rise above mere diplomatic and social categories in dealing with the war. They erected an elaborate syllogism concerning the spiritual destiny of the United States. One of the propositions in this argument concerned the character of the enemy. After seeing Hitler attack neighbors and articulate bizarre notions of race and culture, few Americans would have denied that the German revolution threatened Western civilization. Archbishop Rummel of New Orleans warned that German totalitarianism threatened to wipe out 2,000 years of Christian culture. The pagan dimension to National Socialism impressed American Catholics even though the church in Germany continued an uneasy existence under Hitler. But it became a short step from considering the political order of the new Germany a threat to Christianity to seeing the entire war as a morality play. A glance at European history, however, would have provided many examples of political systems which had attacked the church and many examples of self-serving definitions of civilization. The existence of an aggressive, anti-Christian, revolutionary political group in Germany could be explained in traditional historical terms. But American Catholics accepted the antihistorical explanation which had been stated so simply by Jacques Maritain: Hitler was really the "anti-Christ." Monsignor Fulton Sheen, a leading Catholic publicist, repeated this theme by insisting that the United States fought, not against Germany, but against the spirit of the anti-Christ, a kind of devil.[18]

A second proposition in the moral syllogism of war used by American Catholics came close to identifying the United States with the "City of God." Ever since John Winthrop and the Puritans had spoken of a "City on a Hill," America had been identified with providential purpose. In 1884 the Catholic bishops at the Third Plenary Conference who affirmed the inspirational character of the Founding Fathers had acted in this tradition. No one should have been surprised during World War II to hear leading Catholic spokesmen identify the nation with the Godhead. Archbishop John J. Mitty explained that the Founding Fathers were all implicit Roman Catholics. His reasoning echoed that of such bishops as John M. Gannon and Joseph M. Gilmore, who stressed the religious character of American democracy. Forgetting that the church taught the moral neutralism of political forms, these men insisted, in Gannon's words, that "democracy is the nearest thing to God on earth . . . as a form of life and government. Democracy is primarily a philosophy of life. It is something social, moral, spiritual; only secondarily is democracy an instrument of government. . . . In its purity democracy really was established by God." Archbishop Spellman of New York told Catholics coast to coast on national radio in March 1942, "Our nation is like a house built upon a rock which is God." Roosevelt's Catholic secretary, William Hassett, deplored the neutralism of church leaders when the issue was "between the swastika and the cross of Christ."[19]

After the propositions that Hitler represented the devil and the United States represented God, the conclusion about the meaning of the war was not difficult. American Catholic spokesmen considered World War II a holy war. As Bishop Sheen expressed it, "This war is not merely a political and an economic struggle, but rather a theological one." Spellman told the troops he visited that they were "sacred instruments" in a modern crusade. "We of American today," announced the American bishops, "fight not only for human values, but also for those that are divine."[20] The joint statement of the American hierarchy of November 14, 1942, explained that the war was being fought between those seeking to enslave the world and the Allies who sought to keep the world free. *America* editorialized that the war was a "struggle between the established Christian order and the revolutionary order of Fascism, Nazism, and Marxism," apparently forgetful of the alliance with Russia.[21]

A more interesting concern is how this theological interpretation of events had spread so rapidly through American Catholicism. Roosevelt's leadership is important, but it should also be recalled that the bishops and their flocks had been trained to think in religious terms. Understanding diplomatic trends as revealing the hand of Providence did not seem strange to mentalities already disposed that way. Catholic exuberance over the nation's cause can also be explained by a sense of embarrassment over earlier isolationist leanings by certain church spokesmen. After having called for a rejection of Europe and for neutrality toward Spain, Catholics

now had to try to prove that they were as dedicated to the war as others.
The attack on Pearl Harbor made it easy for Catholics to adopt a theological interpretation. Hitler seemed to fit the demonic role. Traditional
Catholic teaching about the sanctity of state power helped propel Catholics into Roosevelt's moral consensus.[22]

While such a theology of war, adopted during 1942, could only lead
to disillusionment when later confronted with the reality of politics and
diplomacy, it served well at first. The theology had the positive effect of
releasing a tremendous amount of moral energy for the Allied cause.
Nothing encourages all-out effort so much as the belief that one's salva-
tion is at stake. Consider the impact of the announcement by Bishop
Charles E. Buddy of San Diego that "the Cross and the Flag are the
highest symbols of glory," and his hinting that a martyr's crown awaited
anyone killed in battle.[23] Just as important, the construction of a
theology of war helped to bring the various religious groups of the nation
together. Catholics, long concerned about their acceptance, could now
become active members of a new cultural religion which preached the
scripture of "praise the Lord and pass the ammunition." The crusade
against paganism became the function of Judaeo-Christian civilization.
Rabbi Hyman J. Schachtel of New York praised both the triumph of
Judaism and the triumph of Christ in his call for victory over the Nazi
evil. When Dr. W. E. Garrison of the University of Chicago published
The Year in Religion, 1942, he stressed that the war had brought the
different American faiths closer together. The December 1942 manifesto
by the Federal Council of Churches and the statement by American
Catholic bishops in November 1942 could have been written by the same
men.[24] After decades of interfaith bickering and bigotry, ecumenism was
born in the midst of World War II.

2

As the nation mobilized, most Catholic leaders wondered how they
could be of some aid in the crisis. Organizations and church leaders
answered the call to the colors in different ways. Many clergy joined the
Chaplain Corps to serve the estimated 31 percent of the army which was
Catholic. A National Catholic Community Service group headed by
Matthews of the Knights of Columbus helped the military care for men

in training camps. Catholic schools changed their curricula. Church cere-
monies were changed to conform with air raid schedules. Occasionally
a bishop, such as Buddy of San Diego, would lend a hand in getting
striking workers back on the job. Students and priests at one Jesuit college in Massachusetts helped harvest crops. Some clergymen enrolled in
the civil air patrol, served as air raid wardens, or operated farm tractors.
A few nuns provided good copy by serving as air raid wardens or glider
pilots. Organizations such as the Catholic Daughters of America and the
Knights of Columbus engaged in USO activities, bond drives, and blood
donation campaigns.[25]

All of these activities represented a practical demonstration of the
patriotism of American Catholics. To make sure that non-Catholics got
the point, church spokesmen repeated it. In the words of *Il Crociato*, a
newspaper published by the Italian clergy in Brooklyn, "we are loyal to
God, Church and country." Catholic soldiers, said Archbishop John
Cantwell of Los Angeles, were "writing a new and glorious chapter in the
records of Catholic loyalty and service." The bishops never tired of emphasizing that patriotism was a virtue in Catholic teaching. In a sense,
Catholic spokesmen considered these manifestations of patriotism as
insurance against any future campaign of bigotry toward the church.
Reverend Thomas T. McAvoy remained convinced that groups were
already working to discredit Catholics as profascist. For these reasons
and others he felt that "Catholics must be zealous for their country's
victory." Similarly, the work of Archbishop Spellman and other chaplains
did more than save souls of military men; it immunized them from future
anti-Catholic bigotry.[26]

Such zeal led Catholics to reject compromise and insist upon conformity. If the war was felt to be the apocalypse, temporizing with the
enemy became worse than treason. Total victory seemed necessary. As
the editor of *Ave Maria* quoted a contributor, "If we are not fighting
for our Christian civilization, then the war is not worth fighting at all."
Unrealistic expectations about the peace which would be won emerged.
As one naval chaplain declared, "This is not a war to defend the American
way of life, it is a war to extend the American way of life . . . to the
peoples of the world." The bishops of the United States issued a statement
on "Victory and Peace" in November 1942. After reiterating the theology
of war, they announced that "this conflict of principles makes compro-

mise impossible." Some of the delusions and disappointments of the post-war period were forged in this theology of war.[27]

By approaching war in the manner of a crusade, Catholics created disturbing pressures for conformity. All wars generate such pressure, but when the war assumes a theological dimension, another reason for rooting out heresy is created. To some, it seemed obvious that a war being fought to realize world democracy and Judaeo-Christian principles required a reaffirmation of those principles at home. Reverend James Gillis challenged the United States to live up to the notion of the war as a crusade by cleaning out the domestic life of the nation. He suggested beginning by firing all atheists who held positions as teachers in colleges. The theology of war could easily turn into a witch hunt if expectations remained unfulfilled, as postwar America learned with the appearance of Senator Joe McCarthy.[28]

To set an example, Catholics themselves began to clean house; one of the first casualties was isolationism. Even Father John Ryan, who prided himself on his membership in the American Civil Liberties Union, urged that the government suspend mailing privileges for Catholic isolationist publications such as Father Coughlin's *Social Justice*, Patrick Scanlan's *Brooklyn Tablet*, and Reverend James Gillis's *Catholic World*. Editors of old isolationist magazines and papers argued that their position before Pearl Harbor had validity, but more Catholics listened to such men as M. R. P. McGuire, president of the Catholic Historical Association, who in January 1943 announced to the annual meeting of the association that "it is our moral duty as historians to do all in our power to prevent isolationism from again ruining our efforts to establish a new and better world order." He wondered how "an isolationism almost psychopathic in character all but defeated our effective preparations for war." Bishop Lucey, a leading interventionist before Pearl Harbor, wrote that "enemies of human solidarity in this country await only the end of hostilities to preach again their strange gospel that America does not belong to the family of nations and that our people do not belong to the human race." Dr. Francis E. McMahon, president of the CAIP, predicted that unless the United States rejected isolationism, another conflict would follow. Despite this commentary, Catholics were still suspect in liberal circles. When in November 1943 the American bishops issued a statement entitled "The Essentials of a Good Peace," they expressed misgivings at trends in United States diplomacy. Immediately Max Lerner, writing in *P.M.*, associated the bishops with the outlook of William Randolph Hearst and Senator Burton Wheeler. Benjamin Masse, writing in *America*, denounced Lerner for ignoring Catholic teaching and papal peace plans which were internationalist in scope. When the bishops made their statement on world peace in 1945, they explicitly rejected isolationism as an answer to the problems of American foreign policy.[29]

Catholic spokesmen were in the van of those who warned against allowing the war to make fundamental changes in the domestic social order. Mrs. J. W. McCollum of the National Council of Catholic Women emphasized that its members should work to keep life as normal and traditional as possible. Thoughts that mobilization might upset the family structure caused men such as Monsignor Ready of the NCWC to preach alertness lest Christian social principles be undermined. The American hierarchy's statements during the war warned against dangers to family life arising from permitting mothers to work in industry and from drafting 18-year-olds. The bishops came out against the universal military training bill of November 1944 precisely because they feared the social implications of such a policy. Victory abroad should not be at the expense of repudiating the very Judaeo-Christian social order which gave sanctification to the war.[30]

3

Not satisfied with Apostolic Delegate Cicognani's traveling across the United States converting erstwhile isolationist bishops, American Catholic leaders also worked to have the Vatican conform by cooperating with Roosevelt's diplomacy. Presidential astuteness played a role here. While seeking to overcome American Catholic isolationism, the president had enlisted Vatican support. Now he sought aid from committed American bishops to overcome the neutrality of the Holy See. All during World War II Roosevelt tried to identify the Allied cause with the prestige of the papacy.

Papal neutrality could be embarrassing, as Roosevelt discovered soon after the United States entered the war. In March 1942 the Holy See formally established relations, for the first time, with the Imperial Government of Japan. Coming so soon after the attack at Pearl Harbor, this decision seemed an affront to the United States. Actually, talks between the Vatican and Japan had been going on since early 1922 and the Vatican had spiritual motives behind its move. The pope expected some American criticism, and Monsignor Vonuzzi, assistant to Apostolic Delegate Cicognani, had warned Sumner Welles that formal diplomatic ties between Japan and the Holy See were pending. Not surprisingly, both Roosevelt and Churchill considered this recognition of Japan a triumph for German diplomacy. Harold Tittmann, at the Vatican, lodged a protest; Assistant Secretary of State Welles reported to American clerics that Roosevelt was stunned by the pope's move. Cicognani responded by meeting Welles in March 1942 to assure him that no anti-American sentiment was intended. Actually, Cicognani agreed with Welles that the move was ill-timed. Bishop Hurley of Florida and Monsignor Ready of the NCWC both said that they were "horrified." They offered their services to the Department of State to prevent any recurrence of anti-American diplomacy at the Vatican. Ready urged Roosevelt to convery his personal bitterness to Archbishop Spellman. In his letter to Spellman, Roosevelt dismissed the Vatican excuse that negotiations had been going on for some time. "The fact remains," the president complained, "that the dilemma should not have been created in the first place." Promising official silence, he added, "my heart is torn because it is bound to get out and there will be definitely a bad reaction." Roosevelt proved right in an ironic way as the affair made American church leaders more willing to assist the administration. They were deeply embarrassed when, at the Vatican on April 2, the pope presented a medal to the Japanese Foreign Minister, Yosuke Matsuoka.[31]

This incident helped convince Roosevelt and the leaders of American Catholicism that a diplomatic offensive should be launched to prevent the pope from becoming a pawn of the enemy. The British recalled that after the fall of France in 1940, a Vatican peace offensive had been prevented only through the strenuous objections of Cardinal Primate Hinsley.[32] To prevent recurrences of such interference, Roosevelt decided to have Myron C. Taylor, who had just recovered from surgery, return to Rome. Before departing in September 1942, Taylor met with such Catholic leaders as Ready, Cicognani, Spellman, and Mooney. With advice from the president and the Department of State, they drafted an elaborate memorandum outlining the aims and objectives of the

United States in the war; Taylor was to use this information in discussions with the pope. After stopovers in England and Spain, Taylor arrived in enemy territory on September 19 and received an Italian escort to the neutral territory of the Vatican.[33]

During his stay of nine days in Rome, Taylor held three private meetings with the pope, each lasting close to an hour, and spoke with other Vatican diplomats such as Maglione, Montini, and Tardini. Apparently Roosevelt and American Catholics hoped to obtain the following concessions: they wanted the pope to condemn publicly the atrocities and aggressions of the Axis, thereby giving moral sanction to Allied arms; they hoped to use the pope to convince the Italian government to break with Mussolini and Hitler; Roosevelt sought to prevent the pope from sponsoring premature negotiations on the basis of a compromise peace with Hitler; Taylor had the additional tasks of convincing the Vatican that postwar plans for peace required an understanding with the Soviet Union and quieting Vatican fears of communism. Finally, Roosevelt hoped to have the pope cooperate in Allied plans for the postwar world, including a United Nations organization.[34]

Taylor, when the pope admitted him to his first audience, launched his campaign to enlist the Holy See in the Allied cause. He emphasized the support that American Catholics were giving President Roosevelt. The American government felt that Pope Pius XI's condemnation of the Nazis and Pope Pius XII's peace plan had now become part of the objectives of the Western alliance. Taylor said that the United States was fighting "against the very things which the Popes condemned," and "our conviction of complete victory is one with our confidence in the unwavering tenacity with which the Holy See will continue its magnificent moral leading."[35] He warned the pope not to play into enemy hands by endorsing any compromise peace. Allied intelligence expected the Germans to approach the Vatican as a means of escaping "the inexorable results of defeat in the field." Months before Roosevelt met with Churchill at Casablanca, an American diplomat at the Vatican was saying that the United States would not accept anything less than unconditional surrender. Taylor felt sure his warnings would have weight at the Vatican. The United States was fighting to obtain goals endorsed by the pope, as anyone who read the Atlantic Charter could see. Taylor likewise felt that "due weight will be given to . . . a nation which numbers among its citizens so many millions of devout Catholics and whose government is in such close agreement with principles enunciated by the Holy See."[36]

As his plane left Rome, Taylor thought he had succeeded in neutralizing Vatican diplomacy. The pope had told him that the loyalty of American Catholics was gratifying and that the mutual trust of the president and American bishops, something Taylor had stressed, was a source of satisfaction. More important, Pope Pius had announced that while he hoped for a peace which would take into consideration the "vital needs of all nations," he did not believe in peace at any price. "Despite what any propaganda may say to the contrary," he wrote, "we have never thought in terms of a peace by compromise at any cost." He insisted that no amount of outside pressure would cause him to deviate from his position. He had promised to reject any peace which "gives free rein to those who would undermine . . . the foundations of Christianity and persecute religion and the Church." Looking over Taylor's report later on, J. W. Jones of the European Division of the Department of State wrote that the pope's statement was friendly "and for the Vatican, even enthusiastic."[37]

Only once did a breakdown in this neutralization of Vatican diplomacy threaten, on June 2, 1944, as Allied troops moved into Rome. Elsewhere, the Allies were making ready for the invasion of Europe. The pope issued a statement calling for a moderation of demands and conditions for peace. He affirmed Vatican neutrality, deplored the tendency to blame an entire people for war, and regretted the absence of alternatives between total victory and defeat. Many Americans resented what they felt was an attempt to help Hitler at this time. A Jesuit priest and Vatican expert in the United States, Father Robert A. Graham, hastily wrote to Americans that the pope had not deserted the Allied cause. Graham felt that the pope's speech did not represent anything novel. The pope had called for a just peace in September 1939, September 1943, and at other times. His idea of justice, wrote Graham, did not mean peace at any price. The pope would never approve a peace which permitted Hitler to retain his stolen possessions or allowed him to remain in control of Germany. Neither would he allow war criminals to go unpunished or prevent measures to ensure that Germany did not march again. But did not these qualifications add up to the doctrine of unconditional surrender, something the pope seemed to want modified? Perhaps

Graham's evaluation was accurate, however. When Taylor revisited the pope in February 1945, they discussed chances for a German surrender. The pope said that Germany fought on with the hope of obtaining terms less than unconditional surrender. He seemed to agree that modification of Allied terms was an impossible requirement. Taylor left Vatican City convinced that the pope had approved the Allied policy of unconditional surrender, even as the Russian army was moving across Catholic Poland.[38] A more likely interpretation is that the pope realized that there was no hope of having Roosevelt and Churchill accept less than unconditional surrender and so Pius accepted the inevitable even though he did not like it.

Taylor was accredited to the Vatican throughout the war and made several trips there in the course of which he invariably consulted with the pope. But one must conclude that his mission, which after the war resulted in a book and some considerable public attention, was hardly a major triumph for the Allies. There seems little evidence that the Vatican had much to do with the downfall of Mussolini's government. Similarly, the Vatican failed to satisfy Allied demands for public condemnation of German atrocities. Despite consistent pressure from Tittmann, Taylor, and the British ambassador at the Vatican, the pope never issued an unequivocal condemnation of the Germans. The Vatican, like the Allies, knew of the deportation and executions of Jews and Slavs in occupied nations. Cardinal Maglione always replied to such requests by asserting that the pope had spoken out on many occasions and was working hard to care for refugees, especially Jewish refugees. He felt that it was impossible for the pope to descend "to particulars" because it would get him into politics. (The arguments on this issue have continued to the present day.) The Allies wanted a public statement from the pope in addition to good works. This insistence makes one wonder if the main concern of the Allies in this case was with the fate of the Jews or more with the propaganda value which would accrue from having the pope publicly condemn the Nazis.[39]

Another area in which Vatican-United States cooperation proved ill-fated involved the future of the United Nations. At the outset, Roosevelt had every reason to encourage papal endorsement of the goals of the Atlantic Charter, including an association of nations. The pope became enthusiastic about the concept of a United Nations through conversations with Taylor. Then Taylor had to reverse himself and discourage discussion because the Department of State feared that the Vatican might join the United Nations. Maglione had made such an approach to Taylor. Secretary of State Hull pointed out that the great powers, including the Soviet Union, would have to approve all membership. He predicted that the question would "be likely to raise political controversy in the United States." When the pope brought up the question of Vatican membership in a private audience in October 1944, Taylor put him off. Later, Taylor and Archbishop Spellman both sought to discourage the pope from bringing the Vatican into the United Nations.[40] Unconditional surrender remained the only area of Vatican-United States collaboration, and even in this case the pope seemed to be merely accepting a *fait accompli* rather than endorsing and promoting the Allied terms.

4

Roosevelt's minor victory in having the Vatican agree to unconditional surrender came because he enjoyed the full support of American Catholics. Why did these Catholics become so committed to a principle which had little basis in church teaching and served to minimize the moral role of the papacy during the war? The idea of unconditional surrender grew out of the idealism in America's entry into the war. Incapable of projecting a war for such reasons as the restoration of the balance of power, the president and people sought more noble objectives. Although more sober in their attitude than the generation of 1917, the Americans of 1941 could not resist making a crusade out of their involvement and erecting a theology to defend it. A few days after Roosevelt announced the doctrine of unconditional surrender at Casablanca, Monsignor Sheen expressed a desire for the eradication of Nazism, fascism, and communism. William Agar, a leading interventionist who had worked to break down Catholic isolationism, wrote in *Commonweal* that victory was essential because Judaeo-Christian civilization was at stake. American bishops who had helped Taylor draft his statement for the pope in September 1942 reflected this commitment. As Taylor had told the pope: "Our moral position is impregnable, we are not open to the compromise usual to those who look for merely material gains. . . . We think anything less than unconditional victory will endanger principles we fight for and our very existence as a nation." C. G. Pauling in *Common-weal* condemned attempts to deal with such fascists as Admiral Darlan because "this war is more than a war between armies."[41] Roosevelt's press release at Casablanca seemed a reiteration of the obvious. Arch-bishop Spellman informed the president when he returned to Washington that he was one of the "Great men of history." Elmer Murphy of the *NCWC News Service* wrote that the Casablanca declaration had ratified the spiritual foundation of the war because Roosevelt had brought the ethical dimension clearly into focus.[42]

American Catholic exuberance for unconditional surrender repre-sented the culmination of their march into the Roosevelt foreign policy consensus. The march began before Pearl Harbor and now reached a high point with endorsement of the war as a moral crusade for Judaeo-Christian principles, with no compromise possible. But such a commit-ment could not last even under a masterful consensus politician such as Roosevelt. American Catholics eventually began reconsidering their com-mitment to unconditional surrender because it involved an unacceptable revolution of the social order. Some liberals within the Roosevelt adminis-tration, especially in the Office of War Information, took seriously the talk of the war against fascism and for democracy. Max Lerner, Henry Morgenthau, and Eleanor Roosevelt were committed to the democratiza-tion of Europe as part of the United States war aims. They distrusted Catholic influence. Despite the public assertion of Frances E. McMahon, president of the CAIP, that 99 percent of American Catholics favored unconditional surrender and that they had changed their mind about Franco, doubts lingered among liberals. Had not McMahon himself been fired from his post at Notre Dame for being too outspoken? Eleanor Roosevelt constantly reminded the president that the pope had been pro-Franco and that such Catholic diplomats as Robert D. Murphy and Department of State officials like James Dunn could not be counted on to promote unconditional surrender if it meant overthrowing the old regimes in Europe. Although Roosevelt came to the defense of the pope's wartime diplomacy, he could not deny the problems involved in using the war as a means of restructuring Europe. There is little evidence, however, that his commitment to such a goal approached that of his wife.[43]

Catholics had serious second thoughts about any attempt to democ-ratize Europe. The imposition of American political forms on the world would require social changes. To the dismay of many American Catholics, the revolution for democracy often had anticlerical tones. Frequently, the issue of anticlericalism was confused with anti-Italian feelings. As the British swept through North Africa in 1943, they began a campaign to remove Italian and German clergy. Archbishop Spellman protested these moves to Roosevelt, who took the issue up with Churchill at Teheran. As American and British armies invaded Italy, the Knights of Columbus passed resolutions that "the control of administering the affairs of Italy be retained and placed in the keeping of Roman Catholics in proportion to the Roman Catholic population of Italy."[44]

Catholics became increasingly embarrassed by the talk of revenge. Some publicists asserted that the German people were responsible for the war and must be made to pay. Secretary of the Treasury Henry Morgenthau recommended that Germany be turned into an agricultural area. Catholics began to have doubts. They criticized Morgenthau's approach on two grounds: it rested upon the erroneous idea of national war guilt and it made impossible the realization of the papal plan for a just peace. Quoting Edmund Burke about the impossibility of indicting an entire people, Catholic writers emphasized that the German people had been as much victims of Hitler as supporters of his cause. Some two million German citizens had been imprisoned by the Nazis. Morgenthau's plan had the added drawback of being a direct violation of the Atlantic Charter. Instead of revenge, justice should be sought. Spellman even thought he saw a stiffening of German resistance due to the demand for unconditional surrender. He approached Roosevelt with these worries and received assurances that the Allies did not seek to destroy the German nation.[45]

The administrative board of the NCWC had set up a committee under Archbishop Samuel Stritch of Chicago to promote a papal plan for peace. Pope Pius had issued a set of principles in 1940 and revised them in 1941. Stritch emphasized that according to papal principles, Morgenthau's plan was anti-Christian. Repeatedly, the pope had emphasized that every historic nation has juridical and inherent rights of sovereignty and independence which should be guaranteed by the peace. The papal plan called for a program of disarmament, an international peacekeeping organization, and universal recognition that the needs of one nation can never justify the destruction of another. If all nations would only accept the principles of the natural law, conflict could be avoided. As early as 1943, American church leaders, following this papal program, rejected the concept of demanding retribution from defeated nations. A. J. App, an American professor, argued persuasively in the *Catholic World* that the United States was failing to live up to papal principles. Both the pope and the Committee on Ethics of the CAIP taught that the United States could not continue the war any longer than was necessary to recover its rights. The church could not support a diplomacy of total victory at any price. It was unethical to avoid telling the enemy the terms for peace. According to App, Pope Pius had repeatedly made public his objections to a dictated peace doctrine, although not denouncing the Allied doctrine of unconditional surrender.[46]

Catholics opposed plans to punish all Germans; they did not protest punishment of war criminals. The *Commonweal* recalled that after 1918 Germany had acquitted everyone involved in the war. The establishment of an International Tribunal of Justice drew endorsement from the liberal Father John Ryan, who felt that the good of all nations would be served by forcing the war criminals "to expiate their crimes, according to the canons of retributive justice." It was reasoned that obedience to orders did not absolve a man from personal responsibility for his actions, especially such acts as mass execution of civilians.[47]

The military tactics of total war also helped American Catholics cast off the vision that they were involved in a crusade. Nowhere did modern war challenge ethics more clearly than in the matter of aerial bombing. By the time the United States became involved in bombing raids, there were arguments to deal with the problem of civilian deaths. Some American journalists bluntly pointed out that in a modern industrial war the distinction between civilian and soldier had disappeared. Most Americans agreed that the factory worker was as vital to the war as the soldier. Other observers lamented civil casualties but argued that accidents were unavoidable. General Hap Arnold, commander of the Army Air Force, defended the bombing of enemy cities on the grounds that the Germans had started the practice and said Americans must not be squeamish about civilian deaths. Officially, the president in 1939 had appealed to all belligerents to avoid bombing civilian areas. But he, like the British, became caught up in the dynamics of modern war, which made unrealistic distinctions between military and civilian targets. By August 1941 Roosevelt was complaining to Morgenthau that the British could beat Germany by following the president's advice. He recommended that, when the British sent a large aerial force to bomb military objectives, ten planes "should bomb some of these smaller towns that have never been bombed before." From his own bicycle tours of Germany, Roosevelt knew these towns well and guessed that each of them must have "some kind of factory." Morgenthau replied with unintentional irony, in light of the night bombing practiced by the English, "At least you have got to hand it to the British that they stick to their ethical methods of warfare."[48] The dynamics of warfare would soon lead inexorably to the fire-bomb raids of General Curtis E. Lemay and later to the atomic bomb.

As the war intensified, civilian opposition to such bombing disappeared. In March 1944 when 28 clergymen and writers issued a public protest to the obliteration bombing of German cities, they were met with scorn. Many newspaper editors gratuitously asserted that these 28 men had not been heard from when the Germans bombed Warsaw, Belgrade, and Coventry. Undersecretary of War Robert Patterson denounced the clergymen for giving comfort to the enemy. Such criticism of American war strategy would merely encourage the Germans to expect a soft war.[49]

In the beginning of the war few foresaw such a military development. Everyone seemed satisfied with the decisions to be careful and to warn non combatants. Catholic thinkers admitted that as the methods of warfare evolved so must moral principles. The submarine and the airplane had made old rules of war obsolete. Lawrence L. McReavy wrote in *Clergy Review* in 1941 that the modern economy made most noncombatants partners and targets in the war. Others adopted the rationale of double effect: Catholic ethics provided that one could permit an evil consequence if the same action produced primarily a good consequence. In the case of bombing, the good effect was the destruction of the enemy's war potential and the evil effect was the destruction of civilians. Since the killing of civilians was not directly willed in the bombing and did not have to occur to fulfill the good intention, bombing remained morally legitimate.[50]

This moral position regarding bombing was summed up in a direct appeal to President Roosevelt in September 1942 wherein Pope Pius pleaded for the warring nations to avoid aerial bombardment of civilian areas. If such attacks must continue, he urged, let them with "all possible care be directed only against objectives of military value." American Catholic spokesmen insisted that the means taken to destroy a target should be kept to a minimum of force; if secondary destruction of civilians became intolerable, officials should consider making the locality an open city. The American bishops seemed satisfied that the Roosevelt administration was following these canons. But by the summer of 1944 many Americans began having second thoughts. When the leading churchmen of France appealed to American Catholics to prevent Allied bombs from killing civilians, the bishops replied that they had always urged avoiding civilian destruction and that they had "assurances" from civil and military leaders that every precaution was being taken. Establishment of an American "Commission for the Protection and Salvage of Artistic and Historic Monuments in Europe" convinced many Catholics that their leaders were scrupulous men. Many applauded when the Cathedral of Cologne, a gothic masterpiece, survived an extensive Allied bombing raid. One Catholic pacifist, however, pointed out that the other buildings and houses in the city were totally destroyed.[51]

A few bombing raids had special meaning for American Catholics. The first case involved the bombing of Rome during the Italian campaign of 1943. No sooner had Mussolini brought Italy into the war than the pope became worried about the vulnerability of Vatican City and of Rome. The British made public their intention of retaliating for attacks on London with raids on Rome. These threats remained in force even though Taylor, during his trip to Vatican City in late 1942, sought to prevent a clash between the pope and the Allies. Churchill admitted the sensitivity of bombing the Vatican but refused to make any public commitment because of the inaccuracy of night bombing. Faced with this refusal, the pope turned to Roosevelt. Cicognani approached Assistant Secretary of State Adolf A. Berle about sanctuary for Rome in December 1942; the pope wrote Roosevelt in May 1943. Publicly, the president replied that the Allies would observe Vatican neutrality and continue to avoid needless destruction. Privately, he wrote Cicognani that, while remembering the city's value, "we must recognize that Rome is the center of the Italian government and is of definite use to that government in conducting the war against us." He suggested that the Vatican seek to have Rome declared an open city. Hull objected to the idea because he did not feel that the pope could guarantee it. He feared that protracted negotiations over the issue would interfere with the Allied advance. The British also objected to such a proposal. Roosevelt eventually wrote Cicognani about the Italian government's aggression against its neighbors for twenty years. The president would honor his commitment to the pope about the Vatican but, "should the conduct of the war require it, recognized military objectives in and around Rome cannot be ignored."[52]

Here the matter stood until July 20, 1943, when Allied bombs first fell on the Eternal City. Despite every precaution, including detailed briefings for pilots, a few bombs landed on the Basilica of San Lorenzo, one of the seven major churches of the city. In the course of the Italian campaign, a few more churches were destroyed, including the famed Monte Cassino monastery.[53] The pope sought to moderate these attacks. He publicly lamented the destruction without placing the entire blame upon the Allies.

President Roosevelt was more sympathetic than the British but at the news conference in July 1943, he announced that more bombs would fall unless Rome was declared an open city. The Axis used the city to make ammunition and as a rail center. Roosevelt reminded reporters that hundreds of churches in Britain had been destroyed by the Germans—not that the president intended to pursue a policy of *quid pro quo*. Privately, he again worked toward the notion of an open city, discussing the matter with both General Marshall and Secretary of State Hull. By late August the Italian government had submitted such a proposal. But before the United States could respond, the German army had taken over northern Italy, including Rome. Hull still wanted to pursue the subject and submitted a draft for Roosevelt's consideration on the basis of the initial Italian plan. The plan had been revised because of objections by General Eisenhower. By December 1943 Roosevelt had a chance to discuss the matter with Churchill. They decided it would be "inadvisable to reopen the matter at this time."[54]

When bombs fell on Rome, American Catholics suffered a jolt in their commitment to the war as a crusade. Identification of God and country blurred when American bombers attacked the home of their spiritual leader. They could not accept the attitude of the secular press that because precautions had been taken, because Germans had attacked London, and because human lives were more valuable than relics, the Allies were justified in attacking the Eternal City. To many of them, the city of Rome and the Vatican were synonymous. After supporting the administration and preaching against any lessening of war spirit, the leaders of American Catholicism found it difficult to shift gears. Bishop O'Hara of Kansas City, Archbishop Edward A. Mooney, Bishop Joseph P. Hurley, and other defenders of the administration tended to blame the Italian government for refusing to accept the open city proposal and for using the Vatican as a hostage. Still, Hurley and Mooney both understood that the bombing of Rome had hurt the prestige of the Allies. Confidence in the justice of the Allied cause "has received a deep setback." Hurley even lamented that the bombing had destroyed the national consensus, strong words from a bishop who had been so firm in support of the Roosevelt administration. Mooney had helped create the moral consensus. Now he warned the Allies not to bomb Rome again or the idealism of their cause would be lost. Archbishops Mooney, Stritch, and Spellman met with Roosevelt on September 15, 1943, to discuss the tragedy. The president told them of his intention to approach the Germans with the open city proposal. Yet, this hope soon collapsed in the face of British opposition. Bombs continued to fall on Rome right up to the time Allied troops entered the city on June 2, 1944. General Mark W. Clark then set up his military headquarters in the city. On Washington's birthday in 1944, Spellman lamented that the United States had violated the principles for which it was fighting.[55]

The second bombing tactic which shocked American Catholics and made them doubt the moral superiority of the Allies occurred in August 1945. The atomic bombs dropped on Hiroshima and Nagasaki were the nuclear conclusion to the moral collaboration. Not everyone reacted the same way. Spellman casually wrote in his diary for August 7, 1945: "First atomic bomb fell on Hiroshima. Got inoculations and wrote for passport." A few Catholic sources reacted as expected. Dorothy Day of the *Catholic Worker* came out with a violent attack on Truman and the scientists who had designed the bomb. She felt sickened over the jubilation of the public at having incinerated Japanese. "Perhaps we will breathe their dust into our nostrils, feel them in the fog of New York on our faces, feel them in the rain on the hills of Easton." Reverend James Gillis felt that the United States had "struck the most powerful blow ever delivered against Christian civilization and the moral law." The bomb became a symbol of moral anarchy. *Catholic Mind* called Hiroshima the "original sin of mass destruction." No cause could be justified if it used such means. The editors of the *Commonweal* agreed that the bomb had tarnished the Allied victory and lamented the general lack of moral outrage over its use.[56]

On a more positive side, the bombing experiences of World War II played an important role in the development of Catholic ethics. In June 1942 the editor of *Ave Maria* probably expressed the sentiments of many Catholics when he wrote that he "would go to his death before he would give an order to bomb any city." Yet he admitted that if an Allied aviator asked spiritual advice, he would be told that he could obey orders to bomb a city provided it was a military objective or center of munitions production. The principle of double effect covered the situation; the death of civilians would be accidental. They had been warned to leave. Even the pope seemed to agree.[57]

But the increase of Allied strategic bombing, culminating in Hiroshima, had made such a distinction insecure. As early as 1943 the editors of the *Commonweal* and the *Catholic World* began to see that the notion of precise air raids hitting military targets had been discarded for saturation bombing. Even with the elaborate precautions taken for the bombing of Rome, some destruction of nonmilitary areas had occurred. Precision bombing was a myth.[58] Finally, in September 1944, Father John C. Ford wrote an elaborate ethical condemnation of saturation bombing which came very close to concluding that modern warfare must be condemned by the church. Ford's primary objective was to demonstrate that the principle of double effect could not excuse obliteration bombing. He felt that it was wrong to suggest that one could drop bombs on a city while inwardly withholding the direct intention of killing civilians. Civilian deaths flowed directly from the bombing act. "A man could not, even if he wanted to, avoid the direct willing of an evil effect so immediately consequent upon his action as this is." In the case of saturation bombing, the good effect of destroying military potential came about only as a result of destroying the city itself. The principle of double effect also required that some proper proportion exist between the evil permitted and the good willed. But in this case the evil was certain and widespread while the good came afterwards and appeared problematic.[59]

Ford's argument did not go unchallenged. Some pointed out that modern society made it impossible to distinguish between a civilian and a soldier. Ford replied by demonstrating that, by the American government's own definition of essential and nonessential war work, three-fourths of all citizens in such industrial areas as Boston and New York-New Jersey must be classified as noncombatants. Surely the same ratio applied in such cities as Berlin, Dresden, and Tokyo. Furthermore, it was not necessary to prove a clear dividing line between civilian and soldier in order to condemn saturation bombing. One merely needed to demonstrate that bombing large cities resulted in the death of many people who were clearly not combatants. Refined definitions of who is a soldier and who is not a soldier might be of some importance in a moral assessment of a tactical raid, but not in saturation bombing.[60] Some writers replied that Ford's essay simply proved the irrelevancy of traditional ethical categories in the face of modern war. In total war, enemy cities had to be bombed and one could not distinguish soldiers and civilians. Ford replied that changes in technology did not mean that the morality of the matter had been changed. If modern war could not be fought without the death of innocent civilians, then modern war could never be fought in a moral and just manner.[61]

5

Even if the Allied forces had consistently refrained from bombing civilians and adopted more morally acceptable tactics, other factors would have helped to erase the naive notion that the United States was engaged in a crusade. The wartime alliance with the Soviet Union presented moral difficulties for American Catholics and was even more decisive in turning them against Roosevelt. To appreciate the bitterness over this issue, one must recall the spirit of idealism which Catholics accepted as characteristic of Roosevelt's diplomacy. This spirit was cultivated by the administration. Roosevelt drew a picture of a brave new world. Taylor worked with the American bishops to draft their November 1942 statement "Victory and Peace," which applauded the administration.[62] Catholics accepted cooperation with the Soviet Union because Roosevelt presented the war as a means of redeeming Russia from communism as well as defeating the Axis. No matter what his private estimates, during the Lend-Lease debate the president even had intimated that United States cooperation with Russia would be a means whereby religion would be given a second chance in that land.

Roosevelt was sincere about bringing Russia into more friendly contact with the West. He was convinced that an enduring peace required such a relationship. But he realized that to achieve such a reconciliation it would be necessary to improve the Soviet image in the eyes of many Americans, especially Catholics.[63] This requirement led the president to promote a campaign of reconciliation between the Vatican and Russia. He felt sure that the key to American Catholic suspicions of Soviet Russia could be found in the Holy See. He knew that while Pope Pius might be willing to distinguish between the Russian people and communism, the pope had no illusions about who controlled whom. During the war, Roosevelt and the pope debated communism and the Soviet Union. While Roosevelt sought to break down Vatican suspicions about Russia, Pope Pius sought to dispel what he considered to be presidential illusions about communism. If Roosevelt played up the force of Russian nationalism, Pope Pius emphasized the importance of ideology. If Roosevelt sought to bring Stalin into a community of nations, Pope Pius strove to isolate communism and to prevent its penetration into a war-torn European economy.

All during the war the Vatican maintained a firm Russian policy. Even while muting American Catholic criticism of Lend-Lease, Cardinal Maglione in Rome had insisted that communism was not softening its opposition toward organized religion. Little changed after the United States became the partner of Russia and England. Taylor kept repeating Roosevelt's theme that Stalin had accepted the Four Freedoms and the Atlantic Charter, implying recognition of religious freedom. But before he departed for the United States after his visit in September 1942, he received a long memorandum by Monsignor Tardini which indicated that religious conditions in Russia were as bad as ever. Tardini named individuals who had been imprisoned or had just disappeared.[64]

Roosevelt in April 1943 joined the British in a written argument to mollify the Vatican anti-Soviet posture. The presentation was a rehash of what had been said before, together with a plea for realism. It took the Vatican almost a month to prepare an answer. Apparently Tardini drafted the memorandum and handed it to Harold Tittmann, and the British ambassador on May 30, 1943. The Vatican made the following points: Nazism and communism endangered Christianity because both were materialistic, totalitarian, militaristic, and atheistic; a German victory would lead to a Nazi-dominated Europe, but a Russian victory would have to be shared with the United States and England; an Allied victory would lead to communist control of Europe because England had no large land force and the United States would probably "return to her traditional isolationism." A victory for Russia would enhance communism, making it attractive to the many hungry people of Europe. To consolidate gains, the Soviet Union would remain armed while the democracies returned to business as usual. Tardini's memorandum predicted that people in the democracies would tire of sacrifice. The document concluded that only the disappearance of Nazism and communism would permit Europe to enjoy peace. As for evidence of Stalin's attitude toward religion, the vicious anti-Vatican campaign being conducted by communists in Italy made Roosevelt's optimism appear ill-founded.[65]

Such an interpretation could not be reconciled with the more benign view prevalent in Washington. But the unfolding of the war during 1944 and 1945 served to make the Vatican even more suspicious. On December 29, 1943, the pope spoke privately with Tittmann on the dangers of communist penetration into the Mediterranean and the Balkans. The pontiff thought that the Allies were giving Stalin too good an image, helping his prestige, and advancing communism. Tito's power in Yugoslavia was cited as an example of a trend which might envelop all Europe. As for hope of religious liberalization in Russia, the pope dismissed such illusionary notions. Tittmann appeared ineffective in attempts to explain the American policy of domesticating communism. In the United States Cicognani, the apostolic delegate, sent frequent reports to Secretary of State Hull of Soviet atrocities and attacks against religion in territories occupied by its advancing army. In December 1944 Taylor, recently returned to Rome, reported that the pope was gravely concerned over Yugoslavia, Greece, and Poland. The pope felt that Italy was next on the Marxists' list.[66]

At times, the American effort to better the opinion of the Soviet Union held by high Vatican officials seemed almost naive. The notion that a few written words, agreed to in the midst of a struggle for survival, might become the foundation for a complete reorientation of communist doctrine did not convince the Vatican. Tittmann, Hull, and Welles emphasized the Soviet commitment to the United Nations declaration and to the Atlantic Charter. Taylor and Tittmann continued to respond to Vatican evidence of actual religious persecution in Russia with verbal formulas. Taylor even submitted a proposed statement that he wanted Roosevelt to persuade Stalin to read: "Because of the loyal participation in the defense of the Fatherland by all Russian people under the direction of the constituted authority in the State, the Soviet Government, by interpreting and applying Article 124 of the USSR Constitution publicly proclaims complete freedom of religion, including freedom of worship in all Soviet territory. Any abuse of these privileges, either to organize movements or incite the people toward the overthrow of the Government, will be dealt with in each individual case according to the law." This bizarre suggestion met opposition from both the Vatican and the White House. Vatican officials objected to the final clause in the statement as an invitation to continue persecution. The pope wanted an understanding based on examples and an end to Soviet persecution of the church in the Baltic regions. Roosevelt replied that while he had thought about getting such public assurances from Russia, he had "reached the reluctant conclusion that at this particular moment it would be unwise to raise the issue openly." He feared that Stalin's sensitivity to this question would make it a dangerous one to inject into the discussion then in progress at Dumbarton Oaks on the future United Nations organization. Roosevelt instead suggested that the United States continue "to exert our influence quietly and constantly . . . to use our good offices whenever possible in practical tests of Soviet respect for that principle."[67]

Taylor and Tittmann went on seeking practical examples of increased Soviet liberalism toward religion all during the war. Tittmann reported that the Vatican might be open to receiving a Soviet delegation. When Welles investigated, he found that he was "unable to assure [Tittmann] of a similar interest in such a proposal on the part of the Soviet Government." Taylor appealed to the Department of State for information to help "clarify general doubt regarding religious freedom in Russia." Assistant Secretary Berle could only repeat the old story of how Harriman had sought to change Soviet religious policy as a preliminary to Lend-Lease. Berle reported that there "have been no subsequent developments." The two sides could not even agree to cooperate on humanitarian affairs. The pope hoped to establish an information exchange service for families of prisoners of war. Such a program was established and the United States cooperated. Despite the best efforts of Welles and others, however, the

Soviet Union consistently rejected such a program. Molotov reportedly "brusquely threw it aside saying he did not desire information on Russian prisoners in German hands."[68]

If any chance of a Vatican-Soviet accord ever existed, it was fading in mutual recriminations. From Moscow came a steady barrage of news releases accusing the pope of being profascist and an apologist for Nazi crimes. When Pope Pius released his June 1944 statement questioning the unconditional surrender doctrine, the *Red Star* wrote that the Vatican was trying to revive Catholic fascism. The Vatican replied by accusing Russia of atrocities in Poland and announcing through *Osservatore Romano* that communism and Catholicism were incompatible. Nothing new seems to have emerged in this dialogue-at-long-distance.[69]

Roosevelt had hoped that promoting Vatican-Russian understanding would be a means of maintaining the support of American Catholics for his diplomacy and removing one more postwar irritant. Instead, he found that Vatican suspicions of communist ambitions were being transmitted to American Catholics. Reports of active antireligious hostility from European prelates in areas overrun by the Soviet army reached Monsignor Ready of the NCWC and others. As Joseph J. Gawlina, Military Bishop of the Polish Armed Forces, wrote to Archbishop Stritch of Chicago in September 1942, any concessions made to religious feelings by the Soviets was entirely "out of motives of political expediency" for purposes of influencing American opinion. The notion of religious freedom in Russia, wrote Gawlina, was a "legal fiction." This letter circulated among members of the American hierarchy. Archbishop Edward A. Mooney suggested that Ready give the information to Welles. Ready continued to keep Welles "abreast of the religious situation in the USSR" by forwarding other information as it reached the American bishops.[70]

Even without Vatican encouragement American Catholics would have become suspicious of the Soviet Union, for Red fears were built into American Catholicism. When the United States entered the war, men such as Archbishop Curley of Baltimore, Reverend Gillis of the *Catholic World*, and the editors of *Sign* and *America* spoke of the anti-Christian goals of Stalin. These men and others like them kept up a steady bombardment against the Soviet Union throughout the war. Few articulate American Catholics believed that religious freedom was winning ground in Russia.[71]

Anticommunist beliefs even led American Catholics to become sensitive to subversion at home. Elmer Murphy, author of the *NCWC Washington Newsletter*, expressed the thoughts of many by warning that domestic communism was making large inroads under the cover of the alliance. Murphy had two examples in mind. He wondered who had approved the filming and release of a new movie called "Mission to Moscow," based on the autobiography of the former ambassador to the Soviet Union Joseph E. Davies, which repeated all the popular-front cliches about the peaceful goals of Stalin and Russia. Such blatant procommunist propaganda made Murphy suspect a gigantic communist-inspired campaign to twist American minds. He also found it incredible that Professor Doxey A. Wilkerson of Howard University should have been employed as an education specialists by the Office of Price Administration. Wilkerson was a known communist. Murphy concluded that the government "might well give some attention to eradicating the noxious growth of Communism in the United States." He, Gillis, and other Catholics felt sure that the containment of communist influence would be a major postwar problem.[72]

If such suspicions spelled trouble for Roosevelt's plan of postwar collaboration between the United States and Russia, the president's troubles were partly of his own making. Misunderstanding had begun in December 1941 when Roosevelt had told the American bishops "in victory we shall seek . . . the establishment of an international order in which the spirit of Christ shall rule the hearts of men and of nations." Catholic thinking about the future of the world after the war reflected the universalism of Roosevelt. American Catholic leaders increasingly identified the Atlantic Charter with papal plans for peace. Taylor had told the pope in September 1942 that the United States would work to eliminate "anti-Christian philosophies." The Bishop's Committee of the NCWC felt that the papal peace plan was identical with the secular objectives of the war. As American Catholics came to identify religious and secular goals, a new postwar idea grew. The war was to lead to a *Pax Christiana* achieved by American arms. Was this not what Roosevelt promised? It followed, in the minds of Wilbert O'Neill and Mrs. Robert A. Angelo, presidents of the national councils of Catholic men and women, that the peace conference should be controlled by Christians. No role was assigned to Marxist Russia. The American bishops said the same thing in "On Victory and Peace" in

1942. Only Christianity provided the principles of a true peace. Muench and Sheen agreed that Allied postwar planning would fail unless it followed Christian principles.[73]

By summer 1943 American Catholics began to suspect that Russia was a major stumbling-block to any *Pax Christiana.* The Declaration of Moscow, affirming the United States-Soviet commitment to a postwar international organization, was made on October 30, 1943, but rumors flew of secret understandings between Russia and the West. Few American Catholics were in a better position to do something about their suspicions than Archbishop Spellman. As director of the Catholic Chaplain Corps and as a confidant of the president, he had numerous opportunities to make Catholic fears known. He shared the general anti-Russian bias of his colleagues. He had seen how American aid to Russia received no publicity in that country, how the exchange of military information was always one-way. He brought his suspicions directly to Roosevelt in a private conversation in September 1943. As recorded in Spellman's diary, the discussion revealed Roosevelt's realistic side. The president had no hesitation in telling Spellman that the Allied powers expected Russia to take Finland, the Baltic states, the eastern half of Poland, and Bessarabia as part of the spoils for defeating Hitler. He felt that there was no point in objecting because Russia had too much power and deserved some reward for defeating the Nazi army. He even suspected that communist governments might be imposed upon Germany and Austria. The only hope for France to escape communist domination was to set up a popular-front government. Austria, Hungary, and Croatia, however, would surely be made into Soviet protectorates. Yet the president reassured Spellman that there would be a general softening of this control after ten or twenty years. By that time, Russia would be changed by its contact with European civilization.[74]

These realistic assessments of Soviet plans must have shocked Spellman. He must have recalled with anguish his own contribution to the general understanding that Russia would soften its attitude due to the "Grand Alliance." Only a few months earlier, in March 1943, Spellman had sought to undermine Spanish fears of communism by pointing to "Mr. Stalin's adherence to the Atlantic Charter and other subsequent statements by himself and other leaders . . . that Russia does not wish to possess any non-Russian territory or to impose its form of government."

Now, the president was telling Spellman to expect Russian domination of Central Europe.[75]

Roosevelt had hinted at some postwar expansion of Soviet influence in Europe in conversations with the Vatican. But he had always emphasized that this influence was but a prelude to domesticating communism through Western contact. As the war neared its end, the president spoke bluntly. He even complained to Spellman that the pope was being unreasonable about Russia because of excessive fears of communism. No doubt these words were much on Spellman's mind as he was called to the Vatican to talk with the pope in July 1944. It seems fair to guess that Spellman passed on Roosevelt's hard-boiled assessment of Europe's future. The pope undoubtedly conveyed to Spellman the increasing apprehension of the Vatican about Soviet intentions. Evidence of an antireligious crusade accompanying the advancing Russian army continued to pile up at the Vatican. Cicognani sent frequent reports to Secretary of State Hull, and in December 1944 Taylor reported to Roosevelt that the pope feared that Italy would soon fall to the communists.[76]

Meanwhile, in the United States the united religious front in Roosevelt's consensus was showing signs of collapse. To reassure themselves of the idealism associated with the American war effort, a group of Catholic, Protestant, and Jewish leaders had made a public statement in October 1943, insisting that the United Nations issue a declaration of human rights. Any postwar international organization should guarantee the rights of minorities and promote anticolonialism and economic cooperation. To ensure that these ideals were met, the religious leaders urged that church figures be given power as commissioners at the peace conference. Unfortunately Spellman, who might have qualified for such a post, had already received the disturbing news about the current status of such idealism within the White House. He knew that the president expected to divide the world between the "Big Four," with Russia getting a large slice of Europe. Furthermore, the president expected the major powers to control any postwar international organization. Spellman unquestionably passed this news on to his fellow bishops because on November 11, 1943, the executive committee of the NCWC had issued a statement, "The Essentials of a Good Peace." The bishops explained that the Moscow declaration and the communiques issued after the Allied foreign ministers' meeting of October, despite the commitment to a United

Nations organization, did not "dispel the fear that compromises on the ideals of the Atlantic Charter are in prospect." To forestall such compromises, the bishops decided to make clear the Catholic position about peace. They declared that peace required a recognition of the sovereignty of God and His moral law, and the erection of a United Nations. Such an organization did not mean the end of national sovereignty or world government; it did mean that all nations must recognize the principles of international justice and guarantee basic individual rights to private property and religious freedom. The bishops' vision of peace looked remarkably similar to the basic principles of a Christian culture affected by the American historical experience. The United States remained the key to world peace. Even as the realities of diplomacy became visible in 1944, one author emphasized that hope for the future rested on America which has "been since its inception the greatest moral force politically in the Western world."[77] In November 1944, after more rumors of compromises, the bishops issued another statement, declaring that "we have no confidence in a peace which does not carry into effect, without reservations or equivocations, the principles of the Atlantic Charter." There should be no return to the politics of power; no group of superpowers should dominate the United Nations. No veto should be permitted.[78]

6

The issue of Poland in 1944 and 1945 symbolized the growing distrust of Roosevelt's diplomacy and increased suspicions of the Soviet Union. In the minds of many American Catholics, Poland had become representative of freedom and Christian culture. It had become, in the words of Reverend James Gillis, "the moral condition of victory." The future of Poland became for American Catholics the test of the Atlantic Charter. The concept of World War II as a crusade had been buffeted by the problems of unconditional surrender, the bombing tactics of the Allies, and the intentions of Russia. Now, in the future of Poland, it met another test. Few American Catholic publications adopted the realism of the *Commonweal* in August 1943, whose editor said that since Russia was doing most of the fighting and would have the largest army in Europe after the war, it would have to be granted concessions. The thought of allowing communist Russia to dominate Catholic Poland created panic in many Catholic minds. But according

to Spellman, this is what Roosevelt was contemplating. Cynics such as
Gillis had been predicting a sell-out, hinting that the Allies would treat the
Atlantic Charter as a scrap of paper when it suited their purposes.[79]

Perhaps the most bizarre case of clerical politics emerged from an
attempt to promote Vatican-Moscow reconciliation over Poland in the
spring of 1944. To demonstrate the quirks of history, neither Roosevelt
nor any important American prelate was involved. Instead, the major
figure was an unknown Polish-American priest named Stanislaus Orlemanski of Springfield, Massachusetts. Orlemanski had indicated his sympathy for Russia by organizing a pro-Soviet league of Poles in the United
States. To the surprise of Roosevelt and the Department of State, Orlemanski received an invitation from Stalin to visit Moscow for talks. Although motivation is obscure in the labyrinth of Moscow, Stalin probably recalled Roosevelt's frequent complaints about the political hostility of American Poles to any deal with Russia. Perhaps distrust could
be cleared up through personal diplomacy with a Polish-American priest.
Thus Orlemanski began his strange journey, which would eventually lead
him to an American monastery. He spent twelve days in Russia and spoke
with Stalin twice. At these conferences, the Soviet dictator indicated his
commitment to religious freedom in Russia and to increased contacts with
the Vatican. Stalin's sincerity is impossible to gauge, but such promises
certainly would have helped to undermine American Catholic opposition
to Roosevelt's program for Poland. Orlemanski thought Stalin was being
honest. The priest revealed these proposals to the American press upon
his return to the United States. Four hours later he had been relieved of
his priestly functions and was ordered to a monastary for "rest and
reflection" by Bishop Thomas O'Leary. If Stalin expected Orlemanski
to have some influence on church policy, Soviet intelligence was over-
rated. American church officials, including Ready of the NCWC, called
Orlemanski a "stooge" and the entire affair a "burlesque." Although
shocked and resentful at first, Orlemanski soon apologized to Bishop
O'Leary, expressing regret at the Moscow venture and promising "to
cease and separate myself from all activities which are not in accord with
the rules and mind of the Catholic Church." Stalin undoubtedly smiled
when he read this confession; the procedure seemed familiar. But the
treatment of Orlemanski was also a rebuff to the policies of reconcilation
that Stalin had proferred. The entire affair was bungled from the beginning. If Orlemanski had been more mature, he would have checked with

the hierarchy for instructions before running off to Moscow. Perhaps the Vatican would have refused permission for the trip. More likely, Rome would have insisted upon regular diplomatic channels instead of using the inexperienced Orlemanski. At most, regular contact might have been established, if Stalin was sincere and not just playing American politics to help Roosevelt. Instead of these developments, Orlemanski ended up with a reprimand and Stalin could rightly accuse the church of repulsing his approach. American Catholics remained concerned about Poland.[80]

When in November 1944 the American bishops announced their suspicions about Allied diplomacy, Poland was much on their minds. Meeting in Washington, the hierarchy issued a resolution, "Religious Freedom in Poland and the Baltic States." After mentioning the long Catholic tradition of Poland, the bishops concluded that "American Catholics would ever resent their country's being made a party to the de-Christianization of historic Catholic peoples." By this time, the bishops had become convinced that the United States was failing also in its moral commitment to the Baltic states and retreating from the ideals of the Atlantic Charter. Catholic bishops feared that Poland and its neighbors were going to become mere puppets of the Soviet Union. News of religious persecution in these Russian-occupied areas shocked the men who had lent their moral support to the Allied cause.[81] They refused to view the issue within the larger context of Allied relations and pre-1939 Polish-Russian relations.

Roosevelt always considered such fears hysterical, but he appreciated that misunderstanding about Poland was causing political problems in the United States. Unless something could be done to reassure Catholics about Russia, Roosevelt's wartime consensus would collapse even faster, Catholic isolationism would revive, and the Senate might even defeat plans for a United Nations, to say nothing of the defection of Polish-American voters from the Democratic party. Already in late 1944 both the CAIP and the bishops had condemned plans for the United Nations because it gave too much power to the communists. Roosevelt's fears about these matters probably explain why he decided upon another attempt to have Stalin accept some compromise over the religious issue. No other reason explains Roosevelt's decision to take Edward Flynn on the trip to Yalta in early February 1945.

Few people in the Roosevelt party knew why Flynn, an Irish-Catholic and a leading Democratic figure in New York politics, was coming along on a major diplomatic mission. When planning the finances of the trip,

Grace Tully asked the Department of State to authorize transportation for Flynn to Moscow and several other places in Russia and Europe. Officials at the department complained that they did not know the nature of Flynn's mission but would put up the money if Roosevelt would send them a written request. Despite his desire for secrecy, Roosevelt had already given Flynn a letter for presentation to all United States officials abroad, explaining that the bearer was "engaged in a mission for me which involves a visit to Moscow . . . and also a visit to Italy." On March 10, 1945, Roosevelt authorized the Department of State to cover all of Flynn's expenses.[82] On the voyage to Yalta, the president had hinted about Flynn's presence by facetiously announcing one day at sea that "Father Flynn will say Mass tomorrow morning." James F. Byrnes, director of war mobilization, who was also in the party, guessed that Flynn was along to inquire about the status of the Catholic church in Russia. Flynn stayed four weeks in Russia, during which time he saw Molotov twice and raised the issue which had motivated the trip—Vatican-Soviet rapprochement. According to Ambassador Harriman, Molotov showed "undisguised interest in the subject." Despite such interest and Flynn's interview with "commissars of religion," the ambassador suspected that the Vatican would have to make the first gesture for reconciliation. Still, the visit seemed worthwhile to Harriman. He was sorry to see Flynn catch his plane for Rome, but Vatican officials waited.[83]

Flynn spent only a few days in Rome. He held talks with Vatican officials and conveyed his impressions on the state of religion in Russia. By now newspaper reporters began guessing that Flynn was engaged in negotiating a Vatican-Soviet accord. His subsequent conduct indicates that he had little success in encouraging the Vatican to take the first step. After leaving Rome, he telegraphed Harriman in Moscow that no immediate or dramatic changes would be forthcoming. Roosevelt died before Flynn had a chance to file a full report. It was not until July 3, 1945, that he discussed the matter with President Truman, and by then a new attitude toward the Soviet Union was emerging in Washington.[84]

Roosevelt died on April 12, 1945, and three days later the Catholic bishops of the United States officially ended their membership in his moral consensus. In a statement on world peace, they condemned the proposed voting procedure of the United Nations because it rejected the equality of nations and gave a veto to the superpowers. The alliance of the three superpowers was a poor substitute for the pope's peace of justice. Furthermore, they feared that the United Nations charter might not insist upon individual rights, such as religious liberty. Why had the ideals of Roosevelt failed? "Every day," the bishops wrote, "makes more evident the fact that there can be no meeting of minds between Marxism and democracy." The United States had entered the war to defend democracy. Now Marxism was on the march. After the United Nations charter had been drawn up and signed, the bishops issued another statement in November 1945, "Between War and Peace." They again rejected the charter as a mere alliance of the great powers. No longer could they remain silent and ignore the "profound differences of thought and policy" between the United States and Russia. The Soviet Union continued to impose its ruthless control over the nations of Eastern Europe. Nothing had changed from the late 1930s in American Catholic attitudes toward Russia.[85]

The theology of war had been repudiated; the moral consensus had disintegrated. Roosevelt had been solicitous of American Catholic fears for years, but now a new consensus was emerging around the ideological and political struggle with the Soviet Union. But this is another story. The consensus of World War II had been the product of many historical factors. Pearl Harbor had generated a consensus on the question of a just war. Catholics shared this view. They found it easy to enlist in Roosevelt's crusade, to take his idealism seriously. Catholic theology, which taught reverence for constituted authority, made it easy to accept Roosevelt's leadership. The image of American Catholics as suspended between full citizenship and alien status, an image enhanced by their deviant attitude toward the Spanish Civil War, helped promote enthusiasm for the war. Catholic patriotism in this crusade would be so shining that never again would anyone dare question their Americanism. Catholics also accepted the idea that the United States was different from other countries. The vision of an American mission to the world proved irresistible.

Yet the moral consensus had collapsed, primarily because it existed only on a verbal level. Such impossible dreams must always confront the reality of the windmill, in this case, Russia and Eastern Europe. The crusade had fallen before Roosevelt's concessions to the Bolsheviks. Some scholars lament Roosevelt's failure to remain steadfast in his idealism.

An increasing body of revisionist historical literature laments the removal of the idealistic Roosevelt and the appearance of hard-boiled Harry Truman. These historians argue that Truman's realism was missionary diplomacy, not realistic at all, and helped produce the cold war. They argue that Roosevelt was the true realist in his recognition of Russian needs. Undoubtedly, Roosevelt acted the realist in his treatment of American Catholics and political realities. But in the perspective of the foregoing pages, Roosevelt's idealism also caused problems. His public statements on the Allied war aims failed to prepare Catholics for his subsequent Russian policy. His dream of harmonizing Catholics and Bolsheviks remained unfulfilled. The collapse of Roosevelt's dream for a new democratic world meant great bitterness on the part of Catholics. And the way in which Catholics left the Roosevelt consensus helped ensure that they would adopt the cliches of the cold war. In fact, they had created most of them before President Truman entered office. Whatever the reality of foreign policy or the threat of Russian arms, American Catholics would support their new president in his struggle. Catholics used World War II to promote their integration into American life, to become part of American culture, but integration was a two-way process. A more Catholic America meant an America more conscious of the dangers of communism. Where this would lead, few people could tell in 1945.[86]

NOTES

1. *NCWC News Service:* Dillon quoted in December 1, 1941; Curley quoted in December 9, 1941.

2. Coughlin continued his opposition until silenced by pressure from Archbishop Mooney. See Richard Polemberg, *War and Society* (New York, 1972), p. 47.

3. Mooney to Roosevelt, December 22, 1941, in Raphael M. Huber, editor, *Our Bishops Speak: National Pastorals and Annual Statements of the Hierarchy . . . , 1919-1951* (Milwaukee, 1952), p. 350. For an interesting comparison with how German bishops reacted to Hitler's war, see Gordon C. Zahn, *German Catholics and Hitler's Wars* (New York, 1969).

4. Huber, *Our Bishops Speak*, p. 352.

5. John J. Carigg, "American Catholic Press Opinion with reference to

America's Intervention in Second World War" (M.A. thesis, Georgetown University, 1947), pp. 137, 138, 143; *NCWC News Service,* December 9, 15, 16, 1941.

6. *NCWC News Service,* December 14, 22, 1941. Some observers thought World War II was a continuation of Wilson's crusade for a democratic world. James Reston wrote, "We cannot win this war until it . . . becomes a national crusade for America and the American dream" (G. Perritt, *Days of Sadness, Years of Triumph* [New York, 1973], p. 280.) See also Allan Nevin's comments in Paul Goodman, editor, *While You Were Gone* (New York, 1946), pp. 11, 13.

7. Ryan and Muench quoted in *NCWC News Service*, December 15, 1941; Lucey quoted in ibid., December 22, 1941; ibid., December 16, 1941; Spellman quoted in Robert I. Gannon, *The Cardinal Spellman Story* (New York, 1962), p. 241.

8. *NCWC News Service*, December 15, 1941.

9. Thomas C. Cornell and James H. Forest, *A Penny a Copy: Readings From the Catholic Worker* (New York, 1968), pp. 52-53; T. Maguire, "Catholics and the War," *Sign*, January 1942, p. 323.

10. Memo of conversation of Cicognani with Welles, May 6, 1942, SDF 701.9466a/8½, State Department Files, National Archives, Washington, D.C. (hereafter cited as SDF).

11. *Commonweal,* April 4, 1941, p. 587; Cornell, *A Penny a Copy,* p. 58.

12. Jacques Maritain, "Just War," *Commonweal,* December 22, 1939, p. 199.

13. *NCWC News Service*: December 8, 15, 22, 1941; "The Catholic Church and the Present War," *Sign*, July 1944, p. 691. In another age, theologians and moral critics took another view. Traditional Catholic theology dealing with war has always insisted upon the legitimate right to self-defense and the moral imperative of protecting the public good. Seeking to strike a balance between the need to defend oneself and the dangers of total war, Catholic theology has been affected by the coming of the atom and the missile. The bishops of Vatican II announced that "the fierce character of warfare threatens to lead the combatants to a savagery far surpassing that of the past;" see Walter M. Abbott, editor, *The Documents of Vatican II* (New York, 1966), p. 291. Under such circumstances, Catholic moral theology has moved closer to the posi-

tion that only a defensive war is justifiable, given the existence of modern weapons. Historically, a state could justify war for two other reasons: *ad vindicandas offensiones* ("to punish offenses" against the state), and *ad repentendas res* ("to regain possessions"). Now theologians emphasize only *ad repellendas iniurias* ("to repel injuries" done to the state). See also John C. Murray, "Morality and Foreign Policy: II," *America*, March 26, 1960, p. 766; Paul Ramsey, *The Just War* (New York, 1968), especially Chapter 4, pp. 75-85; and two collections of essays: William Nagle, editor, *Morality and Modern Warfare* (Baltimore, 1960); Robert W. Tucker, *Just War and Vatican Council II: A Critique* (New York, 1970). The Nagle book has an outstanding bibliography on the entire question of ethics and war. FDR called Gannon's public conversion "courageous" (Roosevelt to Mary Norton, September 11, 1942, PPF 5418 Roosevelt Papers, Hyde Park, New York).

14. Cornell, *A Penny a Copy*, p. xiv. Even Vatican II qualified its endorsement of the conscientious objector by including the proviso "that this can be done without injury to the rights and duties of others or of the community itself." The government is called upon to provide for these individuals, but they must "accept some other form of service to the human community," because "governments cannot be denied the right to legitimate defense once every means of peaceful settlement has been exhausted" (Abbott, *The Documents of Vatican II*, pp. 291-292).

15. *America*, June 27, 1942, p. 323.

16. *NCWC News Service*: December 15, 16, 1941; January 11, 1943; February 23, 1943; Samuel Rosenman, *Working with Roosevelt* (New York, 1952), p. 316; for Roosevelt quotes see *New York Times*: December 31, 1942, p. 18; January 6, 1943, p. 23; Robert A. Divine, *Second Chance* (New York, 1971), p. 65 (for Wallace's quote).

17. Quoted in Perritt, *Days of Sadness*, p. 202.

18. Maritain, "Just War," p. 200; *NCWC News Service,* December 5, 15, 1941; Sheen quoted in January 11, 1943.

19. *NCWC News Service*: December 15, 1941; January 18, 1943; February 1, 1943; June 7, 1943; Gannon quoted in July 19, 1943; Spellman quoted in Gannon, *The Cardinal Spellman Story*, pp. 244-246; William D. Hassett, *Off the Record with FDR* (New Brunswick, N.J., 1958), p. 188.

20. *NCWC News Service*: December 29, 1941; Sheen quoted in January 4, 1943; March 15, 1943; Gannon, *The Cardinal Spellman Story*, pp. 231, 244-246.

21. Quoted in *NCWC News Service,* December 22, 1941.

22. Zahn, *German Catholics and Hitler's Wars,* discusses this problem extensively from the perspective of a radical pacifist.

23. Quoted in *NCWC News Service,* June 7, 1943.

24. *New York Times:* December 26, 1942; December 27, 1942.

25. Ibid.: December 19, 1942; December 26, 1942; *NCWC News Service:* December 22, 1941; August 16, 1942; March 2, 1943.

26. *NCWC News Service,* December 22, 1941; Cantwell quoted in January 25, 1943; June 14, 1943; Thomas McAvoy, "American Catholics and the War," *Ave Maria* 55 (May-July 1942), pp. 679-680.

27. *New York Times,* January 25, 1943; *Ave Maria,* July 18, 1942, p. 69; Huber, *Our Bishops Speak,* p. 110.

28. *NCWC News Service,* March 16, 1943.

29. Frederick L. Broderick, *The Right Reverend New Dealer: John A. Ryan* (New York, 1963), p. 260; M. R. P. McGuire, "Some Reflections on the Present World Crisis," *Catholic Historical Review* 28 (January 1943), p. 443; *NCWC News Service,* January 18, 24, 1943; Huber, *Our Bishops Speak,* pp. 355-356, Benjamin Masse, "A Reply to Mr. Max Lerner," *America,* November 27, 1943, p. 204. 204.

30. *NCWC News Service:* July 12, 19, 1943; December 12, 1941; Huber, *Our Bishops Speak,* pp. 112, 234.

31. Tittmann to Hull, March 18, 1942, SDF 701.9466A/19. As early as May 23, 1940, Japanese Minister Ito had discussed with Maglione the prospect of the pope's acting as a mediator in the China war. Maglione reminded Ito that Pope Pius had already approached Roosevelt on that subject without success. If another opportunity arose, Maglione promised action, but he was not optimistic (Maglione notes, May 23, 1940, Pierre Blet, et al., editors, Secrétairerie D'État de sa Sainteté, *Actes et Documents du Saint Siège Relatifs à La Second Guerre Mondiale,* 5 vols., (Citta Del Vaticano: Libreria Editrice Vaticana, 1967-   ), vol. 1, pp. 433-434 (hereafter cited as *Holy See and War*); memo by Welles, March 3, 1942, SDF 701.9466A/4½; Cicognani to Maglione, March 5, 1942, *Holy See and War,* vol. 5, p. 462; memo of conversation between Cicognani and Welles, March 6, 1942, SDF 701.9466A/8½; Tittmann to Maglione, March 11, 1942; March 14, 1942, *Holy See and War,* vol. 5, pp. 485, 487, 488; Welles to Roosevelt, March 14, 1942, SDF 701.9466A/9½; Tittmann to Hull, March 6, 1942, SDF 701.9466a/16; Tittmann to Hull, March 18, 1942, SDF 701/9466a/19; Tittmann to

April 10, 1942, SDF 121.866a/228; Tittmann to Maglione, April 2, 1942, *Holy See and War,* vol. 5, p. 510; *NCWC News Service,* Vatican City, April 4, 1941; Roosevelt to Spellman, March 14, 1942, PSF: Spellman, Roosevelt Papers.

32. Montini's notes, July 25, 1940, *Holy See and War,* vol. 1, p. 470.

33. Taylor memo, October 3, 1942, PSF: Vatican, Roosevelt Papers.

34. Taylor to Pope, September 19, 1942, *Holy See and War,* vol. 5, pp. 681-688; Taylor to Roosevelt, September 29, 1942; PSF: Vatican, Roosevelt Papers.

35. Taylor to Pope, September 19, 1942, PSF: Vatican, Roosevelt Paper

36. Ibid.

37. Pius to Taylor, September 22, 1942, *Holy See and War*, vol. 5, pp. 692-694; also in September 22, 1942, PSF: Vatican, Roosevelt Papers; memo by J. W. Jones, November 4, 1942, SDF 740.00119EW1939/1185.

38. "Vatican Neutrality," *The Catholic Mind* 42 (August 1944), pp. 470-471; R. A. Graham, "What Kind of Peace Does the Pope Ask For?" *America*, June 24, 1944, pp. 315-316; Taylor to Roosevelt, February 28, 1945, PSF: Vatican, Roosevelt Papers; *New York Times*, June 25, 1944.

39. Saul Friedlander, *Pius XII and the Third Reich: A Documentation,* trans. by Charles Fullman (New York, 1966), pp. 122-123; *Holy See and War,* vol. 5, p. 675; Taylor memo of conversation with pope, September 22, 1942, and Taylor memo of conversation with Maglione, September 25, 1942, and Welles to Taylor, October 21, 1942, all in PSF: Vatican and PSF: Taylor, Roosevelt Papers.

40. Taylor memo, September 25, 1942, SDF 840.50/816; Tittmann to Hull, September 2, 1944, SDF 740.0011EW/9-244; Taylor to Hull, September 18, 1944, SDF 500.CC/9-1844; Hull to Taylor, September 23, 1944, SDF 500.CC/9-1844; Taylor to Roosevelt and Hull, October 6, 1944, SDF 500.CC/10-644; Taylor to Roosevelt, October 29, 1944, SDF 840.48 Refugees/10-2944.

41. *NCWC News Service,* March 15, 1943; Taylor to pope, September 19, 1942, PSF: Vatican, Roosevelt Papers; W.M. Agar, "The Future Can Be Ours," *Commonweal,* July 24, 1942, p. 324; C. G. Paulding, "Expediency: Our Policy in Africa," *Commonweal*, January 15, 1943, p. 317. See also R. G. O'Connor, *Diplomacy for Victory* (New York, 1971), who explains unconditional surrender in terms of holding the Allied coalition together.

42. Gannon, *The Cardinal Spellman Story*, p. 252; *NCWC News Service*, February 1, 1943; Tittmann to Hull, March 13, 1943, SDF 033.1166a/9.

43. Joseph P. Lash, *Eleanor and Franklin* (New York, 1971), pp. 913, 918, 919; Morgenthau Papers, Presidential Diary 6, p. 1501 (April 11, 1945), Roosevelt Library; John M. Blum, *From the Morgenthau Diaries*, 3 vols. (Boston, 1959, 1965, 1967), vol. 3, pp. 353-354; *New York Times*, April 25, 1943, p. 25.

44. Gannon, *The Cardinal Spellman Story*, pp. 269-270; Knights of Columbus quoted in *NCWC News Service*, August 23, 1943.

45. F. A. Hermens, "Germany and Christian Peace," *Catholic World* 158 (February 1944), pp. 427-434; *NCWC News Service*, August 30, 1943; F. A. Hermens, "Peacemaking 1945," *Catholic World* 161 (May 1945), p. 125; J. McCawley, "Atrocities: World War II," *Catholic World* 161 (August 1945), pp. 378-385; Louis P. Lochner, "Is There Another Germany?" *Catholic Digest* (February 1943), pp. 87-92; E. M. von Kuehnelt-Leddhin, "Guilty Nations," *Catholic World* 162 (December 1945), p. 203; *NCWC News Service*, June 28, 1943; Gannon, *The Cardinal Spellman Story*, pp. 251, 314.

46. *NCWC News Service*: January 11, 1943; March 22, 1943; A. J. App, "American War Policies and Catholic Principles," *Catholic World* 160 (October 1944), pp. 28-30.

47. Ryan quoted in Broderick, *The Right Reverend New Dealer*, p. 273; "Sound Political Weapon: Punishment of the War Criminals," *Commonweal*, October 16, 1942, p. 604; J. H. Ryan, "Peace with Justice," *Commonweal*, June 11, 1943, p. 197; "War Criminal Trials," *Commonweal*, September 21, 1945, p. 131; "Nuremberg," *Commonweal*, December 7, 1945, p. 181; Abbott, *The Documents of Vatican II*, p. 292.

48. Morgenthau Papers, Presidential Diary 4, p. 952 (August 4, 1941), Roosevelt Library; *New York Times*, June 2, 1943. Churchill made the same appeal but there seems some question of who really started the practice during 1940. See J. McCawley, "Bombing of Civilians," *Catholic World* 162 (October 1945), pp. 11-19.

49. Paul Gallico, "What We talked About," in Goodman, *While You Were Gone*, p. 49; *New York Times*, March 11, 1944.

50. McCawley, "Bombing of Civilians," p. 11; notes by Taylor, September 27, 1942, PSF: Vatican, Roosevelt Papers; *NCWC News Service:* June 8, 1943; July 26, 1943; Ramsey, *The Just War*, p. 73; Lawrence L. Mc-

Reavy, "Reprisals: A Second Opinion," *Clergy Review* 20 (February 1941), p. 138ff; "Tentative Essay in Morals: De Seversky's Strategy," *Commonweal*, August 28, 1942, p. 435.

51. Memo by Pius, September 26, 1942, PSF: Vatican, Roosevelt Papers; "Responsibility: Policy of Bombing only Military Targets," *Commonweal*, September 10, 1943, p. 505; Huber, *Our Bishops Speak*, p. 353; *America*, May 27, 1944, p. 210; Cornell, *A Penny a Copy*, p. 63. Public opinion polls reflected consistent support for bombing. A poll of March 29, 1944, asked, "If the military said we need to bomb historic religious buildings and shrines in Europe, would you approve or disapprove?" On a national scale, 74 percent approved, 19 percent disapproved, and 7 percent had no opinion. Among Protestants, 75 percent approved, 19 percent disapproved, and 6 percent had no opinion. Among Catholics, 63 percent approved, 28 percent disapproved (Hadley Cantrill, *Public Opinion 1935-1941* [Princeton, N.J., 1951] , p. 1069; *New York Times*, April 19, 1944).

52. Tardini to Taylor, September 17, 1941, and notes of Tardini, November 23, 1941, *Holy See and War*, vol. 5, pp. 225, 307; memo of conversation with Cicognani by A. Berle, December 4, 1942, SDF 740. 0011EW1939/26629. Notes of Winant on Taylor-Churchill talks, October 5, 1942, PSF: Vatican; memo FDR to Hull, June 28, 1943, and Hull to Roosevelt, June 28, 1943, in PSF: Vatican; Roosevelt to Cicognani, June 29, 1943, PSF: Vatican; all in Roosevelt Papers. Myron C. Taylor, *Wartime Correspondence Between President Roosevelt and Pope Pius XII* (New York, 1947), p. 85; Taylor to Cicognani, July 9, 1943, Tittmann to Hull, July 15, 1943, and Hull to Tittmann, July 19, 1943, in *USFR 1943*, vol. 2.

53. *NCWC News Service,* July 20, 21, 27, 1943; Gannon, *The Cardinal Spellman Story,* pp. 292-293; see on entire subject SDF: 740.0011EW1939 33780; 740.0011EW1939/33218; 740.0011EW/11-3045. H.L. Matthews, *New York Times* correspondent, actually flew on the Rome raid and wrote that with precision bombing there was no possibility of coming anywhere near that 'Mother Church of the Catholic World' [St. John Lateran] , because "any good bombardier can guarantee to leave unscratched anything half that distance [1,000 yards] from his target" *(New York Times,* July 20, 1943).

54. *NCWC News Service,* July 23, 1943. Roosevelt to Hull, August 30,

1943; Roosevelt memo, September 1, 1943; Roosevelt to Hull, December 7, 1943; all in PSF: Vatican, Roosevelt Papers.

55. Gannon, *The Cardinal Spellman Story*, pp. 291-295; *New York Times*, July 22, 24, 1943; *NCWC News Service*, July 20, 26, 27, 1943; *Newsweek*, August 2, 1943, pp. 66-68. A public opinion poll of April 27, 1943 asked, "Do you think the Allied Airforce should bomb Rome?" On a national level, 37 percent said yes, 51 percent said no, and 12 percent had no opinion. Catholics responded with 24 percent saying yes, 67 percent saying no, and 9 percent with no opinion. Among Protestants, the response was 36 percent yes, 52 percent no, and 12 percent no opinion. No poll was taken after the bombing, but the Catholic press, with the exception of *Commonweal*, was unanimous in condemning the raids. See Cantrill, *Public Opinion*, p. 1069.

56. Gannon, *The Cardinal Spellman Story*, p. 359, who quotes from the diary; Cornell, *A Penny a Copy*, p. 67; James Gillis, "Atomic Bomb," *Commonweal*, August 31, 1945, p. 468; "Atomic Bomb," *Catholic Mind* 43 (October 1945), p. 610.

57. "Morality of Air Blitz," *Ave Maria*, June 1942, pp. 804-805; *NCWC News Service*, June 3, 1943.

58. "Open Cities," *Commonweal*, August 27, 1943, p. 457; James Gillis, "Blue Print for Peace," *Catholic World* 155 (July 1942), p. 390; McCawley, "Bombing of Civilians," pp. 11-19.

59. John C. Ford, "The Morality of Obliteration Bombing," *Theological Studies* 5 (September 1944), pp. 261-309; see also Ramsey, *Just War*, pp. 60-90.

60. Ramsey, *Just War*, pp. 60-90. Some years later the Second Vatican Council came very close to adopting this identical moral position. Earlier, Popes Pius XII, John XXIII, and Paul VI had all condemned total war involving mass destruction of civilian populations. The Council concluded that "any act of war aimed indiscriminately at the destruction of entire cities or of extensive areas along with their population is a crime against God and man himself. It merits unequivocal and unhesitating condemnation" (Abbott, *The Documents of Vatican II*, p. 293).

61. Ramsey, *Just War*, pp. 60-69.

62. Hull to Taylor, November 18, 1942, and Taylor to Pope, September 19, 1942, PSF: Vatican, Roosevelt Papers.

63. Roosevelt's sensitivity to Catholic anticommunism emerged in this

conversation with Leo Crowley in January 1942. When Crowley wondered why Roosevelt would oppose a judicial appointment because it
would mean too many Catholics on the bench, the president turned and
asked if Catholics would support him if he sent United States troops to
fight with Russia (Morgenthau Diaries, Presidential Diary 5, p. 1061
[January 27, 1942]).

64. Memo of conversation of Tardini with Taylor, September 26, 1942,
SDF 861.404/482.

65. Tittmann to Hull, May 7, 1943, SDF 862.20266A/5.

66. Tittmann to Hull, January 11, 1944, SDF 740.0011EW1939/32657;
Tittmann to Hull, May 25, 1943, SDF 740.0011EW1939/29544; Cicognani
to Hull, August 5, 1944, SDF 860C.404/8-544; Cicognani to Hull, Septem-
2, 1944, SDF 740.0011EW1939/9-244; Taylor to Roosevelt, December
12, 1944, SDF 740.0011EW1939/12-1244; Cicognani to Stettinius, Octo-
31, 1944, SDF 870.00/10-3144, and December 6, 1944, SDF 740.0011EW
/12644; Taylor to Roosevelt, July 17, 1944 and August 4, 1944, PSF:
Vatican, Roosevelt Papers.

67. Welles to Tittmann, August 3, 1942, SDF 740.0011EW1939/23496a;
Tittmann to Hull, August 14, 1942, SDF 740.0011EW1939/24145; Taylor
to Roosevelt, August 11, 1944, SDF 740.0011EW1939/8-1144; Roosevelt
to Taylor, August 29, 1944, PSF: Vatican, Roosevelt Papers.

68. Tittmann to Welles, March 23, 1942, and Welles to Tittmann, April
21, 1942, SDF 701.9466a/20; Taylor to Hull and Roosevelt, September
21, 1942, SDF 121.866a/256; Berle to Tittmann, October 14, 1942, SDF
740.0011EW1939/24145; Molotov quoted in Welles to Cicognani, May
27, 1942, and June 24, 1942, SDF 740.00114EW1939/2419¼; Hull to
Standley, February 5, 1943, SDF 740.00114EW1939/3095; see also
James M. Burns, *Roosevelt: The Soldier of Freedom, 1940-1945* (New
York, 1970), p. 232.

69. *New York Times*: February 2, 1944; January 1, 1945; January 3,
1945; February 8, 1945; March 1, 1945. The entire question of an accord
must await the opening of Vatican and Soviet archives.

70. Ready to Welles, November 27, 1942, SDF 861.404/486; Ready to
Welles, January 20, 1943, SDF 861.404/490.

71. "Cooperating with Russia, " *Sign* September 1943, p. 69; James
Gillis, "No Alliance with Atheism," *Catholic World* 156 (January

1943), pp. 390-391; *Catholic World* 160 (October 1944), p. 1; *Catholic World* 155 (June 1942), p. 262; N. S. Timasheff, "Religion in Russia Today," *Catholic Digest* (March 1943), pp. 18-20.

72. Elmer Murphy, "Washington Newsletter," *NCWC News Service:* January 25, 1943; June 7, 1943; June 28, 1943; January 18, 1943; F. Hermens, "Peacemaking," p. 128; James Gillis, editorial, *Catholic World* 155 (August 1942), p. 513.

73. Huber, *Our Bishops Speak*, pp. 111, 232-233; Taylor to pope, September 19 and 22, 1942, PSF: Vatican, Roosevelt Papers; memo of conversation between Maglione and Taylor, September 25, 1942, PSF: Vatican, Roosevelt Papers; *NCWC News Service*: January 18, 1943; March 15, 1943; *New York Times*, January 8, 1943.

74. This remarkable conversation was typed up by Spellman soon after it took place; see Gannon, *The Cardinal Spellman Story*, p. 279, 285-287.

75. Spellman to Roosevelt, March 4, 1943, PSF: Spellman, Roosevelt Papers.

76. Gannon, *The Cardinal Spellman Story*, pp. 299, 315; Cicognani to Hull, September 2, 1944, SDF 740.0011EW1939/9-244; Taylor to Roosevelt, December 12, 1944, SDF 740.0011EW1939/12-1244. Spellman also discussed Allied occupation of Rome; Tully to Roosevelt, July 10, 1944, PSF: Spellman, Roosevelt Papers.

77. Gannon, *The Cardinal Spellman Story*, pp. 284-285; Huber, *Our Bishops Speak*, pp. 115-116; W. M. Bennett, "Churches and the Peace," *Commonweal*, August 11, 1944, p. 396; L. J. A. Mercier, "The Church and the Peace," *America*, July 8, 1944, pp. 369-370.

78. Huber, *Our Bishops Speak*, pp. 123-126.

79. *Catholic World*: July 1942, p. 393; August 1942, p. 513; February 1944, p. 423; "When Mañana Won't Work: Tensions Between the Soviets and their Anglo-American Allies," *Commonweal*, August 27, 1943, p. 455.

80. See John L. Gaddis, *The United States and the Origins of the Cold War, 1941-1947* (New York, 1972), pp. 145-146; *New York Times*, May 1, 14, 15, 1944; Orlemanski quoted in May 17, 1944.

81. Huber, *Our Bishops Speak*, pp. 128-129, 234, 357-359.

82. Roosevelt to all Diplomats, etc., January 22, 1945; Tully to

Roosevelt, March 3, 1945; Roosevelt to Secretary of State, March 10, 1945, PSF: Flynn, Roosevelt Papers.

83. Divine, *Second Chance* p. 251; Roosevelt quoted in James Byrnes, *All in One Lifetime* (New York, 1958), p. 255; Harriman to Roosevelt, March 14, 1945, PSF: Flynn, Roosevelt Papers.

85. Taylor to Roosevelt, March 23, 1945, SDF 866A4611/3-2345; Taylor to Hull, March 31, 1945, SDF 761.66a/3-3145; Taylor to Flynn, April 7, 1945, SDF 761.66a/4-745; *Stars and Stripes* (London edition): February 1, 16, 1945; March 23, 31, 1945; *New York Times,* March 22, 23, 28, 1945.

85. Huber, *Our Bishops Speak,* pp. 126-128, 356-359.

86. Seymour Lipset, "Religion and Politics in the American Past and Present," in *Religion and Social Conflict,* edited by R. Lee and M. E. Marty (New York, 1964), p. 95, points out that the index of religious voting dropped significantly during the war years and hypothesizes that Catholics were reacting to Roosevelt's Russian policy. See also Burns, *Roosevelt: Soldier,* pp. 601-609. For the debate over the origins of the Cold War, see Herbert Feis, *Between War and Peace* (1960) and *From Trust to Terror* (1970); G. Alperovitz, *Atomic Diplomacy* (New York, 1965); A. Schlesinger, Jr., "Origins of the Cold War," *Foreign Affairs* 46 (October 1967), pp. 22-52; M. L. Hertz, *Beginnings of the Cold War* (Bloomington, Indiana, 1966).

BIBLIOGRAPHICAL NOTE

The student of American Catholicism is at a disadvantage in his quest for information because of the deplorable state of church archives. The archives of the National Catholic Welfare Conference (NCWC) operates under a fifty-year rule. Since the organization is barely fifty years old, its holdings are safe for the moment. Few prelates have papers available for research. There is no clearing house for manuscripts. Indeed, the situation has prompted a group of younger historians, led by David O'Brien of Holy Cross College, to seek a more liberal and uniform archival policy for the church in America.

Lacking access to a central depository of American church material, the historian must work through secular channels. The major source of information on the political activities of the period from 1937 to 1945 is the Franklin D. Roosevelt Library at Hyde Park, N.Y., where a staff of experts is ready to provide assistance. Yet, overall, the Roosevelt papers are not very fruitful for material dealing with the political activities of American Catholicism. The president, like most

Americans, was aware of the sensitive national tradition opposed to
the mixing of religion and politics. He wrote of such matters only seldom,
and his writings hardly reflected the extent of his association with religious leaders. A number of years ago a staff from the Catholic University
of America traveled up the Hudson to microfilm those materials in the
Roosevelt collection which touched on "Roman Catholic Church Matters." The journey itself was a testimony to the awareness among Catholics of Roosevelt's importance in the history of the American church.
Yet the three reels of microfilm which resulted from this journey are
disappointing in content. Much more fruitful are the files of the United
States Department of State held by the National Archives in Washington,
D.C. They contain considerable correspondence between men such as
Sumner Welles, Myron Taylor, Harold Tittmann, Monsignor Michael
Ready, Apostolic Delegate Ameleto Cicognani, and others.

Outside of the Roosevelt Library and the National Archives, manuscript material dealing with the political activity of American Catholicism is rather scattered. Of considerable importance is the John A. Ryan
collection housed at the Catholic University Library in Washington. As a
leading publicist and polemicist, Father Ryan's papers are filled with
letters to leading figures of the day. His manuscripts are supplemented by
the smaller collection of William F. Montavon, a leading figure in the
Spanish Civil War debate and an official of the NCWC. Also in Washington,
D.C., the releases of the *NCWC News Service*, available on microfilm, form
another major source of information on Catholicism. Since virtually all
diocesan papers made use of the NCWC service, these releases are vital in
understanding the type of information American Catholics received during
the period. The NCWC gave the most complete coverage to all Catholic
activities. The papers of the Catholic Association for International Peace
constitute another manuscript collection of some interest. This group was
connected with the NCWC and was a leading source of Catholic internationalism. The archives of Marquette University of Milwaukee hold what
material the NCWC has seen fit to release thus far. The record is scanty
for the period immediately before World War II except for an impressive
collection of pamphlets on international problems. Marquette also has
the papers of the leading Catholic pacifist, Dorothy Day.

Other materials on the political life of American Catholics come from
collections of individuals. The papers of Frank Walker at the University

of Notre Dame should be important since he was close to both the leaders
of the church and the president, but they reveal little. Frank P. Walsh, a
leading Catholic layman and New York politician, was a strong supporter
of the president. His papers at the New York Public Library are helpful
in understanding the crosscurrents involved in Catholic attitudes toward
the Spanish Civil War. Senator David I. Walsh of Massachusetts played a
major role in fighting aid to England and Russia, but his papers at Holy
Cross College, Worcester, Massachusetts, are of minor quality. Much more
fruitful for correspondence from Catholics concerned with foreign policy
questions are the papers of Senator Joseph O'Mahoney housed at the
University of Wyoming, Laramie. The papers of Representative John J.
O'Connor at the Lilly Library, Indiana University, are interesting because
of his connection with the anti-Roosevelt faction of American Catholicism.

These primary sources have been supplemented by collections of published documents. Of capital importance here is the series *Foreign Relations of the United States*, published by the United States Department of
State and now complete through World War II. In this series, see especially the volumes for 1939 through 1945. The Department of State also
published a separate volume called *The United States and Italy, 1936-
1946* (Government Printing Office, 1946), which contains the important
documents of United States-Vatican relations. Earlier documents can be
found in Edgar R. Nixon, editor, *Franklin D. Roosevelt and Foreign
Affairs*, 3 vols. (Cambridge, Mass., 1969). Equally important is the still
incomplete collection of Vatican papers dealing with the period of World
War II. Officially titled *Actes et Documents du Saint Siège Relatifs à la
Seconde Guerre Mondiale*, 5 vols. (Vatican City, 1967-) the multivolume
collection is available in both French and Italian. Volume one, which
covers the period from March 1939 through August 1940, has been trans-
lated into English by Gerard Noel and is available under the title *The Holy
See and the War in Europe*. The French edition is complete up through
1942. Other edited collections of value include *The Public Papers and
Addresses of Franklin D. Roosevelt*, 13 vols. (New York, 1938-1950),
edited by Samuel I. Rosenman; *F.D.R.: His Personal Letters*, 3 vols.
(New York, 1947-1950), edited by Elliott Roosevelt; *The War Diary of
Breckinridge Long* (Lincoln, Nebr., 1966), edited by Fred L. Israel;
From the Morgenthau Diaries, 3 vols. (Boston, 1959, 1965, 1967),
edited by John M. Blum.

On the interaction of religion and politics, see the comprehensive work by Anson Phelps Stokes, *Church and State in the United States*, 3 vols. (New York, 1950), which lists occasions when the two institutions infringed upon each other. More interesting for its methodology and conclusions is John H. Fenton, *The Catholic Vote* (New Orleans, 1960). Despite an artificial quality due to a study of episodes rather than trends, Fenton's work does explain how church leadership influences the members. The most thorough sociological analysis of the role of religion in modern American life is Gerhard Lenski, *The Religious Factor* (Garden City, N.Y., 1963). Despite his exclusive focus on the community of Detroit, Lenski's work presents many original ideas on the current state of religion in America. *Religion and Social Conflict* (New York, 1964), edited by Robert Lee and Martin E. Marty, has some equally penetrating essays on the interaction of religion and society; for religion and politics, see especially the article by Seymour M. Lipset, "Religion and Politics in the American Past and Present," pp. 69-126. The best works on ethnic voting are Harry A. Bailey and Ellis Katz, editors, *Ethnic Group Politics* (Columbus, Ohio, 1969), and Moses Rischin, *Our Own Kind: Voting by Race, Creed, or National Origin* (Santa Barbara, Calif., 1960), whose major concern is the 1950s.

Political scientists have yet to fully document the techniques used by domestic pressure groups to influence foreign policy, but a beginning was made by Bernard C. Cohen, *The Influence of Non-Governmental Groups on Foreign Policy-Making* (Boston, 1959), which contains a very helpful bibliography. Other studies which deal indirectly with the question of religion and politics include Ed Levine, *The Irish and Irish Politicians* (Notre Dame, Ind., 1966); William Shannon, *American Irish* (New York, 1964); Ronald E. Magden, "Attitudes of the American Religious Press Toward Soviet Russia, 1939-1941," (Ph.D. thesis, University of Washington, 1964). For background on the theoretical framework of the study, see Dean R. Esslinger, "American German and Irish Attitudes toward Neutrality, 1914-1917: A Study of Catholic Minorities," *Catholic Historical Review* 53 (July 1967), and E. Digby Baltzell, "Religion and the Class Structure," in *Sociology and History*, edited by Richard Hofstadter and S. Lipset (New York, 1968).

Information on the public attitudes of American Catholicism is scattered through a number of sources. A few sound monographs do exist which treat various aspects of Catholic life in the period before World War II. Frederick L. Broderick, *The Right Reverend New Dealer: John A. Ryan* (New York, 1962), is a sympathetic study of that social-minded priest. The importance of Robert I. Gannon, *The Cardinal Spellman Story* (New York, 1963), is due more to the fact that the author had exclusive access to the cardinal's diary than to the critical focus of the study itself. David J. O'Brien, *American Catholics and Social Reform* (New York, 1968), is a first-rate study of the implications of the depression for Catholic thinking. See also George Q. Flynn, *American Catholics and the Roosevelt Presidency, 1932-1936* (Lexington, 1968), and Myron Marty, *Lutherans and Catholicism* (Notre Dame, 1968). More general works include John T. Ellis, *American Catholicism* (Garden City, N.Y., 1956); Andrew Greeley, *The Catholic Experience* (New York, 1967; *Catholicism in America: A series of Articles from "The Commonweal"* (New York, 1954); *The Catholic Church in World Affairs,* edited by Waldemar Gurain and M. A. Fitzsimmons (Notre Dame, 1954); *Catholicism in America* (New York, 1970), edited by Philip Gleason, whose introduction on the eccesiological problems of church history is worth reading. For bibliographies on Catholic history see John T. Ellis, *A Guide to American Catholic History* (1959), and Edward Vollmar, *The Catholic Church in America: An Historical Bibliography* (New York, 1963).

These monographs and collections must be supplemented by contemporary Catholic literature. The reader may want to examine first John J. Carrigg, "American Catholic Press Opinion with Reference to America's Intervention in the Second World War" (M.A. thesis, Georgetown University, 1947), which sketches the foreign policy attitudes of leading religious journals. Among periodicals, the three most widely read journals concerned with foreign policy issues were *America*, edited by the Jesuits, *Commonweal*, edited by New York laymen, and *Catholic World*, edited by the Paulist fathers. Complementing these are a wide variety of periodicals ranging from the erudite offerings of *Thought, Catholic Mind,* and *Ecclesiastical Review*, to the more limited interest of *Ave Maria, Sign, Catholic Action, Columbia, Extension, Social Justice,* and *Pax.* Equally important is the testimony of Catholic newspapers. Beyond the news service provided by the NCWC, the editorial opinions of the following Catholic newspapers provided a geographical cross-section of opinion: the Boston *Pilot*; the Brooklyn *Tablet*; the *Catholic Herald* (Milwaukee);

the *Catholic Messenger* (Davenport, Ia.); the *Catholic Telegraph* (Cincinnati); the *Catholic Transcript* (Hartford, Conn.); the *Denver Catholic Register*; the *Monitor* (San Francisco); the *Tidings* (Los Angeles); the *New World* (Chicago); *Our Sunday Visitor* (Fort Wayne, Ind.); the *Baltimore Review*. Most of these diocesan papers are available on microfilm from the Catholic University Library in Washington, D.C.

The number of standard works increases as one enters the realm of traditional secular history and foreign policy. The literature dealing with the Spanish Civil War is impressive. Recently, three separate studies appeared on the American volunteers for Spain: Robert A. Rosenstone, *Crusade of the Left: The Lincoln Battalion in the Spanish Civil War* (New York, 1969); Cecil O. Eby, *Between the Bullet and the Lie* (New York, 1969); and Arthur H. Landis, *The Abraham Lincoln Brigade* (New York, 1967). For information on American Catholicism and the Spanish Civil War, see F. Jay Taylor, *The United States and the Spanish Civil War* (New York, 1956); Allen Guttmann, *The Wound in the Heart: America and the Spanish Civil War* (New York, 1962), and, also by Guttmann, *American Neutrality and the Spanish Civil War* (Boston, 1963), edited for the D. C. Heath series. Guttmann and Taylor add to our knowledge but both share a liberal bias which colors their interpretation and presents a number of difficulties in their understanding of American Catholics. A similar viewpoint is manifested by Richard P. Traina, *American Diplomacy and the Spanish Civil War* (Bloomington, Ind., 1968), who presents a very thorough study of how policy was formulated by the Department of State. The most recent scholar of American Catholics and the Spanish affair is J. David Valaik, whose articles, "American Catholic Dissenters and the Spanish Civil War," *Catholic Historical Review* 53 (January 1968); "Catholics, Neutrality, and the Spanish Embargo, 1937-1939," *Journal of American History* 54 (June 1967); "American Catholics and the Second Spanish Republic, 1911-1936," *Journal of Church and State* 10 (Winter 1968), should be consulted. Valaik shares the same pro-Republican viewpoint presented by Taylor and Guttmann. R. M. Darrow, "Catholic Political Power: A Study of the Activities of the American Catholic Church on Behalf of Franco During the Spanish Civil War, 1936-1939," (Ph.D. thesis, Columbia University, 1953), is a first-rate work and much more realistic than either Taylor's or Guttmann's in interpreting American Catholic behavior and the actions of Roosevelt. A thorough bibliography for the war can be found in Hugh Thomas, *The Spanish Civil War* (New York, 1961), the best general history in English.

Our understanding of isolationism in the 1930s has been enhanced by Manfred Jonas, *Isolationism in America, 1935-1941* (Ithaca, 1966). Other works on the same subject which were consulted with profit include Selig Adler, *The Isolationist Impulse: Its 20th Century Reaction* (New York, 1957), somewhat encyclopedic and dull; Mark Chadwin, *The Hawks of World War II* (Chapel Hill, 1968), which is a first-rate study of the actions of radical interventionists; Wayne Cole, *America First* (Madison, Wisconsin, 1953), a standard work; Walter Johnson, *The Battle Against Isolation* (Chicago, 1944), a propaganda tract by an interventionist; William L. Langer and S. Everett Gleason, *The Challenge to Isolation* (New York, 1952), a very thorough work which has been accused of being official history. Also important for its methodology is Leroy N. Rieselbach, *The Roots of Isolationism: Congressional Voting and Presidential Leadership in Foreign Policy* (Indianapolis, 1966). For Catholic isolationism, see James O'Gara, "The Catholic Isolationist," in *Catholicism in America*, edited by *The Commonweal*. F. Fensterwal, Jr., "The Anatomy of American 'Isolationism' and Expansion," *Journal of Conflict Resolution* 2 (June and December 1958), is really a weak general sketch.

The study of Roosevelt and the coming of World War II has provided considerable historiographical literature. Most of the major questions and issues are covered in James M. Burns, *Roosevelt: The Soldier of Freedom, 1940-1945* (New York, 1970). Equally useful are William L. Langer and S. Everett Gleason, *The Undeclared War, 1940-1941* (New York, 1953), William Leuchtenburg, *Franklin D. Roosevelt and the New Deal* (New York, 1963), and Robert Sherwood, *Roosevelt and Hopkins* (New York, 1950). *The Secret Diary of Harold L. Ickes*, 3 vols. (New York, 1953-1954), is filled with gossip on American Catholicism but must be used with caution. The bibliographies in the Burns and Leuchtenburg volumes should provide the interested student with a good introduction to the literature. Cordell Hull, *Memoirs*, 2 vols. (New York, 1948), cannot be ignored but occasionally distorts the sequence of events. There are a number of more detailed works on particular phases of Roosevelt's foreign policy. The most important for the present study are the following: Robert A. Divine, *The Illusion of Neutrality* (Chicago, 1962), the standard work on neutrality legislation; by the same author, *The Reluc-*

tant Belligerent: American Entry into World War II (New York, 1965), a somewhat sketchy survey; Raymond H. Dawson, *The Decision to Aid Russia, 1941* (Chapel Hill, 1959), an excellent monograph based on government documents; Warren F. Kimball, *The Most Unsordid Act: Lend-Lease, 1939-1941* (Baltimore, 1969), an excessively detailed account; Donald F. Drummund, *The Passing of American Neutrality, 1937-1941* (Ann Arbor, Mich., 1955), a standard treatment; Fred L. Israel, *Nevada's Key Pittmann* (Lincoln, Nebr., 1963), in which the author's obvious antipathy for his subject makes the work less useful than it could have been.

For an understanding of United States-Vatican relations, there is no substitute for a study of the documents in the National Archives and the collection of papal papers being edited by the Vatican. There are, however, a few studies which present parts of the story. On the mission of Myron Taylor, see the following works: Martin F. Hasting, "United States-Vatican Relations: Policies and Problems" (Ph.D. thesis, University of California, 1952), a solid study but rather too broad in scope; Ida T. Bucci, "United States-Vatican Relations and the Taylor Mission" (M.A. thesis, Georgetown University, 1949), based on public sources and little else; Alex Karmarkovic, "The Myron C. Taylor Appointment: Background; Religious Reaction; Constitutionality" (Ph.D. thesis, University of Minnesota, 1967), an unsatisfactory work based on rather narrow documentation. Of some value is Myron C. Taylor, editor, *Wartime Correspondence Between President Roosevelt and Pope Pius XII* (New York, 1947), in which the major public and banal exchanges have been published in convenient form but which ignores the important historical dialogue.

There are a number of other monographs on general Vatican diplomacy which are valuable in filling in the diplomatic picture. Camille M. Cianfarra, *The Vatican and the War* (New York, 1944), a provocative memoir by a *New York Times* journalist who spent many years at the Vatican; Saul Friedlander, *Pius XII and the Third Reich: A Documentation* (New York, 1966), which gives insights on German attitudes toward Taylor's mission; R. A. Graham, *Vatican Diplomacy* (Princeton, 1959), a scholarly study of the principles and guidelines of the international relations of the Holy See; Anne (O'Hare) McCormick, *Vatican Journal, 1921-1954* (New York, 1957), another memoir by a New York journalist; Peter Nicholas, *The Politics of the Vatican* (London, 1968), a general survey of Vatican politics by an objective Englishman; Thomas B. Morgan, *The Listening Post* (New York, 1944), a firsthand account by a reporter stationed on Vatican Hill for 18 years; William Phillips, *Ventures in Diplomacy* (Portland, Me., 1952), the somewhat disappointing memoirs of the American ambassador to Italy and friend of President Roosevelt.

Some first-rate studies are available on the ever-pressing problem of modern war and ethics: see especially Paul Ramsey, *The Just War* (New York, 1968), a solid book by one of America's leading Protestant theologians; William Nagle, Jr., editor, *Morality and Modern Warfare* (Baltimore, 1960), a collection of essays which focuses more on the postwar period, but includes a very comprehensive bibliography compiled by Noel J. Brown; John K. Ryan, *Modern War and Basic Ethics* (Milwaukee, 1944) an older Catholic work which presents the traditional position of the church; Gordon Zahn, *German Catholics and Hitler's Wars* (New York, 1969), which challenges the traditional Catholic approach because of what Zahn concludes was an ethical failure of the German hierarchy. For an updated view, consult Walter M. Abbott, editor, *The Documents of Vatican II* (New York, 1966), and Robert W. Tucker, *Just War and Vatican II* (New York, 1970).

A number of miscellaneous works were consulted with profit. For public statements by the American hierarchy see Raphael M. Huber, editor, *Our Bishops Speak: National Pastorals and Annual Statements of the Hierarchy of the United States, 1919-1951* (Milwaukee, 1952). A convenient guide to Catholic literature is the *Catholic Periodical Index, 1939-1945* (New York, 1945), which unfortunately has gaps in its coverage. For biographical data, see *American Catholics Who's Who* (Detroit, 1934-) and *The Official Catholic Directory 1940* (New York, 1940). Hadley Cantrill, editor, *Public Opinion, 1935-1946* (Princeton, 1951), provides a convenient collection of the major polls conducted during the period. For statistical data on voting and the Catholic population, see The American Institute of Public Opinion, *The Gallup Political Almanac for 1948* (Princeton, 1948); U.S. Bureau of the Census, *Religious Bodies, 1936*, 2 vols. (Washington, D.C., 1941); Edwin S. Gaustad, *Historical Atlas of Religion in America* (New York, 1962). Readers interested in more detailed information on documentation are advised to consult the appropriate footnotes.

INDEX

ABOUT THE AUTHOR

George Q. Flynn is associate professor of history at Texas Tech University, Lubbock, Texas. He did his undergraduate work at Loyola University of the South and received M.A. and Ph.D. degrees from Louisiana State University. He taught previously at Seattle University, Indiana University and the University of Miami. Areas of special interests include United States history in the era of Franklin D. Roosevelt, the homefront during World War II, and historical methodology.

His book *American Catholics and the Roosevelt Presidency, 1932-1936* was published in 1968, and he has contributed many articles to scholarly journals in the field.